Local Citizenship in Recent Countries of Immigration

Local Citizenship in Recent Countries of Immigration

Japan in Comparative Perspective

Edited by Takeyuki Tsuda

LEXINGTON BOOKS

A Division of
ROWMAN & LITTLEFIELD PUBLISHERS, INC.
Lanham • Boulder • New York • Toronto • Oxford

LEXINGTON BOOKS

A division of Rowman & Littlefield Publishers, Inc.
A wholly owned subsidary of The Rowman & Littlefield Publishing Group, Inc.
4501 Forbes Boulevard, Suite 200
Lanham, MD 20706

PO Box 317
Oxford
OX2 9RU, UK

British Library Cataloguing in Publication Information Available

Library of Congress Cataloging-in-Publication Data

Local citizenship in recent countries of immigration : Japan in comparative perspective /
edited by Takeyuki Tsuda.
    p. cm.
Includes bibliographical references and index.
ISBN-13: 978-0-7391-1192-5 (cloth : alk. paper)
ISBN-10: 0-7391-1192-2 (cloth : alk. paper)
ISBN-13: 978-0-7391-1193-2 (pbk. : alk. paper)
ISBN-10: 0-7391-1193-0 (pbk. : alk. paper)
1. Immigrants—Japan. 2. Immigrants—Government policy—Japan. 3. Citizenship—
Japan. 4. Social integration—Japan. 5. Japan—Emigration and immigration. 6.
Immigrants—Cross-cultural studies. 7. Citizenship—Cross-cultural studies. 8. Social
integration—Cross-cultural studies. 9. Emigration and immigration—Cross-cultural
studies. I. Tsuda, Takeyuki.
JV8722.L63 2006
325.52—dc22   2005028083

Printed in the United States of America

♾™ The paper used in this publication meets the minimum requirements of American
National Standard for Information Sciences—Permanence of Paper for Printed Library
Materials, ANSI/NISO Z39.48–1992.

CONTENTS

Part I

INTRODUCTION

CHAPTER 1

Localities and the Struggle for Immigrant Rights: The Significance of Local Citizenship in Recent Countries of Immigration

TAKEYUKI TSUDA

INTRODUCTION: RECENT COUNTRIES OF IMMIGRATION IN EAST ASIA AND SOUTHERN EUROPE

In recent decades, Japan, South Korea, Italy, and Spain have joined the growing array of advanced industrialized nations that import large numbers of foreign workers. None of these countries experienced any large-scale immigration until the 1980s[1] because their earlier labor demands could be successfully met by *internal* migration from poorer regions, increased utilization of previously untapped labor sources (women and the elderly), the mechanization and rationalization of production, and relocation of factories abroad. In fact, all of these countries had been prominent *exporters* of migrant labor in the past, when they were less industrialized than labor-importing countries.[2] However, in the 1980s they all made the

---

[1] This does not mean, of course, that they have never experienced significant immigration in the past or that immigration has never been important for their past nation-building (see Tsuda and Cornelius 2004 for the Japanese case).

[2] Hundreds of thousands of Japanese emigrated to the Americas from the late nineteenth century to the mid-twentieth century, creating large communities of Japanese descendants in the United States and Brazil. There was also substantial Japanese emigration to Asia during the period of Japanese imperialist expansion before World War II. During the same period, close to three million Koreans emigrated to China, central Asia, and Japan. In recent decades, many Koreans have emigrated to the United States. Both Italy and Spain have long histories of emigration to the Americas and more economically developed countries in Western Europe.

transition from countries of net emigration to countries of net immigration. Nonetheless, these recent countries of immigration do not view immigration as part of their national identity or past nation-building process, and their percentage of foreign-born residents remains quite low (between less than 1 percent to 3 percent of the total population) compared to most older countries of immigration.

The reasons why these nations became recent countries of immigration are surprisingly similar. By the 1980s, all were suffering from acute labor shortages caused by rapid economic growth in the 1960s and 1970s. The demand for labor outstripped the supply of domestic workers as previous labor sources (women, the elderly, rural workers) were depleted and negative demographic trends (low fertility rates and rapid population aging) shrunk the working-age population. The growing shortage of workers was exacerbated by a labor market mismatch. Although most labor market expansion in these countries occurred in the informal economy (in low-skilled, low-paying, casual jobs in small and midsize businesses), decades of economic prosperity had created a population of well-educated and socioeconomically mobile youth unwilling to do such 3D (dirty, dangerous, and difficult) jobs.

THE EMERGENCE OF LOCALITIES AS SITES FOR CITIZENSHIP IN RECENT COUNTRIES OF IMMIGRATION

The citizenship status of immigrants is undoubtedly the most precarious in recent countries of immigration. These countries generally grant immigrants fewer rights than do older countries of immigration, for a number of reasons. Because immigrants have only been in these countries for a relatively short period, few have become naturalized citizens or even denizens (permanent residents). In addition, national governments in these countries do not have active social integration programs to grant basic rights and services to immigrants who are not citizens or denizens.[3] Neither the Japanese nor the Korean government has immigrant integration policies, viewing foreign workers strictly as labor power to be regulated and not as people with human needs and rights.[4] Although the governments of Italy

---

[3] In this sense, a government's social integration policies can be considered its citizenship rights policy for immigrants who are not nationals or denizens.

[4] As Castles and Davidson (2000: 206) note, the immigrant rights situation is particularly bad in the Asia-Pacific, which encompasses a number of recent countries of immigration (in addition to Japan and South Korea, they include

and Spain have official social integration policies for immigrants on the books, these have not been seriously implemented.

There are a number of reasons for this neglect of foreign worker rights in recent countries of immigration. Because immigrants are recent arrivals, few in number, and more likely to be sojourners than settlers, they are not considered legitimate, long-term residents. Rather, they are viewed as temporary laborers whose sociocultural and political integration in mainstream society is not yet a pressing concern. In addition, given that they are not yet culturally assimilated, they also lack *cultural* citizenship (the cultural attributes necessary to be considered members of the national community).[5] As a result, immigrants are frequently marginalized from the national community as both temporary sojourners and culturally alien outsiders, not worthy to partake of the rights and social services reserved for members of the nation-state. Finally, these countries tend to have more restrictive immigration policies since they do not yet officially consider themselves to be countries of immigration. However, their strong demand for foreign labor has attracted large numbers of illegal immigrants who are not granted basic legal protections and who suffer the greatest human rights abuses.

Nonetheless, immigrants have become a permanent presence in many local communities in recent countries of immigration as they take up long-term, if not permanent, residence and are joined by their families. Yet the governments of these countries, instead of addressing the citizenship rights and social needs of immigrant settlers and their dependents, have increasingly focused on immigration control and border enforcement in an attempt to keep their foreign populations small and avoid a flood of illegal immigrants.[6] This situation was exacerbated by the terrorist attacks of September 11, 2001, which caused national governments around the world to tighten immigration controls in the name of national security, and later by

---

Taiwan, Hong Kong, Singapore, and Malaysia). These are also countries that do not have strong liberal democratic traditions, compared to the situation in most Euro-American countries.

[5] For discussions of cultural citizenship, see Ong 1996, 1999; Turner 1994: 159.

[6] It is important to remember that immigration control and the social integration of immigrant residents are not necessarily antithetical. In a number of European Union countries, tougher border enforcement has been coupled with more liberal immigrant integration and citizenship policies in an attempt to socially incorporate immigrants who have already become long-term residents.

the subway bombings that foreign terrorists carried out in Madrid in 2004.[7] The Japanese and Spanish governments have also cracked down on illegal immigration in response to the media-fueled public perception that immigrants are undermining public safety by increasing the crime rate.

Because national governments in recent countries of immigration have been largely oblivious to the social needs of immigrants, local governments and institutions have had to deal with the foreigners already residing in their communities. A de facto division of labor has emerged in which the national government is concerned solely with *immigration* policy (the regulation of immigration flows and border control) while local governments and nongovernmental organizations (NGOs) have taken care of *immigrant* policy (the provision of basic services and rights that facilitate the social integration of immigrants). In Japan and South Korea, local governments and/or NGOs have become almost exclusively responsible for providing basic social services to their immigrant residents. In Italy and Spain, the implementation of the national government's immigrant integration policies[8] has been delegated to local governments and NGOs, which have been granted considerable autonomy to develop their own programs. The rights and services that local governments and institutions offer immigrants include employment and housing assistance, language programs, cross-cultural activities, education for immigrant children, health care and insurance, welfare benefits, and local political representation.[9] Immigrants' rights have also been improved in Italy, Japan, South Korea, and Spain through activism—direct political mobilization or through the courts—by local immigrant advocacy groups and the immigrants themselves.

---

[7] The European Union exerted pressure on Italy and Spain to harmonize their immigration policies with other EU member states by increasing external border enforcement. Because of the relaxing of internal border controls within the European Union, Southern European and Eastern European countries on the EU periphery have come under increasing pressure to better control their external borders as the first line of defense against unauthorized immigration.

[8] It is interesting to note that Italy and Spain also have official (though nominal) social integration policies because of policy harmonization pressure from the European Union, which has forced member states to improve access to citizenship and rights for immigrants.

[9] According to Andrew and Goldsmith (1998), this is also the case in older countries of immigration.

THE CONCEPT OF LOCAL CITIZENSHIP

This book explores the emergence of "local citizenship" (cf. Andrew and Goldsmith 1998; Tegtmeyer Pak 2001) among immigrants in Japan, with comparative reference to similar processes in South Korea, Italy, and Spain. Local citizenship refers to the granting, by local governments and organizations, of basic sociopolitical rights and services to immigrants as legitimate members of these local communities. This includes local governments' immigrant social integration programs and policies, immigrant services offered by local NGOs, and local activism to demand and secure basic rights for immigrants. Although this type of citizenship is rarely discussed in the scholarly literature, it has had a significant impact on the lives of immigrants, especially in recent countries of immigration, which makes it imperative to situate local citizenship within broader analyses of immigrant citizenship.

Despite citizenship's inclusionary aspects (the conferral of rights to members of a specific community), in the case of immigration, citizenship seems more exclusionary than inclusionary (Joppke 1999: 630). Immigrants have generally been denied the rights granted to national citizens because of their status as outsiders to the nation-state. Nevertheless, the lack of *national* citizenship does not mean that immigrants lack *substantive* citizenship (the actual possession of rights) since the nation-state has also conferred rights on its non-national foreign residents.[10] Immigrants who have become permanent residents—referred to as denizens (Hammar 1990)—hold rights comparable to those of national citizens in many liberal democracies.[11] Legal immigrants who are not denizens have also enjoyed a more limited set of rights, and certain liberal democracies have offered some basic rights even to illegal immigrants (although these latter two categories of immigrants have sometimes been referred to as "marginens").

Thus immigrants' access to rights has come to depend more on residence in the nation-state than on the possession of national citizenship (Brubaker 1989; Jacobson 1996: 70–72). Therefore, we need to conceptualize citizenship more broadly than in terms of inclusions and exclusions (national citizens versus noncitizens). If we think in terms of *formal* citizenship

---

[10] As Brubaker (1989) notes, many immigrants have rights as well as access to labor markets and social services without possessing national citizenship.

[11] A number of scholars have argued that this has eroded and devalued national citizenship. See, for example, Abraham 2002; Jacobson 1996: 38–41; Schuck 1989.

(rights that the nation-state formally grants to individuals),[12] citizenship appears to comprise gradations of rights, with national citizens enjoying the most rights and unauthorized immigrants enjoying the least.

However, as mentioned above, most foreign residents in recent countries of immigration have not yet become national citizens or even denizens, nor have they been granted rights and services by the national government through social integration programs. Unlike their counterparts in more advanced countries of immigration, the immigrants' mere residence has been insufficient for them to be considered as members of the national community, whose basic rights are guaranteed by the nation-state. Nonetheless, their lack of formal citizenship rights does not mean that they are deprived of substantive citizenship rights, because other institutions and organizations besides the nation-state confer rights on immigrants based on their membership in non-national communities.

Although the nation-state has been the predominant framework used in analyses of immigrant citizenship,[13] it has become a less important source of immigrants' citizenship rights in recent decades (cf. Holston and Appadurai 1999: 2) as non-national organizations—both supranational and subnational—have begun to challenge its status as the exclusive purveyor of citizenship. The result is an increasing discrepancy between the formal citizenship rights granted by nation-states and the possession of substantive citizenship rights.[14] In this manner, citizenship has become somewhat delinked from nation-states, making it possible for immigrants to enjoy considerable rights even without formal citizenship.

When scholars consider non-national forms of citizenship, they invariably refer to rights granted to immigrants by global organizations such as the United Nations, which have produced numerous international conventions relevant to migrant worker rights.[15] These broadly inclusive forms of

---

[12] Formal citizenship is also referred to as juridical citizenship.

[13] According to Adrian Favell (2001), this has also been true for the analysis of immigrant social integration policy.

[14] Conversely, the discrepancy between formal citizenship and substantive citizenship is also illustrated by the situation of indigenous ethnic minorities, who are national citizens but cannot properly exercise their rights because of discrimination and socioeconomic marginalization.

[15] The most significant of these are the United Nations International Convention on the Protection of the Rights of Migrant Workers and the Members of Their Families, the UN Convention on the Status of Refugees, and the UN International Convention on the Elimination of All Forms of Racial Discrimination. The articles in most of these conventions are so idealistic that the immi-

postnational or global citizenship (see Bauböck 1994; Bosniak 2001; Jacobson 1996; Soysal 1994) are seen as challenging—and ultimately superseding—the more limited formal citizenship rights offered by the nation-state. Although international organizations nominally guaranteed the rights of immigrants as members of a global community,[16] the real power of such international human rights regimes remains weak. Unlike the case for national citizenship rights—which are enforceable by the judicial, police, and bureaucratic institutions of the nation-state—there is no global enforcement mechanism that can guarantee the postnational/global citizenship rights conferred upon migrant workers under international conventions. Despite the ratification of numerous bilateral labor agreements (see Miller 1992), an international migration regime has yet to emerge (Zolberg 1992).[17] Therefore, nation-states remain the only political actors that can enforce international human rights regimes. Yet only thirty[18] of the world's two hundred countries—and none of the major countries of immigration—have ratified the United Nations convention on migrant rights. Although many more governments have ratified the UN conventions against racial discrimination and on the status of refugees, few have seriously enforced the provisions of such international conventions (cf. Castles and Davidson 2000: 18–19; Loescher 1993; Guiraudon and Lahav 2000: 167–68).[19] As a result, postnational/global citizenship is often not a form of substantive citizenship.

---

gration policies of virtually all liberal democracies are in serious violation of them.

[16] For other scholars, global citizenship is based on a global consciousness among individuals as members of the human race, which causes them to mobilize for global issues such as human rights, the environment, nuclear nonproliferation, or worldwide socioeconomic, ethnic, and gender equality (see Falk 1994; Linklater 1998; Stennbergen 1994; Urry 2000).

[17] This contrasts with the emerging international and regional regimes for economic trade and finance, which are based on binding multilateral treaties and agreements between countries—such as the General Agreement on Tariffs and Trade (GATT), the North American Free Trade Agreement (NAFTA), and the European Union—and also have international enforcement mechanisms—such as the World Trade Organization (WTO), the European Union, and the International Monetary Fund (IMF, which is a de facto enforcement mechanism that compels developing countries to adopt Euro-American free trade principles as a condition for economic aid).

[18] Eleven of the thirty are original signatory nations.

[19] Few countries have overhauled their domestic laws to bring them into compliance with the international conventions they have ratified. Also, such con-

A more substantial form of supranational immigrant citizenship involves the rights offered by regional organizations, such as the transnational citizenship extended by the European Union. However, even the European Union (where this type of citizenship is most developed) has no regional policy enforcement mechanism (Geddes 2000: 31), and individual member states have not seriously implemented the European Union's migrant and human rights conventions. Only the European Convention on the Protection of Human Rights is legally binding on signatory nations and has a supranational judicial enforcement mechanism — the European Court of Human Rights, which has had some impact on member states (Guiraudon and Lahav 2000; Hammar 1992: 259). Although a regional European citizenship is emerging, its rights remain quite limited, and they do not apply to immigrants who are not EU nationals (see Koslowski 2000).

Nonetheless, international and regional human rights regimes have directly affected the rights that nation-states grant to immigrants. This impact has come through domestic NGOs, advocacy groups, and legal practitioners that fight for migrant rights through the courts by appealing to international conventions their governments have ratified but not fully enforced (cf. Guiraudon and Lahav 2000: 171–75; Gurowitz 1999 and in this volume; Sassen 1998: 51–52, 58, 69–71; Seol and Skrentny n.d.). Although supranational human rights regimes and norms may cause national governments to expand the range of rights offered to immigrants, they are not necessarily eroding the significance of formal citizenship, as some scholars have claimed (see Jacobson 1996). Because both transnational and postnational/global citizenship depend on the nation-state for their implementation and enforcement, they basically exist only as another type of formal citizenship.

Instead of focusing exclusively on supranational citizenship as an alternative to formal citizenship, I argue that we need to seriously consider subnational forms of citizenship. In fact, *local* citizenship is a more viable and independent type of non-national citizenship for a number of reasons. First, in contrast to transnational and global citizenship, the local citizenship rights and social services conferred on immigrants by local governments and NGOs are actually enforced — by city and state ordinances, local law enforcement officials, and the courts. Second, national governments sometimes delegate considerable authority (and resources) to local gov-

---

ventions are often only partially ratified or ratified with "reservations" or "interpretive declarations."

ernments and NGO service providers to run their own immigrant integration programs, as in Italy and Spain. Third, in some cases where a national
government has neglected the social integration of its immigrant residents
(as in Japan and Korea), local authorities have shown considerable
autonomous and independent policy initiative by offering the immigrants
in their local communities the citizenship rights and services denied by the
nation-state.[20] Therefore, even in the absence of formal citizenship, immigrants have been able to enjoy considerable substantive rights in certain
localities.

As a result, local citizenship has become a viable alternative that expands—and at times supersedes—the more restrictive citizenship of nation-
states. Although scholars have examined various causes for the expansion
of immigrant rights in recent decades—including judicial activism and the
courts, client politics (political lobbying by immigrant advocacy groups),
political mobilization, liberal democratic norms, and international human
rights regimes (Guiraudon 1998)—very few have looked at the role of local
governments and institutions. Even when the state has marginalized immigrants from the national community as non-citizen outsiders, immigrants have been incorporated into local communities as residents and
members entitled to rights—that is, as local citizens.[21] As Joseph Carens
(1989) has argued, governments have a moral obligation to offer citizenship to immigrants who are legitimate members of society.[22] Although they
are frequently socioeconomically marginalized, it is undeniable that both
legal and illegal immigrants make important economic and civic contributions to local communities as workers, taxpayers, consumers, and residents
and as ethnic and institutional participants.

---

[20] It is important to remember that local governments (especially in areas with
high concentrations of immigrants) are sometimes more restrictionist and
anti-immigrant than the national government because they must shoulder
much of the social and welfare costs of immigrants (cf. Money 1999: chap. 3).
As a result, they are sometimes less willing than the national government to
grant rights and services to immigrants. A case in point was California's
Proposition 187, which denied education, health care, and social services to
undocumented immigrants (but was eventually overturned by the courts).
[21] According to Andrew and Goldsmith (1998: 110), "citizenship [is] a mechanism to counter the marginalization and exclusion of increasing sectors of the
urban population."
[22] Carens measures immigrant community membership mainly by length of residence.

As a result, a number of scholars have begun to focus on local cities (rather than nations) as important sites for the negotiation of citizenship and claims-making (Andrew and Goldsmith 1998; Holston and Appadurai 1999; Isin 2000a; Sassen 1999). Although some argue that the modern city is too fragmented and its residents too mobile to create the sense of community that is a prerequisite for citizenship (Dagger 2000), a city's smaller scale and more cohesive nature make it easier to incorporate immigrants as local citizens than is the case in the large and fragmented national communities, where immigrants are likely to be marginalized. As a result, cities remain important in a globalized world, not only as the sites where the financial management and support structures for global capital are concentrated (Sassen 2001) but also as the places where global migrants are incorporated as local citizens. In this manner, cities can be better articulated with and more responsive to global forces (whether involving the economy or immigration) than can the nation-state, and hence they have become increasingly drawn into the governance of the local diversity introduced by globalization.

THE IMPORTANCE OF LOCAL CITIZENSHIP IN JAPAN

Japan has been experiencing significant immigration since the late 1980s,[23] driven by severe domestic labor shortages. The country's immigrant population is very diverse, with foreign workers coming from East and Southeast Asia, Latin America, and the Middle East. The total number of legal and unauthorized immigrants in Japan is close to 900,000, about 800,000 of them unskilled or semi-skilled. Although immigrants represent only 0.71 percent of Japan's total population of 127 million, their current numbers represent a sharp increase from the late 1980s. This population has not declined appreciably despite Japan's decade-long economic recession, demonstrating that the demand for immigrant labor has become structurally embedded.

There are a number of reasons why local citizenship is of particular importance in Japan. The Japanese government has a very restrictive (and disingenuous) immigration policy that has placed many foreign workers in a precarious human rights situation. Few recent immigrants have become citizens or denizens—naturalization remains difficult in Japan, and most immigrants have not resided there long enough to become denizens. Re-

---

[23] See Tsuda and Cornelius 2004 for a comprehensive analysis of why Japan became a recent country of immigration.

cent developments in immigration policy indicate that the national government will remain almost exclusively focused on restrictive immigration control. Moreover, among the recent countries of immigration considered in this volume, Japan has probably done the least to socially integrate its immigrant residents and promote their citizenship rights. As a result, the immigrants' only recourses for gaining citizenship rights and services have been local governments, NGOs, and local activism. In stark contrast to Japan's national government, a number of localities have been quite proactive in incorporating foreign workers into their communities as local citizens.

National Immigration Policy

The Japanese government, which adheres to the myth of Japan as an ethnically homogeneous nation that is not and never has been a country of immigration, has one of the most restrictive immigration policies among advanced industrialized countries. It bases its policy on three fundamental principles:

- *No unskilled foreign workers will be admitted.* Even when confronting a crippling labor shortage in the late 1980s, the Japanese government refused to open its doors to unskilled migrant workers. The revised Immigration Control and Refugee Recognition Act (implemented in 1990) maintained Japan's long-standing ban on unskilled foreign workers and imposed tough penalties on employers and labor brokers who knowingly recruit and hire illegal aliens.

- *The government should facilitate the admission only of highly skilled and professional foreign workers.* While forbidding the admittance of unskilled immigrants, the revised Immigration Control and Refugee Recognition Act expanded the number of legal residence statuses (mainly skilled and professional visa categories) from eighteen to twenty-seven and simplified immigration procedures in order to meet the increasing demand for foreign managerial and technical staff, foreign language instructors, and high-tech workers.

- *All foreigners should be admitted on a temporary basis only.* All foreign workers in Japan are granted temporary visas, and no foreign workers are admitted as permanent immigrants. Nor does the government permit the immigration of family members of foreign workers residing in Japan (except for the Japanese descent *nikkeijin*) because family reunification would encourage foreigners to settle in Japan.

Although the Japanese government has officially prohibited the importation of unskilled foreign labor, it has not been as unresponsive to the economic need for foreign workers as it officially appears on the surface. The Ministry of Justice (responsible for immigration policy) has created various "side-door" mechanisms that enable the legal importation of large numbers of unskilled foreign workers under visa categories officially intended for other purposes. With the front door officially closed to all but skilled and professional workers, over half of the estimated 800,000 unskilled immigrant workers in Japan have entered through a side door.

Japan's company trainee program is one important side door for importing migrant labor. In 2002, 39,067 trainees were residing in Japan, many from mainland China. Shortly after the revised immigration law was implemented, the Ministry of Justice modified by decree the traditional trainee program (formerly restricted to official agencies and large multinational corporations) to enable small and medium-size companies with labor shortages to accept trainees from abroad (see also Komai 1995: 41). As a result, although the program is officially justified as a form of overseas development assistance that enables trainees from developing countries to acquire technical skills at Japanese companies, it is being widely abused as a source of inexpensive, unskilled foreign labor (see, among others, Komai 1992; Miyajima 1993: chap. 5; Oishi 1995). "Trainees" in fact perform jobs that require minimal or no training, and Japanese employers can pay them a low "trainee allowance" because they are not classified as workers entitled to standard wages or to protections under Japan's labor laws.

The most numerically important of Japan's immigration side-door mechanisms is the policy that allows Latin American nikkeijin (individuals of Japanese descent who were born and raised outside of Japan) to "return" migrate to Japan. There are currently over 330,000 nikkeijin immigrants in Japan, mainly from Brazil, but also from Peru, Bolivia, and Argentina. Although the nikkeijin work exclusively as unskilled migrant laborers in small and medium-sized Japanese factories (and were tacitly admitted for this purpose; cf. Kajita 1994: 172), the government officially justifies the policy as an opportunity for the nikkeijin to learn the Japanese language and culture, meet their Japanese relatives, travel the country, and thus explore their ethnic heritage. Therefore, by appealing to ideologies of ethnic ancestry and homeland, the Japanese government has been able to acquire a much-needed, large migrant labor force without contradicting, at least at the level of official appearances, the fundamental principle of Japanese immigration policy that no unskilled foreign workers will be accepted. In addition, because of their common racial descent, government officials assumed that the nikkeijin would be culturally similar to the Japanese and would assimilate smoothly to Japanese society, in contrast to other foreigners (Miyajima 1993: 59; Tsuda 1999a). However, since most of the nikkeijin belong to the second and third generations born and raised in South America, most do not speak Japanese very well and have become culturally Latin American. As a result, they are ethnically marginalized and socially segregated in Japan as foreigners and have become Japan's newest ethnic minority (see Tsuda 2003).

The admission of foreigners on visas for pre-college "students" (*shugakusei*) represents another of Japan's side-door immigration policies. This new visa category was created by the revised Immigration Control Act in 1990 in order to encourage more foreign students to study in Japan. In 2002, there were 47,198 pre-college students registered in Japan, a vast majority of them from China. Although ostensibly in Japan to learn the language or participate in vocational training programs, they can work part-time (20 to 28 hours a week) to support themselves during the academic year and full-time during summer and winter vacations. However, most work illegally in excess of the allowed hours,[24] and many are becoming full-time, unskilled foreign workers, particularly in the service sector (see Komai 1995: 119). Not only are many of these "students" overstaying their visas, a number of them are entering Japan on false documentation, and the "language schools" that accept them are sometimes no more than immigrant-smuggling firms.

A final side-door mechanism for bringing unskilled workers to Japan is the "entertainment" visa. In 2002, there were 58,359 foreigners residing in Japan with entertainment visas. Like the "trainees" and "students," these immigrants are legally admitted under a professional visa category, but most (90 percent, according to Ishihara 1992: 176) actually work as bar hostesses in sleazy nightclubs or as prostitutes. A vast majority are from the Philippines, but smaller numbers also come from other Asian countries. Many of Japan's immigrant sex workers are undocumented female migrants who were deceived and exploited by labor brokers (who often have ties to criminal syndicates) and forced to work as hostesses or prostitutes (see also Oka 1994: 58–59; Sellek 2001: chap. 6). Called *Japayuki-san* (literally Ms. Going-to-Japan), they are held hostage by their labor brokers

---

[24] According to a Tokyo Metropolitan Government survey (cited in Komai 2001: 58–59), 65.1 percent of pre-college students surveyed were working an average of 35.4 hours per week.

and employers, who confiscate their passports and force them to repay the huge debts they incur for being smuggled into Japan. Some receive no wages, work under conditions of sexual slavery and forced confinement, and are threatened with physical violence or punishment. Despite efforts by the Philippine government to reduce the number of Filipina migrant women channeled into the global sex industry and the Japanese government's attempt to regulate bars and nightclubs that employ foreign "entertainers," little has been done to combat this illicit trafficking of women, despite criticism from international human rights groups.

It has become quite apparent that even these side-door policies for importing unskilled foreign workers have not sufficed to meet Japan's labor needs. Because Japan has maintained its restrictive immigrant admissions policy despite the strong domestic demand for foreign labor, many immigrants have simply entered Japan illegally through the "back door" in order to take advantage of the country's abundance of relatively high-paying jobs. In 2004, the government counted 219,418 visa overstayers, over 90 percent of whom are assumed to be in the workforce.[25] However, the total number of illegal immigrant workers in Japan considerably exceeds this number, which does not include those who work illegally in violation of their visa's activity restrictions or are smuggled in clandestinely or with false documentation. Immigrants' use of forged visas to enter through airports has become quite common, especially among Thai immigrants (Sellek 2001: 109). In addition, some immigrants have entered Japan clandestinely by boat, and their true numbers cannot be accurately calculated. In 2002, 8,388 foreigners were apprehended while attempting to enter Japan illegally (6,201 through airports, 2,187 by boat), and this number is estimated to represent only 10 percent of the total number of immigrants smuggled into Japan illegally (Friman 2001: 298). If we factor in these different types of unauthorized immigration, the illegal immigrant worker population in Japan is probably well over 300,000.

Human Rights, Citizenship, and Social Integration

The Japanese government's restrictive immigration policy prohibiting unskilled foreign workers, as well as the disingenuous importation of foreign workers through the side door and back door, have led to serious human rights abuses—"entertainers" who are forced into sex work and

[25] The number of visa overstayers has dropped notably in the last decade by about 70,000.

"trainees" who are exploited as cheap, unskilled laborers. Even the relatively privileged nikkeijin are sometimes deceived by labor brokers, who promise easier jobs and higher pay than are available. Unauthorized immigrants in Japan sometimes toil under poor working conditions, receive low wages, lack standard worker rights and protections, and have no access to adequate medical insurance and care. Those who are apprehended are detained in facilities that do not meet international standards, where they sometimes remain for over two years if they do not have proper documents or sufficient funds to be deported (*Daily Yomiuri*, April 25, 2002).

To date, the Japanese government has done little to improve the human rights situation of these foreign workers. Very few of them have obtained formal citizen or denizen status, which would accord them essential rights and protections. Japan has a *jus sanguinis* ("right of blood") nationality law, and therefore grants citizenship only to the descendants of Japanese nationals.[26] In addition, it is quite difficult for foreign residents to become naturalized Japanese citizens. Although naturalization requirements seem uncomplicated,[27] the paperwork requirements are onerous, discouraging many from applying and causing others to be turned down even before submitting an application (Kashiwazaki 2000: 442–43). In addition, Ministry of Justice officials continue to exercise considerable discretion in determining whether applicants have met the requirements for Japanese citizenship. Even when an applicant's paperwork is in order, these officials have denied citizenship on the grounds that the individual has not demonstrated good moral conduct (for instance, if a person has a previous minor legal infraction such as a traffic violation) or has not shown sufficient indications of cultural assimilation (especially if the applicant refuses to adopt a Japanese name, even though this is no longer legally required). Although a number of Korean Japanese have become naturalized Japanese citizens (most are second- and third-generation descendants of Koreans who im-

---

[26] In the past, Japanese citizenship could only be inherited patrilineally. However, because this discriminated against women, the government amended the nationality law in 1984 and now grants citizenship to those born to either a Japanese mother or father.

[27] The requirements are: five consecutive years of residence in Japan, twenty or more years of age, good moral conduct, economic stability and independence, renunciation of previous nationality, and lack of current or previous membership in subversive, anti–Japanese government organizations.

migrated to Japan before and during World War II),[28] few recent immigrants have been willing or able to naturalize.

In addition, until recently it was very difficult for "newcomer" immigrants to become denizens by acquiring permanent residence (which required twenty years of residence in Japan). In 1998 there were only 93,364 permanent residents (a mere 6.2 percent of the total number of legally registered foreigners in Japan), and a number of these were former refugees or spouses of Japanese nationals. Since then, the Ministry of Justice seems to have relaxed the requirements, taking into consideration an applicant's overall contribution to Japanese society as well as his or her personal situation (such as being married to a Japanese national). By 2002 the number of denizens had increased by 140 percent, to 223,875 (12 percent of the total of legally registered foreigners). The much larger population of "special permanent residents" (489,900 in 2002) comprises mainly Korean Japanese and members of other older immigrant minority groups ("oldcomers"), most of whom immigrated before the end of World War II.

As Christian Joppke notes (2001: 59–60), a nation-state can have restrictive rights for immigrants but grant liberal naturalization opportunities, or it can make naturalization restrictive but grant considerable rights to noncitizen immigrants. Unfortunately, the Japanese government has maintained a restrictive policy toward both naturalization and immigrant rights. Indeed, it seems to be increasingly concerned with maintaining a strict immigration control policy and strengthening border enforcement, and it has given no serious consideration to immigrants' social integration and rights. In the fourteen years since the revised Immigration Control Act was implemented, there has been no discernable shift in the Japanese government's closed-door immigration policy. In fact, a 1999 report issued by the Economic Planning Agency recommended that the government maintain its policy of not accepting unskilled foreign workers (OECD 2000: 214; cf. Sellek 2001: 106–107). In 2000 the Ministry of Justice released a new basic immigration control plan that mainly reiterates current policy directions (despite acknowledging the long-term settlement of immigrant workers in Japan). Therefore, the government is unlikely to consider a liberalization of its immigration, citizenship, or naturalization laws in the near future.

---

[28] However, a good number of Korean Japanese have not naturalized because they feel it would be equivalent to abandoning their Korean identity and heritage.

Indeed, recent policy changes have focused mainly on measures to tighten immigration control in order to reduce illegal immigration to Japan and to address domestic security concerns over international terrorism[29] and the country's rising crime rate (attributed in part to foreigners). In 1998 the government began imposing draconian fines and prison sentences on various types of immigrant smugglers (and those who assist them). New penalties were also implemented against visa overstayers beginning in February 2000. Accompanying these measures, there have been stepped-up inspections at airports and seaports, increased screening of visa applicants[30] and airline passengers, increases in the number of immigration officials, a pilot program to introduce machine-readable visas at Japanese embassies, and biometric scanning to prevent illegal entry by foreigners. The government also plans to institute new laws to crack down on human trafficking. Because of increasing public concern over rising foreigner crime (fueled by exaggerated media reporting), the government has determined to halve the number of illegal immigrants in Japan by mobilizing immigration officers and police as part of a plan (backed by the prime minister and Cabinet) to keep Japan one of the safest countries in the world.

Because of the government's current preoccupation with immigration control, it will be some time before immigrant social integration and citizenship rights will enter the policy-making agenda. In fact, the Japanese government's continued insistence that all foreign workers are strictly temporary has allowed it to avoid providing them with extensive social services and rights. Regardless of the government's official stance, however, immigrants are beginning to settle for the long term, if not permanently, in Japanese society (see Okuda 2000; Sellek 2001: 104–106; Tajima 2000: 361). Immigrant settlement is most advanced among the nikkeijin; many have brought their families to Japan and have been living there for

---

[29] Although Japan appears untouched by international terrorism, there have been recent Al Qaeda threats connected to Japan's decision to send Self-Defense Forces to Iraq. In addition, Japanese authorities recently realized that an Al Qaeda agent had repeatedly and clandestinely entered Japan during 2002–2003, and they arrested a number of foreigners in connection with the investigation. Nonetheless, Chikako Kashiwazaki (2000: 463) argues that the Japanese government has grossly exaggerated the international security threat and has used it as a pretext for maintaining strict control over immigration and citizenship.

[30] Most notably, the Ministry of Justice has tightened screening procedures for pre-college student and entertainment visas, which are widely abused.

years (Tsuda 1999b).[31] Among other foreign workers, the average stay in Japan had already reached five years by 1996, and over half of the immigrants from the Philippines, China, and Thailand wanted to settle in Japan (1996 survey, in Komai 2001: 66–67). Even among visa overstayers, nearly half have been in Japan for at least three years (Komai 2001: 70–71). Highly visible immigrant communities have sprouted in parts of Tokyo and in outlying Japanese industrial cities and towns in Gunma and Aichi prefectures. These populations are supported by a vast array of ethnic businesses, churches, employment agencies, and ethnic media (see Okuda 2000; Okuda and Tajima 1992, 1993; Tajima 2000: 361; Tsuda 2003).

Despite the long-term settlement of immigrants in Japanese society, the economic and social rights that the Japanese government has granted them remain very basic and insufficient. Nominally, Japan's labor laws and protections apply to foreign workers regardless of their legal status. In reality, however, several factors — unscrupulous employers, insufficient reporting and oversight, and fear of apprehension — make foreign workers especially vulnerable to labor law violations (see Terasawa 2000). Most foreign workers are eligible for national or employer-provided health insurance as well as the national pension plan and public housing. However, foreign workers and their employers sometimes are reluctant to join these health insurance programs for a number of reasons, and immigrants who are in Japan illegally are ineligible for the national health plan.

Local Government and Social Integration Programs

Because the Japanese national government has done little to provide basic rights and social services to immigrants, it has been left to local governments to integrate the foreign residents who have settled in their neighborhoods and communities (see Kashiwazaki 2000: 462–63; Tegtmeyer Pak 2000). Municipal governments in cities with large immigrant populations have generally been receptive, providing foreign workers with language classes and translation services, information handbooks and pamphlets, consultation services (for personal, legal, employment, and social welfare issues), public housing, health insurance and emergency medical coverage, assistance with alien registration, and even limited political representation

---

[31] The Japanese government allows the immigration of family members only for the Latin American nikkeijin, who are permitted to bring their spouses to Japan on the same visas, even if they are not of Japanese descent. The right of family reunification has been denied to all other foreign workers.

through foreigner advisory councils (see Miyajima and Kajita 1996; Tegt-meyer Pak 2000 and this volume). In order to promote inter-ethnic interaction and understanding in local communities, a number of local governments have also established international exchange offices, which organize special events, festivals, and cultural activities to bring Japanese and foreign residents together. Although immigrants are not legally obliged to send their children to school, it is widely recognized that foreign children have a right to receive education and local communities have required immigrants to enroll their children in Japanese schools (Sellek 2001: 201). Local schools with large numbers of foreign students have designed "Japanese classes" with specially trained teachers, developed teaching manuals, hired personal tutors and aides, and offered counseling and translation services for foreign students and parents.

Local municipal governments have demonstrated considerable independent policy-making initiative by granting such local citizenship rights and services to their foreign residents (Tegtmeyer Pak 2000: 245). Undoubtedly, this is partly by default, as the national government has effectively withdrawn from this policy domain. Nonetheless, local governments' willingness to take independent action is quite remarkable given that they are pursuing a policy objective that conflicts with that of the national government. By treating foreign workers as settled residents and local citizens, local governments are seemingly challenging the national government, which views immigrants as only temporary labor power. In this, Japan differs notably from Italy and Spain, whose national governments have officially endorsed the social integration of immigrants and delegated to local governments and NGOs the responsibility for crafting and implementing specific programs.

Some scholars have questioned the ability of local governments to provide civic citizenship based on equal rights for all residents (Beauregard and Bounds 2000: 249; Borja and Castells 1997), noting a decline in local governments' power and authority as well as their relative inability to deal with global changes.[32] However, local governments are not merely subordinate service deliverers that merely implement national government poli-

---

[32] Ruppert (2000) and others claim that local governments are losing power and legitimacy because of increasing control by national governments, removal of responsibilities from local to state/prefectural/national governments and NGOs, and a reduction in funding and resources, which has caused a privatization of previous local government functions (cf. Andrew and Goldsmith 1998: 104).

cies. They have become important and independent policymakers in their own right, especially in terms of immigrant social integration (Body-Gendrot and Schain 1992; Isin 2000b: 8–9). Although Japan's relatively centralized governmental system limits independent action by localities in a number of ways (more so perhaps than in some Euro-American countries), local governments have shown considerable autonomy in certain policy areas.[33] Since the 1960s they have engaged in progressive local policy making in areas ignored by the national government or in active opposition to national priorities (Jain 1989; Tegtmeyer Pak 2000: 245; Steiner 1980).[34] Likewise, in terms of immigrant citizenship and social integration, localities in Japan have emerged as innovative policymakers and the main source of rights and services for foreign residents.

There are a number of reasons why local governments have become actively engaged in immigrant social integration policy and citizenship rights despite the absence of local electoral pressure[35] and the lack of support or guidance from the national government (see Tegtmeyer Pak 2000, 2001). Unlike national governments, localities cannot ignore the foreign residents in their midst who have social needs that cannot be neglected without negative social repercussions on the surrounding community. In particular, local governments are concerned about the potential for conflict between Japanese and foreign residents, and they realize that proactive immigrant incorporation policies can do much to relieve local tensions. In addition, local governments are legally responsible for the welfare of all local residents (including foreign ones), and they benefit from immigrants, who support the local economy as workers, consumers, and taxpayers.[36]

---

[33] This is especially true for policies that do not require large amounts of financing from the central government (cf. Samuels 1983).

[34] According to Muramatsu (1988: 125), local governments in this period began to realize that they could confront the central government and began amassing political resources for autonomous action and assertion against the central government. This author argues that when local governments have independent projects they wish to implement, they have been willing to do so even at the risk of being sanctioned for challenging central government policy (1988: 108–109).

[35] Since immigrants have not been granted local voting rights, they are not political constituents whose demands local politicians and officials must satisfy in order to be elected to office.

[36] Tegtmeyer Pak (2000: 268–69) notes that local governments have not implemented immigrant incorporation programs in direct response to the local economic contributions of foreign workers. In fact, there has been little pres-

NGOs and academics representing foreign workers have lobbied local governments for immigrant rights, especially because the national government has been unresponsive in this area.[37] Finally, local governments have created an autonomous policy-making space for themselves by conveniently appropriating and redefining the national government's project of "local internationalization" to include immigrant incorporation programs.[38]

NGO Service Providers and Immigrant Activism

Nongovernmental organizations have also been active in providing services and rights to local immigrant residents. Although local governments have been much more inclusionary of foreign workers than has the national government, their citizenship still has limits because it does not encompass the most marginalized of foreign workers—the undocumented. Local officials feel that their social incorporation programs cannot include illegal foreign workers, who generally do not register with municipal governments and are therefore not considered part of the local community (Tegtmeyer Pak 2000: 250).[39] In fact, under Japanese immigration law, all government officials are required to report illegal immigrants to the Immigration Bureau (Komai 2001: 121). As a result, local NGOs have stepped in to provide undocumented foreigners with basic services and to protect their human rights, thereby granting them a limited form of local citizenship by implicitly recognizing them as legitimate local residents, even if municipal governments have not.

---

sure from local businesses employing immigrant workers to provide their employees with rights and services.

[37] This type of impact that local citizenship movements and NGOs exert on municipal governments has been one important reason why local governments in Japan have engaged in progressive and independent policy making since the 1960s. Body-Gendrot and Schain (1992) note that interest groups have also worked through local governments in the United States and France in an effort to influence immigrant policy.

[38] The national government's local internationalization programs also included funding for localities and the authority to raise funds locally (see Tegtmeyer Pak 2001: 15–16).

[39] The notable exceptions are local schools, which require even the children of illegal immigrants to attend as long as they have local addresses and emergency medical coverage, which some local governments have offered to illegal foreign workers (Sellek 2001: 149–52, 201).

Shipper (2002) counts about two hundred NGOs assisting foreign workers in Japan.[40] Many are volunteer citizens groups supported primarily by donations, foundations, membership and service fees, and local governments. They assist unauthorized immigrants to resolve labor disputes and problems with abusive employers; to gain access to medical services and coverage, education, and housing; and to handle issues related to immigration status, apprehension, and detention. Others are faith-based (mainly Christian) NGOs or women's support groups that protect immigrant women from prostitution, sexual exploitation, and violence (both at work and at home). In addition, Japanese Christian churches have welcomed foreigners into their congregations, providing an informal means of social support. Japanese community labor unions[41] have also been somewhat involved in the defense of migrant workers' rights, interceding in cases of employer exploitation, labor law violations, or workplace accidents. Some professional associations also assist foreign workers. These include medical support groups that offer low-cost treatment, medical information, translation and consultation services, health insurance, and assistance in the case of workplace accidents. Lawyer associations have published human rights handbooks for immigrants and offered legal consultation services to resolve various types of disputes. Although many NGOs primarily assist unauthorized immigrants, they also serve legal foreign residents. Nikkeijin immigrants from Latin America have been active in creating their own NGOs, such as those that Keiko Yamanaka analyzes in her chapter in this book.

Although local governments and NGOs are generally serving two different immigrant constituencies (legal versus illegal foreign workers), their efforts are not mutually exclusive. Local governments support NGO networks (sometimes including financial support), and NGO service providers lobby local governments, request their assistance, and work with them to develop programs (see Tegtmeyer Pak 2000 and in this volume; Shipper 2002). However, Keiko Yamanaka (this volume) argues that local governments have a tendency to rely too much on NGOs for some immigrant service delivery and community outreach, so that grassroots organizations

---

[40] For descriptions of these organizations, see Roberts 2000; Shipper 2002; Terasawa 2000.

[41] Most of Japan's workers are organized in company-specific enterprise unions, not by industry. However, since foreign workers are not formal employees of these companies (virtually all are on temporary contracts), they can only join community unions (Shipper 2002: 20).

end up doing much of the work that is the responsibility of local governments.

Clearly, NGOs are not mere service providers for marginalized foreign residents, but activist organizations that defend and fight for these residents' rights. In this sense, citizenship is not simply a conferral of rights; it has an active, performative dimension in which its boundaries are contested and challenged by marginalized, excluded groups (cf. Chung 2002; Isin 2000b; Marx 1996). Again, local cities have become the primary site for such claims-making and activism because they are where the socioeconomic inequalities produced by global capital are most concentrated,[42] causing disadvantaged and marginalized immigrant groups to mobilize politically for citizenship rights (Marx 1996; Sassen 1999, 2000).

NGOs have struggled to improve immigrant rights in a number of ways. First, by offering rights and services to unauthorized immigrant residents, they have contested and expanded the local government's definition of who is a legitimate community member worthy of local citizenship. Second, they have protected and defended foreign workers whose human rights have been infringed by unscrupulous employers who violate labor laws or force women into prostitution, by husbands who abuse their immigrant wives, by local businesses or landlords that discriminate against foreigners, and by a national government that does not provide health coverage to undocumented immigrants and detains them in inhumane conditions. In addition, NGOs often monitor compliance with laws and regulations that apply to foreign workers (especially in the workplace), helping to ensure that they are properly implemented (see Milly and Lim, both in this volume). Finally, they have fought to expand foreign workers' rights through lobbying of local and national governments, legal action through the courts, appeals to international human rights conventions and organizations, and grassroots political mobilization.

SUMMARY OF THE BOOK

The chapters in this book examine the various dimensions of local citizenship in Japan, with comparative case studies from South Korea, Italy, and Spain. In chapter 2, Chikako Usui provides demographic context for Japan's transition to a recent country of immigration and its future depend-

---

[42] According to Sassen (2001), cities affected by globalization are characterized by both a concentration of the capitalist managerial elite and marginalized, low-income service workers (including immigrants).

ence on foreign workers. After outlining the causes of the country's demographic crisis, which has forced the importation of foreign workers, Usui notes that replacement migration is only a temporary solution. The numbers of foreign workers needed to maintain Japan's demographic balance and support its expanding elderly population are simply too large to be feasible, especially given the social issues raised by immigrant settlement and social integration. For the long term, Japan will have to rely on continued restructuring to a post-Fordist technology and service economy that will increase the labor productivity and carrying capacity of its shrinking working-age population. The country already has the competitive dynamism and human resources to make such a transition possible. Although such restructuring may prevent heavy future dependence on low-skilled foreign workers, Usui also outlines why the demand for immigrant labor has become structurally embedded in Japan and how the government has imported unskilled foreign laborers through various side-door policies. Given the likelihood of future increases in the immigrant population, Usui advises that local communities begin dealing with the serious immigrant integration issues they currently face.

Part II of this volume examines the ways in which municipal governments and NGOs in Japan are transforming foreign residents into local citizens by offering them basic rights and services. In chapter 3, Katherine Tegtmeyer Pak examines the immigrant social incorporation programs that local governments have created in various cities. Although municipal governments have used the local internationalization movement endorsed by the national government to legitimate their local citizenship policies, there is considerable regional variation in these programs. Nonetheless, similar immigrant incorporation programs have arisen across Japan's municipalities because of horizontal policy diffusion and cooperation among local governments, creating some uniformity in this type of local citizenship. Tegtmeyer Pak notes how local citizenship is decoupling substantive citizenship from formal (juridical) citizenship by enabling foreigners to obtain rights even though they lack national citizenship. By serving as strategic arenas for the development of alternative forms of citizenship, localities are allowing immigrants to "overcome nationality." As a result, recent immigrants and their descendants ("newcomers") will be less marginalized than previous immigrant groups (mainly the Korean Japanese "oldcomers"). Although there are limits to local citizenship and questions about whether it can become a true alternative to national citizenship, it promises to remain quite resilient.

In chapter 4, Keiko Yamanaka shifts the discussion to NGO service providers as another means through which localities have promoted local citizenship rights and services. Yamanaka focuses specifically on Hamamatsu City, which has one of the highest concentrations of immigrants in Japan. Although the municipal government envisions the incorporation of foreign residents into its community through services, rights, and multicultural programs, it has relied on local grassroots organizations to do much of the actual service delivery and outreach. Japanese citizen NGOs (many staffed by women who have lived abroad) have run programs to teach the Japanese language to immigrant children and assist them in Japanese schools. Yamanaka also examines an independent effort by Japanese Brazilian nikkeijin to create an informal support network for their children's Japanese schooling and to organize cultural exchange activities with Japanese parents. This effort evolved into a nikkeijin association that (along with other NGOs) asked the local government to support an after-school program to teach Portuguese. However, municipal officials were more interested in having Japanese taught in this program in order to encourage more nikkeijin children to attend Japanese schools. Despite the collaboration between this nikkeijin association and Japanese NGOs, the former has fallen into crisis because of declining membership, inconsistent leadership, and internal fragmentation. Yamanaka concludes by arguing that Japan's local efforts at multiculturalism with regard to immigrants seem to be mainly cosmetic and are actually attempts to contain cultural difference through assimilation and the creation of national cultural homogeneity.

Part III of the volume focuses on the fight for local immigrant citizenship in Japan by activist NGOs and through the courts. In chapter 5, Deborah Milly analyzes the impact of local NGO advocacy organizations on the national government's immigrant policy. Not only have these NGOs lobbied local governments on behalf of foreign workers, they have also pressured the national government to change problematic administrative practices and improve the implementation of laws and programs to better protect foreign workers. Milly looks specifically at the activities of NGOs that are part of the National Network in Solidarity with Migrant Workers, which has used both confrontational tactics (protests, demonstrations, petitions) and cooperative approaches (informal meetings with officials, giving testimony during legislative deliberations). Milly examines how these NGOs have lobbied the national government on three issues: (1) clarification and expansion of the criteria the government uses to grant limited amnesty to undocumented immigrants; (2) better access to medical care and social welfare for legal foreign residents through improved implementation of current programs; and (3) abusive treatment of trainees through widespread employer violations of trainee program regulations. Activist NGOs have monitored local compliance with laws and regulations by informing the government about insufficient implementation of immigrant policies and social welfare programs. Because such problems often result from a lack of coordination between a multitude of relevant national and regional government agencies, the attention that NGOs have drawn to the issue has led to improved communication between localities and the national government and among national government agencies. Nonetheless, Milly concludes that the impact of NGO activism on the national government has been limited and indirect. Despite NGOs' recent gains, the process of securing immigrant rights remains informal and inherently unstable, as well as vulnerable to reversals, as shown by the recent government crackdown on illegal foreign workers.

In chapter 6 Amy Gurowitz considers the international dimension of local citizenship, focusing on legal activism. Given that foreign workers enjoy few legal rights and protections under Japanese domestic law, legal activism for immigrants has relied on international legal norms and rights to expand immigrant rights in Japan. Gurowitz argues that Japan has been sensitive to international standards since the Meiji restoration, when it began modernizing in an attempt to catch up to Western countries. Japan is still under external and domestic pressure to become more globally engaged and responsible—and more receptive to foreigners at home. This has allowed legal activists for foreign workers to invoke the ideology of internationalization, claiming that Japan is not complying with international norms on immigrant rights.

In the past, domestic NGOs successfully lobbied the government to ratify a number of international human rights conventions in order to avoid damaging Japan's international reputation, and this improved the situation of Korean Japanese and other immigrant minorities by forcing legislative changes in domestic law. Gurowitz cites examples in which the courts have found domestic practices toward immigrants inconsistent with international standards or ruled in favor of immigrants by referring to international laws and conventions, including those the country has not ratified or to which Japan is not subject. Gurowitz is uncertain whether this trend will continue, given that external pressures on Japan to internationalize have subsided during its current prolonged economic recession.

Part IV offers comparative case studies of local immigrant citizenship in other recent countries of immigration (in roughly the same order as these issues are dealt with in the chapters on Japan). In chapter 7, Harlan Koff notes that in Italy, like Japan, the national government has focused on immigration control and border enforcement, leaving the implementation of immigrant social integration policies to the localities. Significant regional differences have emerged as a result, depending on various local factors. Although Italians are commonly believed to be hospitable to outsiders, Koff notes that the level of hospitality toward immigrants varies significantly by region. It is precisely in Italy's northeastern regions, where the economic need for immigrant labor is greatest, that the local populace is least tolerant of immigrants and anti-immigrant political parties are strongest. This demonstrates that variations in local hospitality toward immigrants (and the intensity of anti-immigrant politics) cannot be explained by socioeconomic factors. Nonetheless, the northeastern regions also have the most extensive and active immigrant integration programs. In other words, levels of hospitality do not determine local immigrant integration policy, which depends more on regional economic factors. Since the northeastern regions are both economically prosperous and dependent on immigrant labor, it behooves them to offer social integration services to immigrants and they have the economic and administrative capacity to do so. In contrast, Italy's south, which is more welcoming toward immigrants, has neither the economic resources nor the need to provide immigrants with proper services and rights. As a result, Koff concludes, local public tolerance toward immigrants does not assure their social participation or their incorporation as local citizens.

In chapter 8, Belén Agrela and Gunther Dietz analyze a similar distribution of policy competence in Spain, where a national government concerned only with immigration control has left immigrant integration policy to the localities, and especially to local NGOs. Because of pressure from the European Union to tighten external borders—along with a national discourse that portrays immigrants as terrorists, criminals, and a cultural threat—Spain's national government is preoccupied with controlling unwanted immigration to an excessive degree, given the low levels of inmigration to Spain. As a result, the immigrants' social integration has become a secondary priority for the government, allowing local NGO service providers to monopolize this policy domain by developing much more expertise and institutional capacity than shown by governmental agencies at the national, regional, and local levels. Agrela and Dietz observe three general trends in the emergence of this multilevel governance of immigration. The first is increasing administrative decentralization, as local regions with strong ethno-national traditions win autonomy to develop their own immigrant integration policies, which, in turn, have contested and influenced the central government's immigration control and citizenship policies. Second, the state's immigrant service delivery functions have been increasingly privatized to local NGOs, despite the government's recent attempts to recover some control over this administrative domain. Third, the immigrant integration programs of local NGOs have been based on an ideology of multiculturalism that essentializes the cultural differences of immigrants, leading to highly specialized and particular programs tailored to each immigrant group. As a result, NGOs' programs are not well-integrated with the more generalized services offered by governmental welfare agencies, leading to a duplication and downgrading of services. Therefore, the delegation of immigrant integration policy to the localities may have allowed NGOs to develop a kind of local immigrant citizenship in the absence of the state, but the nature of this citizenship remains fundamentally problematic.

In his chapter, Timothy Lim examines how political activism by local immigrants and NGOs has dramatically improved immigrant rights in South Korea, a country where human rights violations against foreign workers were worse than those in Japan. South Korea's disproportionately large population of illegal foreign workers has gained worker protections and native-standard wages. In addition, the most abusive aspects of the "trainee" program that South Korea uses to import unskilled foreign workers have been reformed, and a work permit system has been instituted. Lim argues that these changes are a direct result of unrelenting activist pressure by immigrants and NGOs, both through the courts and through direct political mobilization and lobbying of the national government. Despite considerable initial government resistance (especially among ministries beholden to business interests), there has been a fundamental change in the government's outlook; whereas in the past it facilitated Korean businesses' exploitation of foreign workers, it now feels obligated to protect immigrant rights. Nonetheless, the expansion of immigrant rights in South Korea is not unilinear since the government continues to take abusive action against illegal foreign workers and some recent reforms are still inadequate. As a result, political activism will remain a crucial component in the fight for immigrants' rights.

The concluding chapter discusses the limits of local citizenship and activism, focusing on Japan. Unlike national citizenship, local citizenship rights are not geographically uniform; they vary considerably from locality to locality depending on regions' different historical, demographic, and economic conditions. In addition, foreign residents in Japan and other recent countries of immigration view themselves as temporary sojourners. As a result, they often fail to exercise their local rights and utilize local social services as long-term civic participants, or they do so only in emergency situations. Despite a lack of political mobilization among immigrants in Japan to protest human rights abuses or demand better social services, legal advocates and activist NGOs have fought on their behalf to expand their rights and to reform current laws and policies. However, such efforts have been only partly effective. Because of the limits of local citizenship, the national government must become more engaged in immigrant social integration policy and provide necessary guidance and resources to the localities. Ultimately, what is needed is a coordinated effort between national governments and local institutions to develop citizenship and integration policies that respond to local differences and the needs of various immigrant groups, while also providing a comprehensive and uniform set of services and rights to immigrants across localities.

References

Abraham, David. 2002. Citizenship solidarity and rights individualism: On the decline of national citizenship in the U.S., Germany and Israel. CCIS Working Paper No. 53. La Jolla, CA: Center for Comparative Immigration Studies, University of California, San Diego.

Andrew, Caroline, and Michael Goldsmith. 1998. From local government to local governance—and beyond? *International Political Science Review* 19 (2):101–17.

Bauböck, Rainer. 1994. *Transnational citizenship: Membership and rights in international migration.* Aldershot, UK: Edward Elgar.

Beauregard, Robert A., and Anna Bounds. 2000. Urban citizenship. In *Democracy, citizenship, and the global city*, edited by Engin F. Isin. London: Routledge.

Body-Gendrot, Sophie, and Martin A. Schain. 1992. National and local politics and the development of immigration policy in the United States and France: A comparative analysis. In *Immigrants in two democracies: French and American experience*, edited by Donald L. Horowitz and Gerard Noiriel. New York: New York University Press.

Borja, Jordi, and Manuel Castells. 1997. *Local and global: The management of cities in the information age.* London: Earthscan.

Bosniak, Linda. 2001. Denationalizing citizenship. In *Citizenship today: Global perspectives and practices*, edited by T. Alexander Aleinikoff and Douglass Klusmeyer. Washington, DC: Carnegie Endowment for International Peace.

Brubaker, William Rogers. 1989. Membership without citizenship: The economic and social rights of noncitizens. In *Immigration and the politics of citizenship in Europe and North America*, edited by William Rogers Brubaker. New York: University Press of America.

Carens, Joseph H. 1989. Membership and morality: Admission to citizenship in liberal democratic states. In *Immigration and the politics of citizenship in Europe and North America*, edited by William Rogers Brubaker. New York: University Press of America.

Castles, Stephen, and Alastair Davidson. 2000. *Citizenship and migration: Globalization and the politics of belonging*. New York: Routledge.

Chung, Erin Aeran. 2002. Citizenship, identity, and racial politics: A comparative study of Korean communities in the United States and Japan. Paper presented at the annual meeting of the American Political Science Association.

Dagger, Richard. 2000. Metropolis, memory and citizenship. In *Democracy, citizenship, and the global city*, edited by Engin F. Isin. London: Routledge.

Falk, Richard. 1994. The making of global citizenship. In *The condition of citizenship*, edited by Bart van Stennbergen. London: Sage.

Favell, Adrian. 2001. Integration policy and integration research in Europe: A review and critique. In *Citizenship today: Global perspectives and practices*, edited by T. Alexander Aleinikoff and Douglass Klusmeyer. Washington, DC: Carnegie Endowment for International Peace.

Friman, H. Richard. 2001. Immigrants, smuggling, and threats to social order in Japan. In *Global human smuggling: Comparative perspectives*, edited by David Kyle and Rey Koslowski. Baltimore, MD: Johns Hopkins University Press.

Geddes, Andrew. 2000. *Immigration and European integration: Towards fortress Europe?* Manchester, UK: Manchester University Press.

Guiraudon, Virginie. 1998. Citizenship rights for non-citizens: France, Germany, and the Netherlands. In *Challenge to the nation-state: Immigration in Western Europe and the United States*, edited by Christian Joppke. Oxford: Oxford University Press.

Guiraudon, Virginie, and Gallya Lahav. 2000. A reappraisal of the state sovereignty debate: The case of migration control. *Comparative Political Studies* 33 (2):163–95.

Gurowitz, Amy. 1999. Mobilizing international norms: Domestic actors, immigrants, and the Japanese state. *World Politics* 51 (3):413–45.

Hammar, Tomas. 1990. *Democracies and the nation state: Aliens, denizens and citizens in a world of international migration*. Aldershot, UK: Avebury.

———. 1992. Laws and policies regulating population movements: A European perspective. In *International migration systems: A global approach*, edited by

Mary M. Kritz, Lin Lean Lim, and Hania Zlotnik. New York: Oxfoi versity Press.

Holston, James, and Arjun Appadurai. 1999. Cities and citizenship. In *Cities and citizenship*, edited by James Holston. Durham, NC: Duke University Press.

Ishihara, Takumi. 1992. *Gaikokujin Koyo no Honne to Tatemae: Rodoryoku Sakoku no Ura de Nani ga Okite Iru Ka*. Tokyo: Shodensha.

Isin, Engin F., ed. 2000a. *Democracy, citizenship, and the global city*. London: Routledge.

———. 2000b. Introduction: Democracy, citizenship, and the city. In *Democracy, citizenship, and the global city*, edited by Engin F. Isin. London: Routledge.

Jacobson, David. 1996. *Rights across borders: Immigration and the decline of citizenship*. Baltimore, MD: Johns Hopkins University Press.

Jain, Purnendra. 1989. *Local politics and policymaking in Japan*. New Delhi: Commonwealth.

Joppke, Christian. 1999. How immigration is changing citizenship: A comparative view. *Ethnic and Racial Studies* 22 (4):629–52.

———. 2001. The evolution of alien rights in the United States, Germany, and European Union. In *Citizenship today: Global perspectives and practices*, edited by T. Alexander Aleinikoff and Douglass Klusmeyer. Washington, DC: Carnegie Endowment for International Peace.

Kajita, Takamichi. 1994. *Gaikokujin Rodosha to Nihon*. Tokyo: NHK Books.

Kashiwazaki, Chikako. 2000. Citizenship in Japan: Legal practice and contemporary development. In *From migrants to citizens: Membership in a changing world*, edited by T. Alexander Aleinikoff and Douglass Klusmeyer. Washington, DC: Carnegie Endowment for International Peace.

Komai, Hiroshi. 1992. Are foreign trainees in Japan disguised cheap laborers? *Migration World* 20:13–17.

———. 1995. *Migrant workers in Japan*. Trans. Jens Wilkinson. London: Kegan Paul International.

———. 2001. *Foreign migrants in contemporary Japan*. Trans. Jens Wilkinson. Melbourne, Australia: Trans Pacific Press.

Koslowski, Rey. 2000. *Migrants and citizens: Demographic change in the European state system*. Ithaca, NY: Cornell University Press.

Linklater, A. 1998. Cosmopolitan citizenship. *Citizenship Studies* 2 (1):23–41.

Loescher, Gilbert. 1993. *Beyond charity: International cooperation and the global refugee crisis*. Oxford: Oxford University Press.

Marx, Anthony W. 1996. Contested citizenship: The dynamics of racial identity and social movements. In *Citizenship, identity and social history*, edited by Charles Tilly. Cambridge: Cambridge University Press.

Miller, Mark J. 1992. Evolution of policy modes for regulating international labour migration. In *International migration systems: A global approach*, edited by Mary M. Kritz, Lin Lean Lim, and Hania Zlotnik. New York: Oxford University Press.

Miyajima, Takashi. 1993. *Gaikokujin Rodosha to Nihon Shakai.* Tokyo: Akashi Shoten.

Miyajima, Takashi, and Takamichi Kajita, eds. 1996. *Gaijkokujin Rodosha kara Shimin e.* Tokyo: Yuhikaku.

Money, Jeannette. 1999. *Fences and neighbors: The political geography of immigration control.* Ithaca, NY: Cornell University Press.

Muramatsu, Michio. 1988. *Local power in the Japanese state.* Berkeley: University of California Press.

OECD (Organisation for Economic Co-operation and Development). 2000. *Trends in international migration: Annual report 2000 edition.* Paris: OECD.

Oishi, Nana. 1995. Training or employment? Japanese immigration policy in dilemma. *Asian and Pacific Migration Journal* 4 (2–3):367–85.

Oka, Takashi. 1994. Prying open the door: Foreign workers in Japan. Contemporary Issues Paper No. 2. Washington, DC: Carnegie Endowment for International Peace.

Okuda, Michihiro. 2000. Asian newcomers in Shinjuku and Ikebukuro areas, 1988–1998: Reflections on a decade of research. *Asian and Pacific Migration Journal* 9 (3):343–48.

Okuda, Michihiro, and Junko Tajima, eds. 1992. *Ikebukuro no Ajiakei Gaikokujin: Shakaigakuteki Jittai Hokoku.* Tokyo: Mekon.

———. 1993. *Shinjuku no Ajiakei Gaikokujin: Shakaigakuteki Jittai Hokoku.* Tokyo: Mekon.

Ong, Aihwa. 1996. Cultural citizenship as subject-making: Immigrants negotiate racial and cultural boundaries in the United States. *Current Anthropology* 37 (5):737–62.

———. 1999. *Flexible citizenship: The cultural logics of transnationality.* Durham, NC: Duke University Press.

Roberts, Glenda S. 2000. NGO support for migrant labor in Japan. In *Japan and global migration: Foreign workers and the advent of a multicultural society,* edited by Mike Douglass and Glenda S. Roberts. London: Routledge.

Ruppert, Evelyn S. 2000. Who governs the global city? In *Democracy, citizenship, and the global city,* edited by Engin F. Isin. London: Routledge.

Samuels, Richard J. 1983. *The politics of regional policy in Japan: Localities incorporated?* Princeton, NJ: Princeton University Press.

Sassen, Saskia. 1998. The *de facto* transnationalizing of immigration policy. In *Challenge to the nation-state: Immigration in Western Europe and the United States,* edited by Christian Joppke. Oxford: Oxford University Press.

———. 1999. Whose city is it? Globalization and the formation of new claims. In *Cities and citizenship,* edited by James Holston. Durham, NC: Duke University Press.

———. 2000. The global city: Strategic site/new frontier. In *Democracy, citizenship, and the global city,* edited by Engin F. Isin. London: Routledge.

———. 2001. *The global city: New York, London, Tokyo.* Princeton, NJ: Princ__
University Press.

Schuck, Peter H. 1989. Membership in the liberal polity: The devaluation of
American citizenship. In *Immigration and the politics of citizenship in Europe
and North America,* edited by William Rogers Brubaker. New York: University Press of America.

Sellek, Yoko. 2001. *Migrant labour in Japan.* New York: Palgrave.

Seol, Dong-Hoon, and John Skrentny. n.d. How do international norms affect
domestic politics? A comparison of migrant worker and women's rights in
South Korea. Manuscript.

Shipper, Apichai W. 2002. *Pragmatism in activism: Organizing support for illegal
foreign workers in Japan.* Cambridge, MA: Program on U.S.-Japan Relations,
Harvard University.

Soysal, Yasemin N. 1994. *Limits of citizenship: Migrants and postnational membership in Europe.* Chicago: University of Chicago Press.

Steiner, Kurt. 1980. Toward a framework for the study of local opposition. In
Political opposition and local politics in Japan, edited by Kurt Steiner, Ellis S.
Krauss, and Scott C. Flanagan. Princeton, NJ: Princeton University Press.

Stennbergen, Bart van. 1994. Towards a global ecological citizen. In *The condition of citizenship,* edited by Bart van Stennbergen. London: Sage.

Tajima, Junko. 2000. A study of Asian immigrants in global city Tokyo. *Asian
and Pacific Migration Journal* 9 (3):349–64.

Tegtmeyer Pak, Katherine. 2000. Foreigners are local citizens, too: Local governments respond to international migration in Japan. In *Japan and global
migration: Foreign workers and the advent of a multicultural society,* edited by
Mike Douglass and Glenda S. Roberts. London: Routledge.

———. 2001. Towards local citizenship: Japanese cities respond to international
migration. CCIS Working Paper No. 30. La Jolla, CA: Center for Comparative Immigration Studies, University of California, San Diego.

Terasawa, Katsuko. 2000. Labor law, civil law, immigration law and the reality
of migrants and their children. In *Japan and global migration: Foreign workers
and the advent of a multicultural society,* edited by Mike Douglass and Glenda
S. Roberts. London: Routledge.

Tsuda, Takeyuki. 1999a. The motivation to migrate: The ethnic and sociocultural constitution of the Japanese-Brazilian return migration system. *Economic Development and Cultural Change* 48 (1):1–31.

———. 1999b. The permanence of "temporary" migration: The "structural
embeddedness" of Japanese-Brazilian migrant workers in Japan. *Journal of
Asian Studies* 58 (3):687–722.

———. 2003. *Strangers in the ethnic homeland: Japanese Brazilian return migration
in transnational perspective.* New York: Columbia University Press.

Tsuda, Takeyuki, and Wayne Cornelius. 2004. Japan: Government policy, immigrant reality. In *Controlling immigration: A global perspective,* edited by

Wayne A. Cornelius, Takeyuki Tsuda, Philip L. Martin, and James F. Hollifield. 2d ed. Stanford, CA: Stanford University Press.

Turner, Bryan S. 1994. Postmodern culture/modern citizens. In *The condition of citizenship*, edited by Bart van Stennbergen. London: Sage.

Urry, John. 2000. Global flows and global citizenship. In *Democracy, citizenship, and the global city*, edited by Engin F. Isin. London: Routledge.

Zolberg, Aristide R. 1992. Labour migration and international economic re-
gimes: Bretton Woods and after. In *International migration systems: A global approach*, edited by Mary M. Kritz, Lin Lean Lim, and Hania Zlotnik. New York: Oxford University Press.

CHAPTER **2**

Japan's Demographic Future and the Challenge of Foreign Workers

CHIKAKO USUI

Japan has become a poster child for demographic aging and all its collateral economic, social, and political issues. It has one of the most rapidly aging populations among advanced nations due to long life expectancy, falling fertility rates, and low immigration; and the growth rate of the population, which has declined for the last thirty years, is currently at zero. The population is projected to peak in 2005 at 127.7 million persons and then decline to 105 million by 2050 (United Nations 2001; Ministry of Health, Labor, and Welfare 2002). As Japan's population grows smaller and older, the share of the population that is of working age will continue its decline. In 2000 the working-age population (aged 15–64) constituted 68 percent of the total population, but by 2025 it is projected to drop to 59.7 percent, while the percentage of those over 65 years of age will increase to 26.7 percent of the population. By the middle of the twenty-first century, one Japanese person in three will be over age 65, and more than half the population will be above age 50 (Horlacher 2002: 54).

   The economic recession that began in the mid-1990s has invited anxious views about Japan's ability to produce the output needed to support the baby-boom cohorts reaching retirement age in the early twenty-first century. Many observers worry whether Japan will be able to meet future obligations without wrecking the economy, even though Japan is better positioned than many other advanced countries with regard to pension reform and controlled health-care spending (Campbell 2003, citing OECD report). Since the mid-1980s, Japanese policymakers have reassessed budget priorities and reformed national pension and health-care systems in response to this aging of the population. Reforms include a reduction of future public pension benefits, increases in the age of eligibility for public pensions, increased pension contributions, a raised corporate mandatory retirement age, and the introduction of national long-term-care insurance.[1]

Some demographers and economists have called for open immigration to Japan and a greater infusion of foreign workers to offset the decline in the working-age population as a share of total population. Pointing to the use of foreign migrant labor to adjust for aging populations in Europe and the United States,[2] these experts contend that foreign migration will offset the

---

[1] According to Campbell (2003), Japan went through four phases of welfare state development. First, Japan made its national pension available to everyone (universal coverage) in 1959. Second, pension benefits were expanded during the "old people boom" of the 1970s. Third, the pension system was exposed to possible retrenchment in the late 1970s and early 1980s when conservative policymakers were concerned with future financial implications of following the Western-style welfare model; instead of retrenchment, several incremental reforms (that affect future retirees) took place during this phase. The fourth, current, phase involves a significant expansion of programs to keep frail elderly independent as long as possible. This phase began with the Gold Plan of 1989 and culminated in the introduction of the National Long-Term-Care Insurance program in 1997 (implemented in 2000). Recent and current pension reforms include benefit reduction (20 percent by 2025), increase in retirement age from 60 to 65 (to be implemented in 2013–2025), introduction (in 2002) of an earnings test for ages 65 to 69, elimination of delayed retirement with additional benefits, and no employer contribution to social security during child-care leaves. In addition, the 2000 health-care reform included a 20 percent co-payment for salaried workers (co-pays were zero in 1973–1984 and 10 percent in 1984–2000). Japan's pension expenditures were 8 percent of GDP in 1997 and are expected to rise to 8.5 percent in 2050. Health-care expenditures accounted for 7 percent of GDP (compared to 13 percent in the United States, 11 percent in Germany, 9 percent in Canada, and 7.3 percent in the United Kingdom). Another important point about the aging challenge is that it is a gradual process. It can be managed without undue strain if the economy grows at a steady rate. For example, Schulz (1995) suggests that a 1 percent increase per year in social security obligation is a reasonable adjustment. If Japan were to increase its payroll tax rate from 32.3 percent in 2000 (divided equally between worker and employer) to 46.2 percent by 2050 — that is, 14 percent over 50 years — it would meet its goal.

[2] European countries imported large numbers of (primarily unskilled) foreign workers when their economies expanded rapidly after World War II, not to counter population declines. However, these countries, especially Germany and France, used immigration policies to sustain population growth. West Germany gained 11.2 million people between 1951 and 1984, 7.8 million of them through immigration. France's total population increased by 14.5 million

collateral effects of Japan's aging population, such as a decline in gross domestic product (GDP), depressed domestic consumption and future investment, declining tax revenues, and an imminent fiscal crisis (Hewitt 2003: 5–6). Increasing the size of the working population through migration is expected to counteract these effects of population aging by raising tax revenues, stimulating consumption, and helping finance the social security systems (Tanimura 2000: 3–4; Mori 1997; Martin 2001).

This chapter examines a demographic solution (such as replacement migration or infusion of foreign labor) to Japan's aging dilemma, but it also addresses economic growth as a more fundamental issue of Japan's future. Japan must hasten its transition to a post-Fordist (information technology) economy as a way of growing the economy out of the ill effects caused by demographic challenges. This position emphasizes knowledge-based production that expands the working population's capacity to support its aging counterpart. This knowledge-based economy will stimulate production and meet the growing needs of an older population, raise tax revenues, and provide for a stable social security system. The first position (with more emphasis on demographic solutions) and the second position (with more emphasis on economic restructuring) are *not* mutually exclusive and might best represent a coordinated policy sequence of short- and long-term adjustment. Migration may provide a short-term treatment of the symptoms until economic restructuring can provide a more fundamental cure.

In this essay, "migration" refers to the movement of people to another country temporarily or long term for economic reasons. Different authors use slightly different terms to describe this movement, including making a distinction between departing migration (emigration) and arriving migration (immigration), international migration (as opposed to internal migration), foreign labor migration, and immigration. In the United States, however, the term "immigrants" refers to those with permanent residency with naturalization (U.S. citizenship), while "non-immigrants" refers to foreigners who are granted temporary entry to the United States for specific purposes, such as working or studying (Martin and Midgley 1999).

---

between 1946 and 1983 (Van de Kaa 1992: 6). The United States recorded some 330,000 immigrants annually during the 1960s, 450,000 per year in the 1970s, and 600,000 per year in the 1980s. The United States experienced its most dramatic immigration influx in the 1990s, with nearly a million a year (Martin and Midgley 1999: 5).

THE PROBLEM OF AN AGING POPULATION: TWO MODELS OF RESPONSE

It bears repeating that Japan is one of the fastest-aging and "oldest" industrialized nations (see table 2.1). The proportion of people aged 65 and above will rise from 17.1 percent in 2000 to 26.7 percent in 2025. Population projection is based on estimates of future fertility, mortality, and net migration. The "aged dependency ratio"—the number of working-age members of the population (15–64 years) divided by the number of "aged" dependents (65 years and over)—is a common measure for gauging the capacity of the younger, working-age population to support an aging society.[3] For example, in 2000, Japan had 3.9 working-age persons for each person 65 years of age and older. However, by 2010, there will be fewer than 3 working-age persons per elder person, and by 2025 the figure is predicted to drop to 2 for every person 65 years or older (see table 2.2). Although the aged dependency ratio has become a conventional tool for measuring the impact of population aging on society, it is loaded with assumptions that color its interpretation. The policy strategies addressing the issues of the aged dependency ratio may be contrasted in two models of population aging with different focuses and different assumptions about the components of the aged dependency ratio.

Table 2.1. People over Age 65 as a Percentage of Total Population

	1985	1995	2000	2005	2025	2050
Japan	**10.3**	**14.6**	**17.1**	**19.2**	**26.7**	**31.8**
Italy	12.7	16.8	18.2	22.6	26.1	34.9
Germany	14.5	15.0	16.4	17.8	23.4	28.4
Sweden	17.9	17.6	17.2	17.6	22.5	27.0
France	12.5	15.0	15.9	16.7	21.7	25.5
U.K.	15.1	15.9	16.0	16.4	21.2	24.9
United States	11.8	12.5	12.5	12.6	18.8	21.7

Sources: United Nations 2001: 8, table 2, and 112–43, appendix. Projections for 2005, 2025, and 2050 based on UN's medium-variant projections. For Sweden, United Nations 1998 was also used.

---

[3] Some prefer the terms "old-age dependency ratio" or "age dependency ratio." The use of aged dependency ratio in this essay follows the usage common among social gerontologists such as Robert Atchley.

Table 2.2. Distribution of Age Groups and Aged Dependency Ratio, Japan

Age	2000	2010	2015	2025
0–14	14.6%	13.4%	12.8%	11.6%
15–64	68.1%	64.1%	61.2%	59.7%
65+	17.4%	22.5%	26.0%	28.7%
(15–64)/(65+)	3.92	2.84	2.36	2.06

Source: National Institute of Population and Social Security Research 2002. The aged dependency ratio was calculated by the author.

The first model treats the two population components of the aged dependency ratio as more or less constant or fixed. That is, the working-age population actively participates in the labor force, while those over age 65 do not. This conventional view is the basis for emphasizing a quantitative labor market solution, with various foreign migration practices as the key responses to demographic aging. Policymakers tend to focus exclusively on the aged dependent population and look for external solutions that reduce the burden of the aged dependent population on the working-age population. People of working age are considered more productive and also higher-level consumers than those aged 65 and over (Atchley 2000: 407). Thus an infusion of foreign workers would solve the demographic imbalance and the collateral economic problems of population aging. The demographic components of "working age" and "aged dependent" tend to be viewed in isolation from the rest of society. Demographic dynamics are viewed only in relation to other demographic features, and there is only a demographic solution to a demographic problem, such as an infusion of population into the productive portion of the population through foreign labor migration.

A second model emphasizes a longer-term policy designed to change the carrying capacity of both components of the aged dependency ratio. This model assumes that demographic changes are an intrinsic part of the social organization of society. Demographic patterns have historically been altered by political, economic, and technological changes in society. In this model, the focus is on both the numerator and the denominator of the aged dependency ratio, because expansion of the productivity (carrying capacity) of the working-age and aged populations decreases the level of dependency for the same proportion of elderly. The productivity and consumption levels of the different age components of the aged dependency ratio are assumed to be more variable and dynamic than is assumed in the first model. The logic that a certain ratio of the working-age population will have to support the dependent population is based on the social organization and economic life cycle that characterized the Fordist economy of the twentieth century. In the twenty-first century, industrialized countries are shifting to a post-Fordist economy with new levels of *productive capacity*. Thus it is more appropriate to address the issue of the aging of Japanese society within the context of the changing social organization and transforming productive capacity of the post-Fordist economy (Usui 2001, 2003).

The relationship between the two models may be complementary, but the models vary in level of policy intervention and coordination. In the first model, the parameters of the aged dependency ratio are more or less fixed, at least for extended periods, while the second model treats these parameters as more malleable, dynamic, and amenable to policy intervention. To address Japan's future labor shortage, for example, the first model emphasizes the importance of foreign migration, while the second model focuses on an economic transition that creates a more efficient use of the labor force. These two models may represent a sequence of strategies wherein the first model provides a demographic bridge to the second model of economic restructuring.

Model One: Replacement Migration and More Use of Foreign Labor

The two principal solutions of the first model include "replacement migration" and the infusion of "temporary foreign workers." Replacement migration is designed to directly stabilize population distribution in Japan, while the infusion of temporary foreign workers is intended to offset the unmet needs of the working-age population. The United Nations presented several scenarios in its proposal to use immigration as a solution to the problems associated with demographic aging. According to UN estimates, Japan would need to import over 380,000 immigrants annually to maintain the size of its *total* population (the projected total population that will peak in 2005–2006). This would mean that by 2050 almost 18 percent of the Japanese population would be composed of immigrants or their descendants (Ministry of Labor 2002; Horlacher 2002: 21). To maintain the *working-age* population at its 1995 level, Japan would need 610,000 immigrants annually from 1995 to 2050. In this case, by 2050 one-third of the total population would be made up of immigrants and their descendants (Ministry of Labor 2002). Neither scenario, however, would prevent an aging of the population. In order to hold the ratio of working-age population to older population at its 1995 level (4.8), Japan would have to admit an average of 10 million immigrants per year over the next 50 years (Ministry of Health, Labor, and Welfare 2002: 7; Tanimura 2000: 4). According to Horlacher (2002: 21), such an immigration policy would maintain the age structure but would increase the total population to 818 million in 2050, and 87 percent of that population would be immigrants or their descendants. Clearly, the numbers required for "replacement population" are simply too large to be practical.

The UN report, with its focus on the aged dependency ratio as the policy standard, illustrates the impracticality of open immigration as a solution to Japan's demographic challenge. This leads to the second principal solution offered by the first model: the infusion of temporary foreign workers to address declines in the aged dependency ratio and related labor market issues. Since the 1980s, the number of migrant foreign workers in Japan has increased steadily, and many observers expect Japan's dependence on foreign labor to increase in the future. Policymakers, scholars, and the media have debated the appropriate mechanisms for recruiting and controlling the flows of foreign labor. The problem with the use of temporary foreign workers is twofold. First, there is a need to address the social and cultural integration of foreign workers and their families, because temporary migration often leads to long-term stays beyond original intentions. Second, the policies devised to import temporary foreign workers treat only the symptoms of an aging society and labor market problems; they are not directed toward providing a cure.

A brief comparison of migration patterns and experiences between Europe and Japan reveals both similarities and differences, depending on workers' skill levels. The movement of foreign workers occurs most often at the top and bottom of the labor market in both Europe and Japan. There is little or no substantive movement at middle skill levels.[4] Foreign workers constitute about 4 percent of the aggregate population of Europe; Europeans account for over 60 percent of the total foreign worker population, Africans 16 percent, and Asians 11 percent (Salt 2000). European countries imported a large number of unskilled workers from the 1950s to the early

---

[4] Workers in mid-range skill levels display the least movement in both the European Union and Japan. In the EU, they exhibit the strongest national identity or loyalty to the host country, partly because of the language and certification requirements they have had to fulfill. When they move, they are more likely to experience career demotion than promotion because their certification is not valued as highly in the new country (Kajita 1994: 61).

1970s to meet acute labor shortages in their expanding economies. Workers can now move freely between European Union countries; the most mobile tend to be top-level or "elite" workers, such as business managers/executives, professionals, and technical workers. The free movement of doctors, nurses, and lawyers, among others, has become more feasible as EU countries have begun devising mutual agreements on the transferability of technical skills and licenses.[5]

Over the past two decades, the Japanese government has opened the door to larger categories of foreign skilled workers in an effort to induce new corporate activities and professional services. Japan is moving quickly to increase both the quality and quantity of its business management, client development, legal, and professional accounting services through the addition of foreign workers. Further, it does not limit its nursing sector to domestic professionals; after fulfilling a language requirement and passing national qualifying exams, foreign nurses can work in Japan for a period of four years. Some private firms are training foreign nurses in anticipation of future policy changes that would allow qualified foreign nurses to settle in Japan for the long term.[6] However, the labor market rigidity that discourages mid-career hiring at large firms, language and certification requirements, and Japanese-style management (such as seniority-based promotion) have held down the numbers of foreign professionals and skilled workers despite the government's open admission policies for many of these worker categories.

At the other end of the skills continuum are unskilled foreign workers, whose use has been officially banned in Europe since 1973. Nevertheless,

---

[5] For example, Germany introduced a green card system to make it easier and faster to admit foreign workers skilled in Internet technology in 2000 (Hunger 2002: 5).

[6] According to *Asahi Shinbun* (April 7, 2004, http://www.asahi.com/english/business/TKY200404070213.htm), a Tokyo-based personnel resource service began a program to train English-speaking Vietnamese nurses to cater to the growing needs of *foreign* patients in Japan. Nurses from the Philippines migrate worldwide in large numbers, especially to the United States, the United Kingdom, Singapore, Libya, and Saudi Arabia. These nurses do not receive automatic certifications in the host countries and must meet certain conditions. Ironically, the Philippines is now suffering from a shortage of nurses to care for its own domestic population. In Japan, foreign nurses must overcome both certification and language requirements. Some Japanese civic organizations support language training for Vietnamese nurses and prepare them for qualifying exams.

unskilled workers continue to move within EU member countries (Kajita 1994: 60–61), and these nations are experiencing difficulties in controlling and managing their foreign unskilled workers, especially those who tend to settle long-term as a result of family reunification. Some European countries initially adopted policies to avoid long-term settlement of foreign workers (such as Germany's guestworker schemes). Others continue to restrict the entry of foreign workers (through, for example, seasonal and temporary worker programs in Switzerland) and naturalization (in Germany and Switzerland).[7] In the current enlargement of the EU, nations have responded differently to the flow of migrants from Eastern European states.[8] They have also struggled with issues of social integration (Germany's problem of "public order" in the 1980s under Chancellor Helmut Kohl), social costs, discrimination toward foreign workers, and cultural and political clashes (such as the resurgence of right-wing politics in Germany). Generally speaking, Europe is moving toward opening the doors to skilled workers but closing them to unskilled labor (Hunger 2002). In comparison with traditional countries of immigrant settlement such as the United States, Canada, Australia, and New Zealand, European nations have become countries of immigration only recently; and, with the exception of the United Kingdom and the Netherlands, they have not fully embraced multiculturalism. The European countries' experience demonstrates that the high-minded principles of "multiculturalism" and "transnational ethnicity" are not uniformly espoused.[9] The United States also experienced ethnic

---

[7] For example, after Germany's reunification, the country's foreign population swelled to 7 million, or 9 percent of total population (Hunger 2002: 4). In 1989 Germany tightened the influx of unskilled migrants. Switzerland has used an immigration ceiling system since 1970, with seasonal employment in agriculture, construction, and tourism restricted to 88,000 per year. It also restricts the number of temporary permits for foreign trainees, corporate personnel, and technical workers to 24,000 per year (Ministry of Health, Labor, and Welfare 2002). The overall general trend in Europe is to welcome foreign skilled labor but to close the door to unskilled workers and asylum seekers (Hunger 2002: 13).

[8] For a summary of European Union national stances on immigration, see http://www.workpermit.com/news/2004_02_27_working_restrictions_in_eu.htm.

[9] France, for example, is directly involved in the social integration of migrants to ensure "uniformity," and issues of foreign migration are becoming a growing problem, as demonstrated by the recent controversy over religious expression through dress in schools. Similarly, Germany does not celebrate ethnic diversity or multiculturalism. In contrast, multiculturalism in the United Kingdom

exclusion before accepting multiculturalism after World War II, and it ended open immigration in 1986 in an effort to control the influx of Asian and Hispanic immigrants (Komai 2001).

Taking account of the European experience with foreign workers as well as its own unique circumstances, Japan adopted differentiated entry categories for foreign labor in the late 1980s. At the same time, under international pressures regarding human rights, Japan also moved to close gaps in rights between nationals and non-Japanese with respect to resident status, social welfare benefits, and some voting rights in local elections.

Japan has a relatively small foreign population (excluding those with Japanese citizenship) compared to other OECD countries (see table 2.3). Japan's foreign population stood at 1.6 million in 1999, or 1.4 percent of the total population. About one-third of this foreign population are the "old-comers" (descendants of Koreans and Chinese brought to Japan before and during World War II), who hold special permanent resident status. Foreign workers who had arrived in Japan after 1980 totaled 710,000 in 2002, representing slightly over 1 percent of the labor force (Ministry of Health, Labor, and Welfare 2002). It may be convenient to think of these recent migrants in five major categories: (1) legal skilled workers (100,000 in total, of which 53,000 are entertainers); (2) technical trainees (36,000); (3) working students (59,000, including 38,000 pre-college students); (4) ethnic Japanese from South America (233,000); and (5) illegal workers (280,000).[10] One in three (32.4 percent) of these foreign workers is an overstayer.[11] The number of unskilled foreign workers increased during the bubble economy of the 1980s. In response to the labor shortage of the boom, Japan began importing unskilled labor through a trainee program, instituted in 1986 (discussed below), and a special entry category for pre-college students, established in

---

is rooted in that country's history of granting full citizenship rights to early immigrants from former colonies and Commonwealth countries. The British government promotes migrants' social integration based on the enforcement of "racial equality" laws (Soysal 1994).

[10] Estimates of foreign worker populations differ depending on who is counted: registered foreign special permanent residents, permanent residents, and/or temporary residents. Estimates of the illegal foreign population also vary. In this chapter I use the official figure for the foreign population — 710,000 in 2002 — published by the Ministry of Health, Labor, and Welfare.

[11] Dividing the number of overstayers (232,000) by the total number of foreign workers (710,000) yields 0.327 (32.7 percent).

1990. It also revised its immigration control law and opened its door to Japanese descendants from South America (the *nikkeijin*) in 1990.

Table 2.3. Foreign Population in Selected OECD Countries, Selected Years[a]

Country	1983	1995	1999	Number of Foreign Population in 1999 (millions)
Austria	3.9	9.0	9.2	0.75
Belgium	9.0	9.0	8.8	0.90
Denmark	2.0	4.2	4.9	0.26
Finland	0.3	1.3	1.7	0.87
France	n.a.	n.a.	5.6	3.34
Germany	7.4	8.8	8.9	7.34
Ireland	2.4	2.7	3.1	0.12
Italy	0.7	1.7	2.2	1.25
Japan	**0.7**	**1.1**	**1.2**	**1.56**
Luxembourg	26.3	33.4	36.0	0.16
Portugal	n.a.	1.7	1.9	0.19
Spain	0.5	1.2	2.0	0.80
Sweden	4.8	5.2	5.5	0.49
Switzerland	4.8	5.2	5.5	0.49
U.K.	3.1	3.4	3.8	2.21

Source: Adopted from Tarumoto 2003: 4, citing OECD data.

[a] Excludes immigrants who hold citizenship in the host country or immigrants who have been naturalized. Foreign population (as percentage of the total population) in countries of settlement is as follows: Australia, 23.1 percent; Canada, 18.2 percent; New Zealand, 9.5 percent; and United States, 11.1 percent.

n.a. – not available.

Perhaps somewhat surprisingly, the population of unskilled foreign workers also increased during Japan's decade-long economic downturn that began in the mid-1990s. Although unemployment rates increased steadily in the 1990s—from 2.1 percent in 1991 to 3.4 percent in 1996 and 5.0 percent in 2001—hard-hit Japanese workers did not take migrant jobs, demonstrating that the demand for unskilled workers had become structurally embedded in the economy. This fact is confirmed by the increase in the number of unskilled foreign workers (Mori 1997; Martin 2001). The number of foreign workers rose from 260,000 in 1990 to 710,000 in 2002, or from 0.5 percent of the labor force to 1.3 percent in 2000 (Ministry of Health, Labor, and Welfare 2002: 70).

Foreign investments and the relocation of large manufacturing facilities to Asia have increased pressures on small and midsize subcontractors in Japan to maintain competitive prices and cut labor costs. Companies that are unable to move their operations to lower-cost countries have sought other ways to cut costs, primarily by employing cheap labor. Japan's small and midsize firms have experienced chronic difficulties in filling unskilled jobs, in part because Japanese workers shy away from low-wage, unskilled jobs. Mechanization is one way of coping with such a labor shortage, but small and midsize firms are slow, or simply unable, to make the required capital investments, and some are already quite fully mechanized.

Japanese official policies toward foreign workers aim to import needed foreign labor on a temporary basis (except for nikkeijin) through a mix of open-door and side-door policies across various skill and wage levels. Japan maintains an open door for skilled and professional workers, as well as the nikkeijin, who have no restrictions on length of stay, type of employment, or accompanying family members. Side-door policies involve the conditional (or rotational) admission of unskilled foreign workers via a more tightly controlled and restrictive policy. Because Japan does not officially admit unskilled foreign labor, these are called "side-door" or "back-door" policies. The trainee program (*kenshusei seido*) began in 1986, and the recruitment of nikkeijin began in 1990 after the government revised the immigration control law in 1989.[12] In 1990, Japan added a category for pre-college foreign students (*shugakusei*), allowing them to work part-time.

The trainee program, renamed the Technical Internship Training Program in 1993, involves three years of technical training, up from two years prior to 1997. Trainees spend two years in a work-and-learn program at a company, followed by a one-year internship. The trainee program is the result of government efforts to recruit a pool of inexpensive labor from Asia for small and midsize Japanese firms with chronic labor shortages (in, for example, manufacturing and construction) and firms needing to cut costs in order to survive (as in the textile and clothing sectors). The program is company-run, and workers are rotated back to their home countries, where they can apply their newly acquired technical skills (Kuwahara 1998).[13]

---

[12] The nikkeijin, who represent nearly 50 percent of all unskilled foreign workers in Japan, are by far the largest ethnic group of foreign migrants to arrive after the 1980s.

[13] According to Iguchi (1998), Japan uses trainees in larger numbers than do other OECD countries, with more than 40,000 per year (10,000 funded by the government and 30,000 by private companies). Japan's trainee program fol-

About 20,000 trainees enter Japan each year under the program,[14] and over 80 percent of them are employed in the manufacturing sector (Martin 2001). Sponsoring firms work with brokers who bring the trainees to Japan, where the firms provide the technical training. Trainees receive "allowances" (not wages) that are a fraction (one-fourth to one-half) of the average wage that Japanese workers earn in the manufacturing sector (Martin 2001), and trainees are not permitted to take regular wage jobs.[15] By 2000, Japan had 36,000 registered trainees; most were Chinese (61 percent), followed by Indonesians (12 percent) and Filipinos (8 percent) (Kashiwazaki 2002).[16]

The second side-door policy—the recruitment of pre-college foreign students—is more ambiguous in design. The students, over 90 percent of whom come from Asia (Ministry of Education, Culture, Sports, Science, and

---

lows the U.S. and British tradition in that trainees are expected to transfer their newly acquired skills upon return to their home countries. Trainees are not allowed to do tasks that would undermine the jobs of ordinary workers, and they receive allowances in lieu of wages. In contrast, Germany's trainee programs are based on bilateral agreements. Trainees in France and Switzerland are not allowed to bring their spouse and children, but this is permitted in Britain. Contrary to authors who emphasize the disguised nature of the Japanese trainee programs, Iguchi writes of the important roles they have played in Japanese multinational corporations since the 1960s. They serve to compensate for the lack of basic education among local (foreign) workers and have helped transfer skills in their foreign affiliates or joint-venture companies. Iguchi expects trainee programs to grow in importance among high-tech firms in the future, especially in the area of "co-engineering" (cooperation between the research and development, or R&D, division and the production division).

[14] For example, the figure was 22,268 in 2001 according to JITCO's 2002 report. However, others report a figure of 40,000 trainees per year (see Iguchi 1998).

[15] The initial cost per trainee is estimated at ¥510,000 (about US$4,400) for the receiving firm. The median monthly allowance for trainees was ¥115,000 (about $1,000) in 2001. Kashiwazaki (2002) indicates that trainees received less than ¥120,000 per month in 2000, and only 3 percent of trainees received ¥150,000 or more per month. In the manufacturing sector, males receive between ¥240,000 and ¥280,000 per month on average, and females, ¥190,000 to ¥210,000. Thus, if we disregard wage differences in skill levels, a trainee allowance of ¥150,000 is equivalent to 58 percent of male wages and 75 percent of female wages.

[16] Estimates vary depending on the government ministry. According to the Ministry of Health, Labor, and Welfare (2002), there were 29,749 foreign workers in technical training jobs in 2002.

Technology 2002), are permitted to work part-time (over 20 hours per week). Unlike the foreign students enrolled in Japanese colleges and universities, these students are enrolled in Japanese language schools or other technical training schools. There were just under 40,000 shugakusei in 2000, down from 47,000 in 1993 (Ministry of Health, Labor, and Welfare 2002; Kashiwazaki 2002), and they represent a particularly likely source of overstayers. Overstayers reached their highest level (299,000) in 1993, but their numbers have since declined to 250,000 in 2000 and 232,000 in 2003.[17] Although there have been some requests for "amnesty" in these cases, the Japanese immigration office has granted only a few of them (Tarumoto 2003).

Just as Europe's guestworker programs have shown "there is nothing more permanent than temporary workers" (Martin 2001: 349), Japan has found that many of its "temporary" unskilled foreign workers choose to remain in the country despite government efforts to design policies and programs that prevent overstaying. Moreover, observers have been quick to note problems in Japan's side-door policies with regard to workers' rights (employment protections, minimum wage) and social rights (access to public housing, social welfare benefits and services), topics that are discussed in other chapters in this volume. Japan is not alone in the struggle to control and integrate foreign workers, as the European experience demonstrates. Immigration and migrant incorporation are disruptive processes in any country, and there is no reason to expect Japan to be different.

The challenge is exacerbated by Japan's problems with long-term (permanent) foreign residents — the second-, third-, and even fourth-generation Koreans and Chinese who were forced to emigrate to Japan before and during World War II.[18] Driven by international pressure, Japan began to address the human rights issues of these long-term residents in the 1980s, though the problems are by no means fully resolved. For example, Japan adopted international resolutions on the rights of individuals in 1975 and of refugees in 1982, and it revised the 1965 Japan–South Korea Treaty in 1981

---

[17] There are four common routes for entering Japan and then becoming an undocumented worker: as a trainee, pre-college student, professional entertainer, or tourist.

[18] There are some 1.2 million "foreign long-term residents" in Japan, including 635,000 Koreans and 335,000 Chinese. This group is sometimes called the "oldcomers" (as opposed to nikkeijin who came to Japan in the 1980s) and constitutes a third of the foreign population in Japan. Together with nikkeijin with residency status, the total number of foreign long-term residents was 1.69 million in 2002 (Ministry of Health, Labor, and Welfare 2002).

and 1990 to grant its long-term foreign residents special permanent residence status and rights to social benefits (such as public housing and health insurance coverage). In addition, Japan relaxed its fingerprinting system in the 1980s and abolished it in 1992. In the 1990s, some local governments (including the cities of Kawasaki, Osaka, and Kyoto) granted all foreigners (not only foreign permanent residents) the right to hold public-sector jobs (including managerial positions), despite opposition from the Ministry of Home Affairs (Komai 2001: 131).

Political incorporation is yet another unresolved issue in Japan, one that is complicated by the presence in the country of North and South Koreans. Long-term foreign nationals in Japan do not have political participation rights (just as permanent residents of the United States do not). North Korean nationals in Japan (including those born and raised there) still consider themselves to be North Korean nationals residing temporarily in Japan, and thus they oppose political incorporation in Japan. In contrast, long-term residents from South Korea see themselves as such, and they have demanded political incorporation at the local—though not the national—level (Kajita 1994). Since 1993, some Japanese cities and prefectures (such as Osaka and Shiga) have recognized these rights.

The status of those entering Japan since the 1980s—including both skilled and unskilled workers—has improved thanks to the recognition of worker rights under the Labor Law, the imposition of penalties on employers for human rights violations, and, in some instances, local political rights. These improvements resulted from Japan's official recognition of certain rights for long-term residents of Korean nationality. For example, in 1982 the government abolished restrictions on non-nationals' eligibility for public housing, public finance, national pension programs, and child and family allowances. Foreigners who are not covered by health insurance in their workplace can join the national service run by local government. In 1989 the government instituted a penalty for employers who hire undocumented workers. In 1991 it established the Japan International Training Cooperation Organization (JITCO), changed the work status of trainees (they can now work for wages, including overtime), and granted trainees protection under the Japanese Labor Standards Law (that is, labor protections equal to those for Japanese workers, including workers' compensation and minimum wages).

In sum, Japan has developed a mix of flexible mechanisms since the mid-1980s to assist industries dealing with a prolonged recession and global competition. Rather than creating a uniform, long-term policy for dealing with foreign workers, Japan has evolved a differentiated entry strategy, opening doors to nikkeijin from Latin America while restricting conditions and periods of entry for trainees and pre-college students from Asia.

These differentiated entry categories will enable officials to make adjustments in the course of an uncertain economic future. Primary among the uncertainties is the fear of a large-scale influx of unskilled workers from the relatively poor Asian countries that surround Japan. Continued trade and investment in Asia will increase the migration pressures on Japan. Additionally, there is a sophisticated migration infrastructure in place (including labor brokers, foreign government policies to send workers abroad, support systems to finance global migration) that can send a large number of migrants from Asia to Japan. Further, China will intensify international migration pressures due to its oversupply of males (a result of the female infanticide associated with China's one-child-per-family policy) (Martin 2001). Fear of uncontrolled mass migration flows from populous neighbors will lead Japan to maintain its rigid stance and more closely monitor its side-door immigration channels — though this will be an uphill battle.

Japan will need to strengthen policies that facilitate the integration of its steadily increasing foreign population. Tokyo is home to a concentration of Chinese in Shinjuku and Toshima districts. There are concentrations of both North and South Koreans in Adachi, Shinjuku, Arakawa, and Kawasaki City; Filipinos in Adachi, Taito, and Minato; and Thai in Toshima and Shinjuku (Kajita 1994: 96–97; Komai 2001). A trend since 1990 has been the appearance of factory towns with foreign workers. The small subcontractor firms that rely on foreign workers are concentrated in Shizuoka and Aichi prefectures, outside Tokyo. There seems to be a dispersal of foreign workers to localities rather than a concentration in large urban centers (Kajita 1994: 100). Kawasaki City, home to many Koreans, once contemplated creating a Korea Town as part of the city's revitalization efforts (Komai 2001), but questions about the project's feasibility and disagreements between North and South Koreans stymied the initiative (Kajita 1994).

As Japan moves to accommodate these populations, local communities are facing new challenges of coexistence and social and cultural integration. In the labor market, companies have so far assumed responsibility for the treatment of trainee workers without creating a serious segregation of foreign workers. At present, education policy is the most pressing area. Local communities lack educational programs and services for foreign workers' children in primary and secondary schools. Japan has not accepted many foreign children into the country, and thus it is not well prepared for this challenge. To complicate the issue, the life of a foreign worker is dictated primarily by economic (labor market) considerations, and he — and his family — will move whenever a better job is found. Unless there is a critical mass of foreigners, it is also difficult for local communities to develop programs. Nevertheless, some communities — such as Oizumi-cho in Gunma Prefecture, Hamamatsu City, and Ota City — have developed innovative approaches that can serve as models to other communities (Komai 2001; Kajita 1994). Despite worries about Japan's insularity, there is little reason to question Japan's ability to adapt.

Model Two: State Policy Shift from a Fordist to a Post-Fordist Economy

Current policy discussions often frame the issue of population aging as a cause of economic problems. This focus distracts attention from the fact that it is the economy and active workers' carrying capacity (productivity) that determine whether population aging is in fact an issue. Demographic aging should be viewed in the context of the capacity of the long-term economy to support its members. The qualitative restructuring of the economy from a Fordist to a post-Fordist one — increasing its capacity to carry a dependent population, along with the labor, social welfare, and education policies to facilitate such a transition — is crucial to the issue of an aging population. Marginal increases in economic growth rates go further toward addressing the burden of population aging than do marginal decreases in the growth rates of the dependent population (Schulz, Borowski, and Crown 1991: 107–108; Schulz 1995). Relatively small increases in economic growth have the potential to substantially moderate the deleterious impacts of demographic factors. Thus a practical policy intervention is economic, rather than demographic, in nature.

Sociologists and some economists use the Fordist/post-Fordist distinction to discuss the transformation of modern economies ("old economy" and "new economy" are sometimes used in similar fashion). "Fordist" refers to an industrial organization system associated with the Ford Motor Company of the early twentieth century (Jaffee 2001; Myles 1990). A Fordist economy is based on mass-production technology and mass consumption, with products having relatively long life cycles. Worker skills, once acquired, have a long life cycle of attending to routine operations, and a worker's productivity level remains relatively static throughout his or her working life. The auto, steel, and rubber industries are good examples of the leading sectors in this type of industrial economy. In the Fordist economy, "retirement" (dependent population) is a socially created category for managing workforce turnover (Myles 1990: 271).

A post-Fordist economy, in contrast, is oriented to continuous innovation and the application of information technology. The economy is geared to the flexible production of selective goods and the consumption of a variety of goods. Goods and services have short production life cycles and require continuous innovation. Correspondingly, workers must adjust to the flexible production system by constantly upgrading their skills and seeking multiple careers over their lifetimes. Payoffs for an educational investment do not last a lifetime; new career junctures require additional education and training. The computer software, telecommunications, and information-based service industries represent the leading sectors of this type of economy.

Japan's challenge of demographic aging and the country's use of foreign migrant workers (and immigration more generally) as a mechanism for coping with the shrinking population are more appropriately viewed within the context of the transformation in the productive capacity of national economies. The transformation is analogous to the qualitative changes in the number of farmers it takes to feed a population (Myles 1990: 282). At the beginning of the twentieth century, it took more than a third of the U.S. labor force (37.6 percent) to feed the nation (Ford 1988: 40). Innovations in farm technology, improved seed, and better organization have geometrically increased farmers' capacity to support the population. Today the agricultural sector is less than 2 percent of the U.S. labor force. The expanding manufacturing and service sectors absorbed displaced agricultural workers while at the same time increasing the agricultural sector's capacity to supply the rest of the (dependent) population with food. Analogously, future innovations in worker productivity will support ever-increasing numbers of "dependents" in a post-Fordist economy. It is not the ratio of the working population to the dependent population but rather the economy's output that largely determines whether an aging population becomes a problem.

Successful transformation from a Fordist to a post-Fordist economy depends on the application of information technology and the production of selective, high-quality goods and services with relatively short life cycles. As life cycles of job skills become shorter, workers require frequent retraining and career changes. Flexible movement of workers, including the acquisition of skills for short-term projects, is needed in the new economy based on increased employment fluidity.[19]

According to Myles, there are two types of flexibility: dynamic flexibility and static flexibility. Dynamic flexibility (as defined by Cohen and Zysman and cited in Myles 1990: 284) refers to firms' ability to steadily increase productivity through improvements in production processes and product and service innovations. Static flexibility is the firm's change in productive capacity through worker layoffs or lower wages (reliance on cheap labor) in reaction to shifting market conditions. Dynamic flexibility requires skilled workers, provides high wages, and creates employment stability; static flexibility is based on unskilled, low-wage workers and a disposable labor force. Moreover, dynamic flexibility is based on strategic planning, incremental innovation, and adoption of new technology and innovation; static flexibility is based on more passive reactions to market conditions. In any post-Fordist economy, the mix of skills and wage contracts varies between industries in the same country and also between countries. For example, Myles (1990: 285) discusses cross-national differences in service industries. He points out how the United States and Canada developed large labor markets in consumer services with low skill requirements and low wages, while the Scandinavian countries developed large state industries requiring high skills with high wages. The expansion of the Scandinavian welfare industries contributed to increases in female employment and family income security. Myles concludes that "there is nothing intrinsic to a service economy dictating that it will be dominated by low wage, low skill jobs and intermittent employment" (Myles 1990: 288). His example suggests that dynamic flexibility applies to services as well as manufacturing. In addition, the distinction suggests that dynamic flexibility requires coordinated industrial and social policy, whereas static flexibility is based more on reactive solutions in a market-dictated economy.

For workers, the life-course regime of the post-Fordist economy does not necessarily mean career disruptions with periods of unemployment or premature retirement. Rather, the employment lives of workers may involve intermittent periods of extended paid leave from work for child care

---

[19] Examples of such economic restructuring include shifting labor from industries and firms with redundant labor to emerging industries with job training, promoting start-up companies in new industries by providing start-up capital and making appropriate changes in bankruptcy laws, diversifying the forms of employment (full-time and part-time work, contractual work), and improving work conditions through new technological equipment.

or care giving in old age and well-paid part-time or temporary work. The Netherlands, for example, significantly reduced its unemployment rate, restrained wage increases for regular workers, and increased part-time employment. Disparities in wages and benefits between full- and part-time work disappeared, and by 1997 part-time work accounted for close to 40 percent of Dutch employment (Omata 2000: 4).[20]

Japan's successful shift to a post-Fordist economy rests on the expansion of new industries (such as information technology–related sectors, health care, education, and social welfare industries) and the modernization or disappearance of existing inefficient sectors or their transformation into more promising industries. The process involves diversifying types of employment, boosting start-up companies, and dealing with mismatches between job offers and job seekers. In theory, this process involves a mix of jobs with different skill levels. Whether Japan will require a larger pool of foreign unskilled labor rests on corporate and government capacity to upgrade job skills and wages while achieving productivity gains through new technology.

Social welfare industries are a good example of such a mix. The "human washing machine" now in use in some nursing homes, robotics home care, complete health-care systems with Internet technology, and telematics provide promising developments in how traditional nursing and elder care are delivered.[21] Robotics has a relatively long history of product development in Japan, including robotic pets, security robots, and robotic house-maids, and the sales of these devices are expected to increase from US$4 billion currently to $14 billion in 2010 (Brooke 2004). Economic affluence has generated a growing desire for independent living and an emphasis on the quality of life among the older population. Caregivers have also created demands for innovative products in a wide variety of goods and services in

---

[20] In the U.S. economy, which expanded robustly in the 1990s, job creation came in information technology (IT) industries, information-related services, and wholesale and retailing. Helped by information technology, start-up companies multiplied dramatically. Policies adopted by the Clinton administration promoted such growth (especially through deregulation and various supports for venture capital) and reduced the employment mismatch through worker retraining programs.

[21] The "human washing machine" improves productivity and efficiency as well as increasing privacy for care receivers and lessening the work burden for nurses. Robotic pets are designed to provide the elderly with conversation and companionship, and the increasingly popular security robots make them less vulnerable.

special niches. Image sensors attached to the bath, toilet, stove, refrigerator, and even diaper; video-phones in community health centers; and Global Positioning System devices in cell phones are just a few examples of these new developments (Holroyd 2004). Development in material science and technological devices are improving the hygiene and comfort of older persons, transforming the nature of custodial care. The use of a wireless diaper system, for example, enables care workers to know when a diaper needs changing (Belson 2000). Thus social welfare industries are poised to develop dynamic flexibility features and achieve productivity gains across a wide range of worker skill levels.

Recent studies also counter the prevailing image of Japan as a stalled economy that lacks technological innovation and is resistant to change. Holroyd and Coates (2003) point to highly competitive Japanese firms in emerging industries in Internet services, m-commerce, and e-commerce.[22] Japanese firms have responded creatively to the challenge of demographic aging by addressing seniors' needs through the "silver market," "asset industry," or commerce of aging—including in medical services and equipment, real estate, construction, financial services, cosmetics, furniture, foods, travel and education, and robotics. It is estimated that the business potential of the "silver market" will rise from 21 percent of total consumption expenditures in 2000 to 26 percent by 2010 (Holroyd 2004: 5).

The government has deregulated the business environment to induce entrepreneurial and start-up activities and to attract venture capitalists by providing support functions in the areas of business management, client development, legal services, and professional accounting services. To stimulate educational infrastructure, the government recently established graduate programs that are comparable to professional schools in the United States. It has also initiated adult education programs to address employment mismatches and mid-career changes, and it has worked with small and midsize firms to facilitate job training and reemployment of workers to alleviate the mismatch problems. Thus important institutional reforms are under way in the workplace and in education to increase employment fluidity and labor mobility.

To raise the carrying capacity of the economy, Japan should consider a better utilization of female talent, especially middle-aged women. Changes in the female labor force will contribute to a reconceptualization of the aged dependency ratio. The post-Fordist economy is a service-oriented economy,

---

[22] These companies include DoCoMo, NTT's mobile Internet subsidiary, J-Phone, and KDDI.

and the female population represents an educated but underutilized labor force that might supply vital labor to the expanding service economy. Mobilizing this potential female labor force would make the working-age population more productive. And increasing middle-aged women's years of labor force participation would make the working-age group even more productive. Realizing this strategy will require corporate and government reform in family and employment policies to assist women in their child-rearing responsibilities (Usui 2003).

In short, Japan's future hinges on whether growth industries will emerge and raise economic productivity and whether labor market fluidity will accommodate these new industries. Some authors maintain that the key to sustaining a healthy economy is continued economic growth rates of 2 to 3 percent (Schulz 1995; Campbell 2003: 14). Japan's demographic dilemma has more to do with restructuring the economy and institutions to raise economic output than with measures to moderate the ill effects of demographic aging through immigration.

CONCLUSION

The aged dependency ratio has been used to justify the importation of foreign workers in greater numbers in order to adjust the population imbalance that demographic aging has created in Japan (the first model discussed above). I suggest that replacement migration is impractical and may provide only short-term relief by sustaining marginal and labor-intensive industries in a struggling economy — and no fundamental cure to the gap between a growing dependent population and the economy's capacity to support it. In the second model discussed in this chapter — which emphasizes productivity-enhancing social and institutional changes in the context of the societal transformation from a Fordist to a post-Fordist economy — the productivity of the different components of the aged dependency ratio is more malleable and dynamic than generally assumed. It is not the ratio of the working population to the dependent population but rather the economy's carrying capacity that largely determines whether an aging population becomes a problem. The challenge of demographic aging can be managed without undue strain if the economy grows at a steady rate and growth is accompanied by collateral policies that restructure and reorient labor, welfare, and educational institutions (Campbell 2003; Schulz 1995; Usui 2003; International Institute for Applied Systems Analysis 2003).

The distinction between Fordist and post-Fordist economies shifts our focus to the social organization of manufacturing and service industries.

Future increases in the numbers of foreign workers will depend on the mix of static and dynamic flexibility based on the use of information technology. In Japan, social welfare industries are quickly expanding, but there is no reason to expect future industries to be filled entirely with low-wage, low-skilled foreign labor. A post-Fordist economy oriented to dynamic flexibility will provide high-skill jobs, a variety of employment forms, and employment stability. Recent studies show that social welfare industries are poised to develop dynamic flexibility features through the use of productivity-enhancing devices, making new jobs attractive to domestic workers.

Japan's future labor force (and society at large) will certainly include more foreign workers with diverse ethnic backgrounds and nationalities. Although the number of foreign workers has not increased as much as some economists predicted a decade ago, it is now time to strengthen social and cultural integration of these workers and their families at the local level. The small towns and cities that have attracted foreign workers provide many examples of successful promotion of coexistence between foreigners and natives. Further, recent studies suggest the importance of local government, the local community, and "intermediate organizations" (volunteer associations, nonprofits, and advocacy groups) in mediating and facilitating the satisfaction of these people's needs (Kajita 1994; Komai 2001). The 1998 Law for the Promotion of Specified Nonprofit Activity and the 2001 granting of tax privileges to nonprofit organizations should improve the incorporation of foreign workers. In addition, the media stories now present foreign and illegal workers in a more sympathetic light, and this should help educate the Japanese public about these groups. And ongoing institutional changes will provide yet another foundation for Japan's transformation to a post-Fordist society.

Ultimately, the challenge of aging—declines in the working-age population and a burgeoning dependent population—rests on Japan's ability to make a swift transition to a post-Fordist economy as a way of growing the economy out of the deleterious impacts of demographic changes. Population aging requires adjustments in markets, corporate practices, and government policies, but it should in no way be interpreted as a bankrupting of Japan's economy. Japan's future does present cause for concern, but our focus must remain on the long-term issue of an aging society in the context of the changing social organization and transformation in productive capacity of a post-Fordist economy.

References

Atchley, Robert C. 2000. *Social forces and aging.* 9th ed. Belmont, CA: Wadsworth Thompson Learning.

Belson, Ken. 2000. These oldies look golden to Japan. *Business Week* (international edition), July 17. http://www.businessweek.com/2000/00_29/ib3690152htm.

Brooke, James. 2004. Japan seeks robotic help in caring for the aged. *New York Times,* March 5. http://www.globalaging.org/elderrights/world/2004/japaninvention.htm.

Campbell, John C. 2003. Population aging: Hardly Japan's biggest problem. *Asia Program Special Report* 107:10–15. Washington, DC: Woodrow Wilson International Center for Scholars.

Ford, Ramona L. 1988. *Work, organization, and power.* Needham Heights, MA: Allyn and Bacon.

Hewitt, Paul. 2003. The gray roots of Japan's crisis. *Asia Program Special Report* 107:4–9. Washington, DC: Woodrow Wilson International Center for Scholars.

Holroyd, Carin. 2004. Commerce of aging. Presented at the Association of Japanese Business Meeting, Stockholm, July 9.

Holroyd, Carin, and Ken Coates. 2003. *Japan and the Internet revolution.* UK: Palgrave.

Horlacher, David E. 2002. Aging in Japan: Causes and consequences (Part I: Demographic issues). Interim report IR-01-008/February (revised and updated version, August 2002). www.iiasa.ac.at. Luxembourg: International Institute for Applied Systems Analysis.

Hunger, Uwe. 2002. Germany's immigration and integration policy: Previous patterns and future directions. Paper circulated at the conference Reluctant Hosts? Japan as a Future Country of Immigration in Comparative Perspective, Center for Comparative Immigration Studies, University of California, San Diego, La Jolla, October 18–19.

Iguchi, Yasushi. 1998. Challenges for foreign traineeship programs in Japan. *Japan Institute of Labor Bulletin* 37 (10). http://www.jil.go.jp/bulletin/year1998/vol37-10/04.htm.

International Institute for Applied Systems Analysis. 2003. The graying of the Japanese economy. *Options,* summer, pp. 2–10.

Jaffee, David. 2001. *Organization theory.* New York: McGraw Hill.

Kajita, Takamichi. 1994. *Gaikokujin rodosha to Nihon* (Japan and foreign workers). Tokyo: Nihon Hoso Shuppankai.

Kashiwazaki, Chikako. 2002. Japan's resilient demand for foreign workers. *Migration Information Source* (Migration Policy Institute). http://www.migrationinformation.org/feature/display.cfm.

Komai, Hiroshi. 2001. *Foreign migrants in contemporary Japan.* Trans. Jens Wilkinson. Melbourne: Trans Pacific Press.

Kuwahara, Yasuo. 1998. Japan's dilemma: Can international migration be controlled? In *Temporary workers or future citizens? Japanese and U.S. migration policies*, edited by Myron Weiner and Tadashi Hanami. New York: New York University Press.

Martin, Philip L. 2001. The role played by labor migration in the Asian economic miracle. In *Population change and economic development in East Asia*, edited by Andrew Mason. Stanford, CA: Stanford University Press.

Martin, Philip L., and Elizabeth Midgley. 1999. Immigration to the United States. *Population Bulletin* 54 (2).

Ministry of Education, Culture, Sports, Science and Technology. 2002. *White paper: Educational reform for the 21st century*. Tokyo: Government Printing Office.

Ministry of Health, Labor, and Welfare. 2002. *Gaikokujin koyo mondai kenkyukai hokokusho* (On the problems associated with employment of foreign workers: A report by the study group appointed by the Ministry of Health, Labor, and Welfare).

Mori, Hiromi. 1997. *Immigration policy and foreign workers in Japan*. New York: St. Martin's Press.

Myles, John. 1990. States, labor markets, and life cycles. In *Beyond the marketplace: Rethinking economy and society*, edited by Roger Frieland and A. F. Robertson. New York: Aldine de Gruyter.

National Institute of Population and Social Security Research. 2002. www.ipss .go.jp.

Omata, Naohiko. 2000. Recent employment and income conditions in Japan. *Tokyo Mitsubishi Review* 5 (9). http://www.btm.co.jp/html_e/databank/rev0009e.htm.

Salt, John. 2000. Europe's migration field. In *Demographic and cultural specificity and integration of migrants*. Bingen, Germany: Network for Integrated European Population Studies.

Schulz, James. 1995. *Economics of aging*. New York: Auburn House.

Schulz, James H., Alan Borowski, and William H. Crown. 1991. *Economics of population aging: The graying of Australia, Japan, and the United States*. New York: Auburn House.

Soysal, Yasemin N. 1994. *Limits of citizenship: Migrants and postnational membership in Europe*. Chicago: University of Chicago Press.

Tanimura, Chieko. 2000. Immigration of nikkeijin to ease the Japanese aging crisis. Unpublished paper. Department of Economics, Simon Fraser University.

Tarumoto, Hideki. 2003. Multiculturalism in Japan: Citizenship policy for immigrants. *International Journal of Multicultural Society* 5 (1):88–103.

United Nations. 1998. *The sex and age distribution of world population*. New York: United Nations.

————. 2001. *Replacement migration: Is it a solution to declining and ageing populations?* New York: United Nations.

Usui, Chikako. 2001. The misplaced problems of aging society: Crisis or opportunity? *International House of Japan Bulletin* 21 (1):42–55. Published in Japanese as Koreikashakai o meguru gokai, *Kokusai Bunkakaikan kaiho* 12 (1):54–65.

————. 2003. Japan's aging dilemma? *Asia Program Special Report* 107:16–22. Washington, DC: Woodrow Wilson International Center for Scholars.

Van de Kaa, D. J. 1992. *The demographic consequences of international migration.* The Netherlands: Netherlands Institute for Advanced Study in the Humanities and Social Sciences.

Part II

MAKING IMMIGRANTS INTO LOCAL CITIZENS:
SOCIAL INTEGRATION PROGRAMS IN JAPANESE CITIES

CHAPTER 3

Cities and Local Citizenship in Japan: Overcoming Nationality?

KATHERINE TEGTMEYER PAK

International migration captures our attention because it makes citizenship visible. For people who are citizens of nation-states that have settled territorial boundaries, full suffrage rights for all adults, and broad recognition of civil rights, the precise definition of citizenship may never become personally salient. International migration triggers debates, however, that highlight the boundaries and content of citizenship, as the presence of non-nationals reminds the public of the rights, duties, and sense of membership that national citizenship bestows upon those who hold it. As the advanced industrial democracies have confronted immigration over recent decades, some, like Great Britain, have reinforced the boundaries around national citizenship; others, including Germany, have eased access to this institution.

Japan unexpectedly returned to debates about international migration in the late 1980s, after decades of ignoring its imperial history of immigration. Though entry control policies have been increasingly fluid and susceptible to political contestation since then, citizenship has not been widely debated within the national government. Yet Japanese citizenship is being quietly changed, at the level of local governance. As the incorporation programs quickly crafted by a few progressive cities responding to the influx of newcomers deepen and spread throughout Japan, the boundaries around national citizenship are being loosened. Other chapters in this volume explain why we can expect the number of immigrants to Japan to continue to increase in future years; the purpose of this chapter is to explain why it is highly likely that immigrants to Japan and their descendants will be substantially less marginalized within Japanese society than were their predecessors of the early and mid-twentieth century.

Local incorporation programs are key components of the wider trend in Japan to push the institution of citizenship beyond a tightly limited concept of nationality, where juridical citizenship status matches up perfectly to the substantive rights and duties of citizenship and again to the cultural identity of national citizenship. Local incorporation programs articulate and promote a vision of citizenship that includes many persons who do not possess juridical citizenship. The people behind the policies are attuned to citizenship debates in other advanced industrial democracies; this chapter argues that those interested in generalized accounts of contemporary citizenship and identity must take their efforts into account as well.

The essay proceeds in three sections. The first reviews the empirical situation with regard to local incorporation programs crafted by the sixteen municipalities involved in the Committee of Localities with Concentrated Foreign Populations and by the six largest designated cities: Yokohama, Osaka, Nagoya, Sapporo, Kobe, and Kyoto. The second shows that a generalized theoretical perspective on cities and citizenship allows for informative comparisons between events in Japan and in other advanced industrial democracies. The concluding section considers alternative conceptualizations of these events, questioning whether local citizenship is capable of providing a path for community membership that moves beyond nationality.

LOCAL INCORPORATION POLICIES

Within several years of the emergence of the new international migration to Japan, some local governments took it upon themselves to fashion a response, to find a way to help the newcomers adjust to life in Japan. Research I conducted in the mid-1990s in four Japanese cities found that these cities were reaching out to their non-national residents under the guise of "internal internationalization" (*uchinaru kokusaika*) (Tegtmeyer Pak 2000a). Even though the national government held to its stringent denial of Japan's emergence as an immigration country, internal internationalization rhetoric came to signal the development of incorporation policies by local government. The combination of specific programs pursued has varied by city and prefecture. In the first half of the 1990s, the most common incorporation policies dealt with the language barriers that many recent migrants faced as they began to build lives in Japan. By early appearances, such efforts appeared uncontroversial or even, to impatient observers in Japan's activist community, wildly insufficient responses to serious economic and legal problems faced by foreign migrants (Tegtmeyer Pak 2000b).

Other interested observers, however, appreciated the potential significance of local incorporation programs as a departure from Japan's institutionalized citizenship regime. Academic researchers have analyzed the developing trend from a variety of perspectives. Much of the writing by Japanese researchers serves the dual purposes of intellectual analysis and political action. This burgeoning community of immigration specialists is bringing debates about denizenship, multiculturalism, and post-national membership into practice while advising local and national government and writing opinion pieces for the national media.[1] Such interest in the early initiatives reinforces the trend, because it gives the local government officials overseeing these policies new ideas, some measure of legitimacy from the connection with a lively academic debate, and, in many cases, direct allies willing to cooperate in related research and serve on advisory councils.

Accordingly, local incorporation policies are no longer as dependent upon the result of contingent histories that made particular cities prone to experimentation in the face of increasing foreign populations. Three factors combined to support the early crafting of local incorporation policies: a pragmatic stance toward a locally visible problem, a history of progressive policy making in particular cities, and the coincidence of available political space created by loosely defined internationalization efforts (Tegtmeyer Pak 2000a).[2] A decade later, we now have evidence that a fourth factor familiar to students of local politics in Japan is in operation, namely, the tendency of new policies to spread horizontally across Japan's localities.

---

[1] A few examples of academic work by scholars who actively cooperate with local governments in crafting incorporation programs include Ebashi 1993; Kashiwazaki 2003; Komai 1997; Kondo 2001; Miyajima 2000; Tanaka 1996; Watadô 1996; Yamawaki, Kashiwazaki, and Kondo 2001.

[2] Kashiwazaki (2003) also presents a four-case comparative study of the sources of incorporation policies ("foreign-resident policy," in her terms). Her analysis confirms the importance of contingent local histories: all three cities in her study — Takatsuki, Toyonaka, and Osaka — adopted these policies because of a strong local history of zainichi Korean activism (as in Kawasaki in my study). The two smaller cities also relied upon the normative prescriptions of human rights discourse. Osaka was further motivated by its image as a global city. Kashiwazaki's fourth case, Kanagawa Prefecture, likewise has seen incorporation policy in part through the lens of the political demands of resident Koreans. Kanagawa has also, however, been quicker to respond to recent immigration because of the legacy of 1970s Governor Nagasu's emphasis on *minsai gaikō*, or people-to-people relations, as opposed to international relations.

Three kinds of horizontal policy links have emerged. The first is direct cooperation, exemplified by the Committee for Localities with a Concentrated Foreign Population (CLCFP; *gaikokujin shūjū toshi kaigi*) which unites sixteen cities in their efforts to deal with immigration issues.[3] Member cities were moved to action in response to the new immigration of the 1990s, most particularly the influx of *nikkeijin* from Brazil. Brazilians comprise the largest group of registered foreign residents in each member city.[4] As shown in table 3.1, opposite, the percentage of local residents who are not Japanese nationals is remarkably high in most member cities, averaging almost 5 percent at a time when the rate for the country as a whole is 1.5 percent (Houmusho Nyukoku Kanri Kyoku [Ministry of Justice, Immigration Bureau] 2004). Although member cities account for only 2.5 percent of Japan's total population, 6.5 percent of registered foreigners in Japan live in one of the sixteen communities.

To date the Committee has met six times and issued two major declarations that target national-level policies. In its first public statement—the "Hamamatsu Declaration"—the Committee dedicated itself to working on local policy with resident foreigners, in recognition of their "important role as critical partners" valued for their contributions to the local economy and culture (Gaikokujin Shuujuu Toshi Kaigi [Committee for Localities with a Concentrated Foreign Population] 2001). The "Declaration" calls upon prefectural and national authorities to reform public education, national health insurance, and the foreigners' registration system to better meet the needs of their foreign residents and promote cooperative local societies. After meeting with representatives of seven national agencies, the Committee reaffirmed its earlier requests while also calling upon the national government to create an office to coordinate policies affecting foreign residents (Gaikokujin Shuujuu Toshi Kaigi 2002).[5]

---

[3] When the Committee was formed in May 2001, there were thirteen member cities. As of April 2004, there were sixteen, hailing from six prefectures (Toyota-shi 2004): (1) Aichi Prefecture: Okazaki, Toyohashi, and Toyota; (2) Gifu Prefecture: Kani, Ōgaki, and Minokamo; (3) Gunma Prefecture: Oita and Ōzumi; (4) Mie Prefecture: Suzuka, Ueno, and Yokkaichi; (5) Nagano Prefecture: Iida; and (6) Shizuoka Prefecture: Fuji, Hamamatsu, Iwata, and Kosai.

[4] Brief accounts of the CLCFP's early history and meeting schedule can be found in Toyota-shi 2004 and Yamawaki, Kashiwazaki, and Kondo 2001.

[5] The Committee's justification for the policy preferences features prominently in an *Asahi Shinbun* column written under the aegis of their think tank, the Asahi Asia Network (AAN). In a February 2004 article, AAN contributing

Table 3.1. Population of CLCFP Member Cities, April 1, 2004

City	Total Population	Registered Foreign Population	Non-Nationals as Percent of Total Population
Hamamatsu	601,878	23,149	3.84%
Iwata	91,284	4,801	5.26%
Kosai	44,719	2,710	6.06%
Fuji	242,772	4,900	2.02%
Toyohashi	375,360	16,776	4.47%
Toyota	358,244	12,031	3.35%
Ōgaki	153,737	5,531	3.59%
Kani	97,900	5,323	5.43%
Minokamo	52,073	4,345	8.34%
Yokkaichi	296,959	7,739	2.64%
Suzuka	196,349	7,873	4.00%
Ueno	62,850	3,313	5.27%
Oita	152,067	7,935	5.21%
Oimachi	42,354	6,356	15.00%
Iida	109,090	3,244	2.97%
Okazaki	351,467	9,317	2.65%

Source: Toyota-shi shakai-bu jijishinkou-ka (Toyota City Municipal Community Development Division) 2004.

The second type of horizontal diffusion comes from the influence exerted on separate local governments by other institutional actors that are themselves organized on a national basis. One example is the separate networks between nongovernmental organizations (NGOs) involved in immigration issues throughout Japan. Because NGOs view part of their task to be lobbying local governments, they provide an additional conduit for the spread of similar policy practices across the country (Tegtmeyer Pak 2000b). Jichirō, the All Japan Prefectural and Municipal Workers Union, is another source of influence in this policy area. It was one of the first organizations to declare that "foreigners are local residents, too" in the early 1990s. In its most recent policy statement, Jichirō recommended sixteen concrete steps that localities should take to realize the slogan, including:

writer Kosuge Koichi advanced the creation of a "Foreigners' Bureau" at the national level to coordinate incorporation policies nationwide (Kosuge 2004).

endorsing petitions calling for local suffrage for foreigners; the creation of local consultative councils "like that adopted by Kawasaki"; ending discrimination by landlords; guaranteeing that all foreigners, regardless of legal status, receive wages and other compensation due from employers; provision of supplementary pension funds to foreigners who do not qualify for the national pension; and a full range of cultural and educational activities to promote mutual understanding among all local residents (Zen nihon jichi dantai roudo kumiai [All Japan Prefectural and Municipal Workers Union] 2003). Mindan, the main organizational representative among the *zainichi* Korean community aligned with South Korea, has also made local governments a target of lobbying activity, particularly with regard to their campaign for local suffrage for permanent residents of Japan (Mindan 2003).

The third type of horizontal dynamic behind the wider institutionalization of local government's role in Japan's migration politics is municipalities' tendency to adopt innovations created elsewhere, or what would be called "best practices" in the United States. Kawasaki is arguably the best-known innovator in this policy area; planning documents for the incorporation programs of other local governments in Japan repeatedly reference Kawasaki favorably. In particular, Kawasaki's 1996 creation of the Kawasaki City Representative Assembly for Foreign Residents was a pivotal development in the increasing popularity of incorporation programs. Although Osaka City and Osaka Prefecture had created consultative councils several years earlier, their membership was comprised of "experts," with half of the seats going to Japanese nationals (Higuchi 2000; Osaka City 2004a). Kawasaki's program was crafted with an eye toward European examples, especially the consultative council created in Frankfurt, Germany.[6] It was the first such council in Japan comprised entirely of resident foreigners, and as such it captured the attention of the press while galvanizing sympathetic participants in immigration debates across Japan.[7]

---

[6] During interviews conducted in 1995 and 1996, city officials in Kawasaki related the process of planning for the Council, which included European trips by city officials and cooperating Japanese academics. Daniel Cohn-Bendit, a well-known activist and Green Party politician in Germany and France, also came to Kawasaki in the early 1990s to speak about incorporating non-nationals at the community level. See Andersen 1990 for a history of consultative councils in Europe.

[7] See also Han 2004 for an in-depth account of the formation and operation of the Kawasaki Assembly for Foreign Residents.

Japan's largest cities play an especially prominent role in influencing other municipalities because they have long enjoyed more power within the hierarchies of Japanese intergovernmental relations (Kitayama 2001).[8] Their adoption of incorporation policies will likely prove an equal, if not greater, source of influence over other localities in the coming decade than will networking between cities, as in the case of the CLCFP, that see themselves as facing similar objective situations in terms of growing foreign populations. We can also expect these cities to have a greater potential for influencing national policy, although the extent to which they will exercise it remains to be seen.

These cities are also crucial sites for the future of incorporation policies simply because they are home to a significant portion of the foreign population in Japan. Approximately 10 percent of Japan's total population and 26 percent of registered foreigners in Japan live in one of the six largest cities—Yokohama, Osaka, Nagoya, Sapporo, Kobe, and Kyoto (Statistics Bureau 2002). As shown in table 3.2, among these six cities, the number of registered foreigners as a percentage of the local population ranges from a high of 4.6 percent in Osaka to a low of 0.5 percent in Sapporo. In addition to differences in population size, these cities vary in terms of the national composition of their foreign resident population, as shown in figure 3.1. Osaka, Kyoto, and Kobe have been the heartland for ethnic Koreans since the imperial period. Yokohama also has been known as a gathering place for foreign residents in Japan beginning earlier in the Meiji era and continuing through the imperial and postwar periods. It continues to be an important destination for newcomers who have arrived since the late 1980s. By contrast, a higher proportion of Sapporo's and Nagoya's foreign residents are newcomers, rather than third- or fourth-generation descendants of former colonial subjects.

The differences in their target populations affect the mind-set of local-level policymakers. Different national groups demonstrate distinct levels of organization as communities, with permanent resident Koreans being by far the best organized, as we would expect. Strong academic interest in

---

[8] The thirteen largest cities in Japan include the "designated cities" (*seirei shitei toshi*) granted special autonomy in important policy-making functions under the Local Autonomy Law. As of 2004, these cities included Yokohama, Osaka, Nagoya, Sapporo, Kobe, Kyoto, Fukuoka, Kawasaki, Hiroshima, Saitama, Kitakyushu, Sendai, and Chiba. ("Tokyo" is not a city, administratively speaking, but rather the name of the special national capitol district that operates at the same mid-level of government as do prefectures.)

nikkeijin means that local policymakers have a wealth of information available about the specificities of their socioeconomic situation in Japan. To a lesser degree, this is also the case with the Filipino and Chinese populations.

Table 3.2. Population of Largest Japanese Cities

City	Total Population	Registered Foreign Population	Non-Nationals as Percent of Total Population
Yokohama[a]	3,534,492	66,780	1.9%
Osaka[b]	2,619,335	120,178	4.6%
Nagoya[b]	2,121,113	53,882	2.5%
Sapporo[a]	1,861,652	8,580	0.5%
Kobe[c]	1,515,864	44,708	2.9%
Kyoto[b]	1,466,978	43,710	3.0%

Sources: Kobe City 2004; Kyoto City 2004; Nagoya City 2004; Osaka City 2004b; Sapporo City 2004; Yokohama City 2004.
[a] March 2004 data; [b] 2002 census data; [c] October 2003 data.

Figure 3.1. Most Common Nationalities of Registered Foreign Population in Large Japanese Cities (percentages)

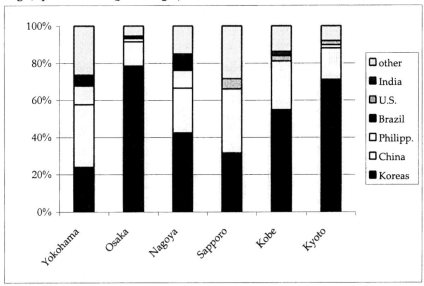

Sources: Kobe City 2004; Kyoto City 2004; Nagoya City 2004; Osaka City 2004b; Sapporo City 2004; Yokohama City 2004.

Despite these differences, however, the content of the cities' incorporation programs shows striking similarity. Six basic types of initiatives are now common: (1) initiatives mitigating language barriers; (2) other incorporation policies; (3) cultural outreach through nonprofit foundations dedicated to internationalization; (4) research and continuing debates on the appropriate scope of incorporation initiatives; (5) advocacy for reforms at the national level; and (6) creation of alternative forms of political participation. The data presented below on these large cities were gathered by Web-based searches for relevant materials; these searches were conducted from March through August 2004.

Initiatives Mitigating Language Barriers

All six of the cities examined in this study have extensive programs to target language problems (see table 3.3). Although English continues to be first among foreign languages, Portuguese, Chinese, and Korean are also used extensively. The cities translate information about local governmental services and other aspects of daily life in their cities into a total of fifteen different languages. All but Yokohama have English translations available at the top page on their main Web site; Osaka also has buttons directing visitors to Korean, Chinese, and French pages on the top page. In addition to the foreign language Web page usage listed in table 3.3, Osaka, Nagoya, and Kobe post separate pages that provide information on daily life in English, Korean, Chinese, and Portuguese. Osaka's page also has a Spanish version, and Kobe's also offers Spanish and Vietnamese.[9] Nagoya's "Nagoya News" page particularly stands out because it is regularly updated with event announcements, messages from public officials, and updates on social welfare services. The link to "Nagoya News" is featured prominently, in English, on the top page of the city's Web site. Interpretation/translation and consultation services are offered by all six cities to help foreign residents negotiate social welfare programs, employment issues, and personal legal situations (especially with regard to immigration procedures), although Sapporo's program is very limited in comparison with the other five cities. Finally, all of the cities offer free or heavily subsidized Japanese language classes at several locations.

---

[9] Although it does not offer a "living guide" Web page, Sapporo does have foreign-language pages dedicated to tourist information in English, Chinese (both mainland and Taiwanese versions), and Korean.

Table 3.3. Language-Related Incorporation Policies

	Lifestyle Pamphlets, Guides & Maps, City Policy Information[a]	Web Site Languages	Japanese Language Classes	Interpretation, Translation, Consultations	Other
Yokohama	27 documents: E (25), C (19), K (19), S (18), P (15), T (3), Cm (2), Th (1), L (1)	HP: J[b]; IC: J, E; CC: J, and limited E, C, K	Yes, at International Center	Yes, at International Center	Public signs
Osaka	13 publications, most in C, K, E, S, P; other languages included occasionally	HP: J, E, K, C, F; IC: J, E, C, K, P, S; CC: J, limited E	Yes, at ward offices and International Center	E, K, C, S, P, by phone, at ward offices, and at city hall	FM Radio: J, C, K, E; Natural emergency video: E
Nagoya	101 documents: E (98), C (29), K (23), S (22), P (24), T (8), F (2), plus 1 each for Tw, Th, I, G	HP: J, E; IC: J, E, C, K, F, P, T; CC: J only	Yes, at International Center	Yes, at International Center and by phone	Public signs: E; FM Radio: E, P, C, S, K
Sapporo	Unclear. Volunteer group coordinated by International Center meets monthly to translate existing information into English.	HP: J, E (more limited); IC: J, E; CC: J only	Yes, at International Center	Limited. Volunteer system registers translators for cultural events. Twice-yearly consultations on visa procedures, J, E	Public signs: E

Kobe	At least 8 publications: 1 in J & E only, others in E, K, C, V, P, S	HP: J, E IC: J, E (but have online lifestyle guide in J, E, C, K, V, P, S) CC: J, E	Yes	Yes, at International Center in E, K, C, V, P, S	Extensive plans for distributing information in case of natural disasters Public signs in multiple languages Multilingual cable TV broadcasts
Kyoto	6 publications: 2 in J, E, K, C, S; 4 in J and E only	HP: J, E IC: J, E, C, K, S CC: J only	Yes, at International Center	Yes, at International Center	FM Radio: J, C, K, E

Sources: Kobe City 2004; Kobe kokusai kyouryoku kouryuu sentaa (Kobe International Center for Cooperation and Communication) 2001; Kobe-shi bousai kaigi (Kobe City Natural Disaster Protection Council) 2003; Kyoto-shi kokusai kouryuu kyoukai (Kyoto City International Foundation) 2002; Kyoto-shi kokusaika suishin shitsu 1999; Nagoya City 2004; Nagoya Kokusai Sentaa (Nagoya International Center) 2002; Nagoya-shi Shichou-shitsu Kokusai Kouryuu-ka (International Exchange Section) 2003; Osaka City 2004a; Sapporo City 2004; Sapporo Kokusai Puraza (Sapporo International Communication Plaza Foundation) 2003, 2004; Yokohama-shi kokusai kouryuu kyoukai (Yokohama Association for International Communications and Exchanges) 1999.

a It is possible that Osaka, Sapporo, Kobe, or Kyoto may have more documents available in foreign languages than I was able to determine through my Web-based research. I could not find reports for those four cities equivalent to those available for Yokohama and Nagoya, which compiled information about this point for the entire city government. For Yokohama and Nagoya, the reports specified exactly which documents were available in each language; reports on translation activities for the other city referred in general to "*tagengo jōhōka*" ("translation in multiple languages") but did not specify which languages or documents were being used. Accordingly, my count for those cities is based on documents I could access through repeated searches of city Web sites and other reports.

b Yokohama's top page varies by time of access. In one version, a visible link to English pages appears in the upper right corner of the page; in the second version no such link is present.

Table 3.4. Additional Incorporation Policies

	Financial Support to Non-National Residents	School-Age Education Activities
Yokohama	Scholarships to foreign exchange students.	Active recruitment of foreign teachers to present international exchange education to elementary students, since 1987.
Osaka	Scholarships to foreign exchange students. Provision of small number of apartments for foreign exchange students. Monthly allowance for disabled foreign residents. Monthly allowance for elderly foreign residents who are ineligible for national pensions.	Guidance counselors to support ethnic clubs in public schools. Establishing ethnic clubs at public schools. Special materials for teaching Japanese as a second language for schoolchildren. Clubs for schoolchildren to use their native languages. Support for public school teachers to study abroad.
Nagoya	Scholarships to foreign exchange students. Provision of small number of apartments for foreign exchange students.	Special Japanese language teachers and texts for foreign children. Intensified counseling services for foreign children. Translated guides for entering public school.
Sapporo	Provision of small number of apartments for foreign exchange students.	Cultural outreach, including JET teachers, exchange visitors.
Kobe	Scholarships to foreign exchange students from less developed countries. Public housing dedicated for foreign exchange students, single and with families.	Multicultural Children's Center. Loans educational materials, provides support staff to help individual children adjust to Japanese schools. Telephone and in person consultations on education issues.
Kyoto	Support for foreigners without access to national pensions. Minimal monthly assistance for national health insurance fees for foreign exchange students paying for their own studies.	Staff member at each school dedicated to promoting foreigners' education. Formal commitment to antidiscrimination program in public school, including full teaching of Japanese colonial policy, Korean culture, and so on.

Sources: Kobe kokusai kyouryoku kouryuu sentaa (Kobe International Center for Cooperation and Communication) 2001; Kobe-shi jinken kyouiku/keihatsu konwakai 2003; Kyoto-shi kokusaika suishin shitsu 1999; Nagoya City 2002; Nagoya-shi Shichou-shitsu Kokusai Kouryuu-ka (International Exchange Section) 2003; Osaka City 2002, 2004a; Sapporo City 2004; Yokohama-shi kaigai kouryuu kyoukai (Yokohama Association for International Communications and Exchanges) 2002; Yokohama-shi kokusai kouryuu kyoukai (Yokohama Association for International Communications and Exchanges) 2003; Yokohama-shi kyouiku iinkai (Yokohama City Board of Education) 1999.

Other Incorporation Policies

Two other kinds of policies serve to incorporate non-Japanese nationals into the community and economy in the six cities: direct financial support and school-age educational programs. All six cities are active in both areas, as shown in table 3.4. All provide some financial assistance to foreign exchange students living in their community, although there are considerable differences in the content of other financial programs.

In addition to these specific initiatives, the cities further contribute to the incorporation of foreign residents by supporting nongovernmental organizations that reach out to this population. All of the cities strive to promote networking between NGOs involved in incorporation activities, while Kobe and Sapporo go so far as to provide them with direct financial assistance.

Cultural Outreach through International Centers

Each city supports an international center incorporated as a nonprofit foundation (*zaidan hōjin*), following Ministry of Home Affairs orders in 1988.[10] Most centers have staff that they hired directly, but they also include some bureaucrats forwarded from agencies within the municipality, a mix that allows for considerable integration of their activities with those of the city government proper. Thus, for example, international centers usually participate heavily in the efforts to mitigate language barriers. Table 3.5 shows that in all of the cities except Yokohama, the cultural activities that are folded into the understanding of "internal internationalization" — and consequently linked with incorporation initiatives more directly targeted at immigration issues — are managed jointly by the city government and the international centers. International centers typically coordinate "international understanding" promotion programs, overseas study trips for students and local officials, and social events to bring non-national and Japanese residents together. International centers also provide public spaces for these activities, and they include on their staffs young

---

[10] Kashiwazaki (2003) recounts the planning that led the Ministry of Home Affairs to involve itself in internationalization programs. See also Jichisho 1988 for original language of the order to the prefectures. In the 2001 reorganization of the national bureaucracy, the Ministry of Home Affairs was folded into the new Ministry of Public Management, Home Affairs, and Posts and Telecommunications.

foreigners hired as "coordinators of international relations" recruited through the national government's Japan Exchange and Teaching Program. Overall, the activities of the international centers are the most similar across cities, which is to be expected given their close ties to the national government.

Table 3.5. Cultural Activities

	Cultural Activities	Responsible Organization
Yokohama	CIR, IE, OS, OX, PS, SC, SE	YOKE (International Center)
Osaka	CIR, EM, HS, IE, OS, OX, PS, SC, SE	City government; I-House Osaka (International Center)
Nagoya	CIR, HS, IE, PS, OS, OX, SC, SE	City government, Mayor's Office; NIC (International Center)
Sapporo	CIR, HS, IE, OX, PS, SC	City government, General Affairs Bureau; Sapporo International Communication Plaza (International Center)
Kobe	CIR, IE, PS, SC, SE	KICC (International Center); City government effort involves multiple divisions
Kyoto	CIR, HS, IE, PS, SC	City government, General Affairs Bureau

KEY   CIR = "coordinators of international relations" through Japan Exchange & Teaching Program; EM = production of educational media; HS = homestay for foreign visitors; IE = international understanding education; OS = overseas study for city officials; OX = overseas exchange programs; PS = public space for "international" events; SC = sister-city exchanges; SE = social events with foreigners

Sources: Kobe kokusai kyouryoku kouryuu sentaa (Kobe International Center for Cooperation and Communication) 2001; Kyoto-shi kokusaika suishin shitsu 1999; Nagoya Kokusai Sentaa (Nagoya International Center) 2002; Nagoya-shi Somu-kyoku Kikakubu Kikakuka (Nagoya City General Affairs Bureau Planning Section) 2001; Osaka City 2004a; Osaka Kokusai Kouryuu Sentaa (International House Osaka Foundation) 2004; Sapporo City 2004; Sapporo Kokusai Puraza (Sapporo International Communication Plaza Foundation) 2003; Yokohama-shi kokusai kouryuu kyoukai (Yokohama Association for International Communications and Exchanges) 2002, 2003.

Research on the Appropriate Scope of Incorporation Initiatives

The most common research activity pursued by local governments consists of surveys of foreign residents to assess social needs and the demand for incorporation programs. Cities also occasionally survey their Japanese residents to measure public support for providing such programs. Additional examples of related research conducted by these six cities over the past few years include Osaka's project investigating a Korean language curriculum for use at public schools and Sapporo's survey of almost two hundred local nongovernmental and nonprofit organizations involved in international exchange activities (including organizations working with migrants) (Osaka City 2004a; Sapporo Kokusai Puraza [Sapporo International Communication Plaza Foundation] 2003).

Advocacy with the National Government

The most common form of advocacy is for a city council to petition the national government to grant local suffrage rights to long-term foreign residents. The quest for local suffrage has been a central issue for the civil rights movement by Korean residents in Japan since 1987 (Mindan 2004). In 1994, led by Mindan, permanent Korean residents and their Japanese allies targeted local government councils as potential allies in their efforts to gain voting rights, asking them to sign a petition requesting the national government to change its stance on this issue. An October 1994 ruling by the Fukui District Court that granting local suffrage would not violate the Constitution garnered national press coverage, adding legitimacy to the campaign. As of April 2004, 46 percent of local municipalities and prefectures had signed the petition; all six of the cities under discussion are among them (Mindan 2003).

Moreover, several towns have invited their foreign residents to vote in local referenda. And Osaka's policy plan for "foreign national citizens" explicitly commits the city to lobby the national government to continue easing the burden of the foreigners' registration system (Osaka City 2004a). The plan also points out that the city has been hiring foreign nationals to public positions in the areas of general office work, welfare policy, and technical skills since 1997. Kyoto's internationalization promotion plan affirms the need to press the national government to treat non-nationals equally with regard to national health care and pension programs (Kyoto-shi kokusaika suishin shitsu 1999).

Creation of Alternative Forms for Political Participation

All six of the cities mention the need to involve their foreign residents in local government policy making. Osaka, Kobe, and Kyoto have taken concrete steps to provide distinct institutions to ensure that participation of some kind exists.[11] As mentioned above, Osaka created its consultative body for foreign residents in 1992; it started meeting in 1994 (Osaka City 2004a). Known as the *Osaka-shi gaikokuseki jyūmin shisaku yushikisha kaigi* (Osaka Expert Committee on Foreign National Residents' Policy), the group is composed of up to twenty members chosen by the mayor to serve two-year, renewable terms. According to Higuchi, half of the members should be non-Japanese; however, the formal explanation of the Committee does not include this restriction (Higuchi 2000). As of April 2004, the Committee had twelve members, six with non-Japanese names (Osaka City 2004a).

Kobe's consultative council, the *Gaikokujin shimin kaigi* (Council of Foreigner Citizens), began meeting in 2003. It has ten appointed members; eight are foreign residents and two are academics with related research specialties (Kobe City 2004). The Council, which liaises with Kobe's city government through the International Division of the Daily Life, Culture, and Tourism Bureau, is charged with reporting on resident foreigners' opinions of city government by January 1, 2005.

Kyoto's consultative council, *Kyoto-shi gaikokuseki shimin shisaku konwakai* (Kyoto Council for Foreign-National Citizens' Policy), began its quarterly meetings in 1998 (Kyoto City 2004). The mayor has set membership at twelve or fewer, with seven seats going to foreigners selected by the mayor's office from a pool of applicants, plus five Japanese academics or NGO members.

JAPANESE LOCAL CITIZENSHIP IN COMPARATIVE CONTEXT

Cities frame the programs detailed in the previous section in a striking rhetoric of local citizenship. Yokohama, Nagoya, Sapporo, Kobe, and Kyoto declare that the policies reviewed here are dedicated to the needs of "foreigner citizens" (*gaikokujin shimin*) or "foreign-national citizens" (*gaikokuseki shimin*). Osaka and the sixteen municipalities of the Committee for Localities with a Concentrated Foreign Population target "foreign-national

---

[11] Nagoya's Human Rights Policy Promotion Plan refers to the need for a consultative council of some sort, but I could find no indication that one has been created, nor could I find information about the status of that plan (Nagoya City 2002).

residents" (*gaikokuseki jyūmin*). All three phrases emphasize foreign residents' status as legitimate members of the local community. All three phrases de-emphasize the significance of national citizenship as the basis for receipt of services from local government.

To students of comparative immigration politics, the goals espoused by Japanese municipalities appear as one more piece of evidence in support of claims that we are witnessing a widespread trend among advanced industrial democracies to decouple substantive citizenship from juridical citizenship. To students of comparative urban studies, the fact that it is the municipal governments that are promoting an alternative definition of citizenship affirms claims that urban areas are home to the most intriguing developments in citizenship institutions across the world. My goal in this section is to show why local-level responses to immigration in Japan should be considered in comparative context.

"Citizenship" is a complicated term. As used by contemporary social theorists, it may invoke one or more of four distinct institutions and practices: juridical, substantive, cultural, and participatory citizenship.[12] The four dimensions of citizenship are linked, which explains why they are sometimes conflated. Distinguishing them analytically is necessary, however, because each dimension plays out differently in political practice and policy making. The distinctions are particularly useful when comparing one society to another, because the ways in which each dimension of citizenship is articulated and the ways in which they are combined vary with spatial and historical setting.

- *Juridical Citizenship.* Juridical citizenship comprises the formal, legal status managed through governmental techniques such as passports, identity cards, and family registers. Until the 1990s, juridical citizenship was of little interest to policymakers and scholars. At that time,

---

[12] Political philosophers Will Kymlicka and Wayne Norman divide citizenship into two concepts, "citizenship-as-legal-status, that is, as full membership in a particular political community; and citizenship-as-desirable-activity, where the extent and quality of one's citizenship is a function of one's participation in that community" (Kymlicka and Norman 1994). Anthropologists James Holston and Arjun Appadurai offer a more empirical definition, distinguishing between formal citizenship, "membership in the nation-state," and substantive citizenship, "the array of civil, political, socioeconomic, and cultural rights people possess and exercise" (Holston and Appadurai 1999). See also Rothschild 1999 for an extensive bibliography of notable scholarship that is particularly strong on sources addressing substantive citizenship.

growing uneasiness with the ambivalent legal status of long-term resident foreigners in post-civil-rights-era liberal democracies peaked. Heated political debates have produced significant changes in the methods for acquiring citizenship in Great Britain, Germany, France, and the United States (Hansen 1999; Schuck 2000). The disintegration of the Soviet Union triggered a parallel debate in successor states as they struggled to specify legitimate, yet politically palatable, procedures for granting juridical formal membership to the ethnically diverse populations within their territories (Laitin 1998).

- *Substantive Citizenship.* Substantive citizenship refers to the contract-like relationships of rights and obligations that bind states and societies together. T. H. Marshall famously divided substantive citizenship into three categories of civil, political, and social rights in his explanation of liberal states. In contemporary liberal democracies, the most deeply institutionalized rights include freedom of speech and assembly, universal adult suffrage, national pensions, unemployment insurance, and public education. Recent debates about substantive citizenship have refocused attention on the other half of the relationship, questioning whether those receiving various entitlements are fulfilling their obligations to state and nation.

- *Cultural Citizenship.* The third dimension of citizenship captures the sense that sharing membership in a polity can underpin individuals' sense of social and cultural belonging. One reason, then, to value juridical citizenship is for its supposed ability to support an integrated collective identity or "common culture" (Kymlicka and Norman 1994). Cultural unity, in turn, is valued because it facilitates the smooth social relations necessary for productive industrial economies (Gellner 1964, 1983). Feminist and multicultural theorists doubt the beneficial effects of cultural unity, however, observing that citizenship should be differentiated so as to ameliorate the oppression of groups historically different from mainstream conceptions of the "universal" citizen (Kymlicka 1995; Kymlicka and Norman 1994; Pateman 1970; Young 1990). Policies regarding public education curricula, affirmative action, and autonomous regions within states typically validate particular preferences regarding citizens' identity.

- *Participatory Citizenship.* This fourth dimension of citizenship is normative. Many strands within Western political philosophy hold that persons who participate in public, associational life realize the richest dimensions of human existence. Participating in politics generates happiness and good character traits like civility and self-restraint. When citizens possess these traits, good government is possible. Praise for nongovernmental organizations, volunteerism, community-based associations, and cooperative workplace relations in democratic societies rests upon the conception that the best citizen is one who is engaged in communal life (Putnam 2000; Putnam, Leonardi, and Nanetti 1993).

Participants in immigration policy debates throughout the world invoke all four dimensions of citizenship in justifying their preferred outcomes. Take the key question of what to do with long-term non-naturalized immigrant populations. Naturalization might be imperative if one believes that possession of juridical citizenship contributes to collective identity or if one thinks that the right to vote is a necessary component of participatory citizenship. On the other hand, the reluctance of some immigrant populations to naturalize is often taken as evidence of the inequities that result from undifferentiated citizenship: seeing that they do not fit into the cultural identity that maps onto juridical citizenship, the argument goes, some immigrant populations choose to forgo whatever benefits accrue to those possessing that status.

The core question about immigrant populations in many democracies, however, is whether the decoupling of substantive citizenship from juridical citizenship over the past three decades is an acceptable development. Yasemin Soysal (1995) argues that juridical citizenship is passé, given that states caught up in globalized human rights discourse no longer limit benefits like labor protection, health care, or social welfare payments to legal citizens. James Hollifield (1992, 2000) points additionally to the effect that international regimes and globalizing labor markets have in eroding state sovereignty in immigration policies. Such arguments concur with the broader argument about the decline of the nation-state. Other scholars, such as Christian Joppke (1999), retort that such benefits were never so limited as Soysal supposes, and furthermore that, to the extent that states grant substantive rights to migrants, they do so as a consequence of domestic political processes and judicial activism. Setting aside these debates over the causes and consequences of the decoupling of juridical and substantive citizenship, it is clear that Japanese policymakers have sufficient external examples to follow (if they choose to do so) of societies that grant their noncitizen populations extensive access to public housing, education, health care, welfare, civil rights like freedom of speech and association, and even local suffrage.

But why would it be policymakers at the local level who are making such decisions? An interdisciplinary field of scholars argues that cities throughout the world are serving today as "the strategic arena of the development of citizenship," harkening back to the historic importance of European cities and Greek city-states in political theory and the practice of citizenship (García 1996; Holston and Appadurai 1999; Sassen 1999).[13] Urban residents struggle over economic crises, living conditions, property relations, and social roles by claiming "rights to the city" (Holston 2001). Writing about urban-poor social movements in Brazil, Holston observes that the "rights-discourse of democracy" gives people a language for claiming resources "not in the name of national citizenship ... but because they are city residents."

A worry for political theorists is that while urban residents need access to literal and figurative public space in order to foster their political skills and thus effectively realize their claims, such space is being challenged by neoliberal economic forces (Beauregard and Bounds 2000; Brodie 2000; Sassen 2000, 2001). Local governments are not seen as capable of assuming supporting roles in the preservation of public space; in fact, for theorists like Brodie, city governments are seen as a potential threat to the preservation of participatory urban citizenship. For others, the disjuncture between city as urban space and city as governmental apparatus is simply too wide to be breached (Dagger 2000). Contemporary municipal governments are too fractured, too large, and too disconnected from their populations to be of much use to democracy.

Yet empirical studies suggest otherwise. Returning to anthropologist Holston, we read an account of city bureaucrats in Oceanside, California, puzzling out a response to Latino migrants' violation of city ordinances restricting open-air food vending (Holston 2001). Faced with a decision on the fate of vital economic and cultural activities within this community, city officials saw their options as a choice between "rul[ing] these noncitizens undemocratically or establish[ing] civic participation and democratic practice among them" (Holston 2001). The officials chose the "democratic" path; practically speaking, this meant that they negotiated an exception to

---

[13] The etymology of the English word reveals the historical importance of cities as the setting for institutions of citizenship; likewise, the Japanese term *shimin* echoes Western political history and thought. See Prak 1999 for an account of urban citizenship historically.

the zoning regulations in recognition of cultural differences. In theoretical terms, the officials' decision involved all four citizenship dimensions. First, they chose to ignore juridical citizenship by declining to inquire into the legal status of the Latino residents living in their city. Second, we see a combination of substantive and cultural citizenship in the decision to recognize a "right" to economic activities prohibited to other city residents on the grounds that cultural differences justify different treatment. Finally, the officials were committed to fostering civic participation and democratic practice among all residents under their authority; in short, they were striving to create good participatory citizens.

The Oceanside officials are not alone. Municipal governments throughout Europe and North America are recognizing the local citizenship of migrant populations living in their communities. In recent years, several large collaborative research projects have sought to trace, and even encourage, cooperation between city governments and local nongovernmental actors. The Metropolis Project based in Canada, the United Nations' Management of Social Transformations (MOST) Programme's study on Multicultural Policies and Modes of Citizenship in European Cities, and the Ethnobarometer project on "Migrant Integration in Selected European Cities" all document extensive efforts on the part of local governments to address how to integrate immigrants into citizenship practices at the community level (Koff 2003; Rogers and Tillie 2001; Metropolis Project 1998).

In Japan, cities' use of the term *shimin* is a deliberative counter to the term *kokumin*, which the 1947 Constitution used to designate those persons holding Japanese citizenship. Substantive citizenship rights in Japan are frequently, though not exclusively, referred to as *shiminken*. Moreover, *shimin* is the term used to refer to civil society and social movements, the bastion of "authentic" democratic participatory citizenship. Since the early postwar decades, intellectuals and politicians on the left have used the language of civil society to suggest an alternative to the state's preferred understanding of citizenship in their push for participatory democracy (Saeki 1998). Leftists have seen the dominant citizenship construction as undemocratic because it orients the population firmly toward the state, which has presented itself as the ideal representative of a unified majority imagined to envelope the entire national community. Minority groups, the disabled, and women were ceded little space for making claims because doing so revealed disunity. And foreigners, whether long-term residents or newly arrived migrants, had absolutely no grounds for claims-making. The multidimensionality of citizenship was denied in this conception: persons possessing legal status as Japanese nationals *all* received rights and ful-filled obligations on an equal ground, because the circle of cultural belong-ing encompassed *all* persons with juridical citizenship. Participation was not a problem, because the state could benevolently guide the united, har-monious citizenry.

Using the term *shimin* breaks the perfect mapping of one type of citi-zenship upon all the others. Cities refer to the demands of human rights and internationalization policies, which are endorsed by the national gov-ernment, to naturalize and legitimize their initiatives. Looking behind Japanese local government rhetoric of local citizenship for *gaikoku-jin/gaikokuseki shimin*, we find references to participatory, cultural, and substantive citizenship dimensions parallel to those traced across the lib-eral democracies. All of the designated cities reviewed above, with the partial exception of Sapporo, explain their incorporation policies in similar terms.[14] A commitment to fostering participation as the way to create a multicultural society (*tabunka shakai zukuri*) is expressed by Yokohama as follows:

> Our goal is to encourage people from various cultural back-grounds living here to come together to recognize each other's cultures so that they can revolutionize individual consciousness and change the community, thereby building a multicultural society that eliminates discrimination and prejudice against foreigners and protects basic human rights (Yokohama-shi kokusai kouryuu kyoukai [Yokohama Asso-ciation for International Communications and Exchanges] 2003).

Osaka indicates its goal of providing services thusly:

> Internationalization has progressed to the extent that we see interactions between people of different nationalities and ethnicities in the community, at work, and at school. Issues have arisen related to foreigners' access to welfare, health care, housing, employment, and education. Differences in

---

[14] Although Sapporo uses the term *gaikokujin shimin* liberally in its policy documents and on its official Web site, reading further, one finds an older version of internationalization that suggests that the major intention of city policies is to enrich the lives of the Japanese nationals who are resident in Sapporo by making the city more charming.

language, culture, and daily customs leave foreign residents socially isolated and vulnerable to conflicts, so we seek to create an environment where they can live comfortably and receive public services [shimin saabisu] without stumbling over language differences (Osaka City 2004a).

Finally, using language from Nagoya, we see the commitment to crafting collective community identity through incorporation programs:

We aim to make the city easy for foreigner citizens to live in, so that they are fully accepted as members of the community, able to comfortably go about their daily lives without inconvenience or trouble (Nagoya-shi Somukyoku Kikakubu Kikakuka [Nagoya City General Affairs Bureau Planning Section] 2001).

The message in all of these statements is that lack of juridical citizenship does not matter. Foreigners living in the cities managed by these governments should be recognized as having a role in the community equal to that of residents with Japanese citizenship. Kobe presents it most clearly: in planning documents for rebuilding after the 1995 earthquake, the city government declared its intent to "overcome nationality" as well as ethnicity. "We want to plan for a Kobe that is appealing to foreigners, to make an environment where being a foreign citizen is not a disadvantage in any area of life, including one's profession, child raising, enjoyment of nature, social life, amusements, or cultural pursuits" (Kobe-shi fukkou/kasseika suishin konwakai [Kobe City Restoration and Rejuvenation Promotion Council] 2004). The initiatives put in place in Japanese cities over the past decade contribute to the air of excitement about the potential for a more open, perhaps more democratic, local citizenship as an alternative to national-level juridical citizenship that is closed on the grounds of national identity, ethnicity, and race.

OVERCOMING NATIONALITY: PROMISE OR ILLUSION?

Before succumbing to the excitement over this marked rhetorical shift, however, we must consider the grounds for doubting that the promise to overcome nationality will be fulfilled. Assertions that the promise is only an illusion could come from two main perspectives. First, it might be that the promise will fade because of limitations in local governments' will and capacity. Second, it may be that the programs will founder in the face of national structures and beliefs.

With regard to the motivations of municipal authorities, we must consider the possibility that most of the political support for incorporation policies stems from fear.[15] Self-interested bureaucrats may be hiding their fear of social disruption and their desire to continue controlling the local population behind a more palatable facade of human rights and multicultural citizenship. With the numbers of foreign migrants having increased so drastically in the past two decades, local officials may have lost their faith in the continued viability of marginalization and taken recourse in containment. Perhaps they are imagining that resident foreigners will be content with the language and cultural policies, and the alternative forms of political participation, and thus ignore the continued existence of discrimination and prejudice in Japan.

The skepticism about local government capacity is twofold. First, it may be that local governments, whether sincere or not in their commitment to local citizenship, are unable to muster the necessary resources to reach very many foreign nationals. And because many newcomers do not envision staying in Japan for the long term,[16] they do not take steps to integrate into the community, making it even harder for local governments to reach them. Overcoming resistance to social incorporation (or participatory citizenship!) is no easy task even for highly motivated actors.

Second, local governments may prove unable to maintain their relative insulation from public opinion in adopting incorporation policies. To date, ordinary Japanese residents of these cities have tolerated these programs, even though they did not request them. It may be that Japan will experience a backlash against foreign migrants in the future, similar to those that have occurred in other liberal democracies.

Turning to national structures and beliefs, even local governments that are sincerely committed to their stated goals must contend with the continued power of national citizenship and the organizations that protect it. The cultural content of national citizenship is strong: many, if not most,

---

[15] Susan Pharr reminded me of this point during a presentation of an earlier version of this chapter at the Reischauer Institute for Japanese Studies, Harvard University, in February 2003.

[16] From studies of international migration in other settings, academics know that even though such sentiments often prevail, they cannot be taken as trustworthy predictions of whether individuals will stay or immigrant enclaves will persist.

Japanese people affirm the image of a homogenous, harmonious Japan. Convincing them that a multicultural Japan is a desirable goal will require sustained effort. Moreover, national political actors like the Ministry of Justice and the Ministry of Education, Culture, Sports, Science, and Technology have long-standing institutional missions that commit them to preserving the dominant sense of the nation. Sociologist Tarumoto Hideki cautions that the national state will prevail because it continues to dominate politics in Japan. Human rights and internationalization may not provide sufficiently weighty anchors for the effort to reform an exclusive citizenship regime that has been in place since the end of World War II (Kashiwazaki 2003; Tarumoto 2003).[17] The resilience of national citizenship as an institution extends beyond Japan. In his assessment of findings from the United Nations' MOST project on local citizenship in Europe, political scientist John Crowley (2001) argues that we have yet to compile good evidence for the existence of distinct local political spheres or local political fields. Instead of serving as an alternative to national citizenship, the kind of political activity being referred to as "local citizenship" is no more than a symptom of the continued exclusionary nature of national citizenship. Important political efforts must still be directed toward the national level.

CONCLUSION

Time will tell whether local incorporation programs can "overcome" national citizenship in Japan (or anywhere else). Yet as necessary as it is to seriously consider the objections raised above, it is clear that a great deal has changed in Japan. Japan's tight closure to international migration is over. The refusal of public institutions to imagine cultural, ethnic, and racial differences as potentially positive factors in society is over. The activist community seeking increased substantive rights, cultural recognition, and political participation is more vocal than ever before. Moreover, each of the objections raised above can be countered, even if not definitively dismissed. Some local government support for incorporation policies undoubtedly stems from fear rather than wholehearted commitment to human rights, multiculturalism, and internationalization. Irrespective of the mixed motives behind their creation, though, the policies still stand. Ordinary Japanese citizens may not have sought local citizenship for foreign

---

[17] Note, however, that Tarumoto thinks that lobbying by foreign actors can be very influential, as in the repeated interventions by the Republic of Korea on behalf of the zainichi Koreans.

residents, but they now find it being promoted by their city governments, taught to their children at school, and claimed by their neighbors, employees, and co-workers who do not possess Japanese nationality. As for the central government's power over and against local government initiatives, there are plentiful examples of local policies shifting the course of national policies in the past forty years or more. Moreover, the national government is no longer a monolith united behind a singular perspective or set of interests with regard to immigration or immigrant policies. Perhaps that is the strongest lesson to be drawn from this essay: where there was long silence, there now exists a debate with many voices expressing opposing ideas about Japanese citizenship and immigration policy.

References

Andersen, Uwe. 1990. Consultative institutions for migrant workers. In *The political rights of migrant workers in Western Europe*, edited by Z. Layton-Henry. London: Sage.

Beauregard, Robert A., and Anna Bounds. 2000. Urban citizenship. In *Democracy, citizenship, and the global city*, edited by E. F. Isin. London: Routledge.

Brodie, Janine. 2000. Imagining democratic urban citizenship. In *Democracy, citizenship, and the global city*, edited by E. F. Isin. London: Routledge.

Crowley, John. 2001. Afterward: Citizenship and its modes. In *Multicultural policies and modes of citizenship in European cities*, edited by A. R. a. J. Tillie. Aldershot: Ashgate.

Dagger, Richard. 2000. Metropolis, memory, and citizenship. In *Democracy, citizenship, and the global city*, edited by E. F. Isin. London: Routledge.

Ebashi, Takashi. 1993. *Gaikokujin wa Jumin desu: Jichitai no Gaikokujin Jumin Shisaku Gaido* (Foreigners are local citizens: A guide to local government policies for foreign local citizens). Tokyo: Gakuyo Shobo.

Gaikokujin Shuujuu Toshi Kaigi (Committee for Localities with a Concentrated Foreign Population). 2001. Hamamatsu Sengen oyobi Teigen [Hamamatsu Declaration]. Hamamatsu, Japan.

———. 2002. Gaikokujin shuujyuu toshi tokyo kaigi ni okeru 14 toshi kyoudou apiru (Appeal from 14 cities of the Tokyo meeting of the Committee for Localities with a Concentrated Foreign Population). Tokyo.

García, Soledad. 1996. Cities and citizenship. *International Journal of Urban and Regional Research* 20 (1):7–21.

Gellner, Ernst. 1964. *Thought and change*. Chicago: University of Chicago Press.

———. 1983. *Nations and nationalism*. Ithaca, NY: Cornell University Press.

Han, Seung-Mi. 2004. From the communitarian ideal to the public sphere: The making of foreigners' assemblies in Kawasaki City and Kanagawa Prefecture. *Social Science Japan Journal* 7:41–60.

Hansen, Randall. 1999. Migration, citizenship and race in Europe: Between incorporation and exclusion. *European Journal of Political Research* 35 (4):415–45.

Higuchi, Naoto. 2000. Political participation of foreign residents. Paper read at the conference Differences and Convergences of Immigration Politics of Japan and Europe: National and Local Levels, Public and Private Spheres. Rikkyo University, September 13.

Hollifield, James F. 1992. *Immigrants, markets, and states: The political economy of postwar Europe.* Cambridge, MA: Harvard University Press.

————. 2000. The politics of international migration: How can we "bring the state back in"? In *Migration theory: Talking across disciplines,* edited by by C. Brettell and J. F. Hollifield. London: Routledge.

Holston, James. 2001. Urban citizenship and globalization. In *Global city regions: Trends, theory, policy,* edited by A. J. Scott. Oxford: Oxford University Press.

Holston, James, and Arjun Appadurai. 1999. Introduction: Cities and citizenship. In *Cities and citizenship,* edited by J. Holston. Durham, NC: Duke University Press.

Houmusho Nyukoku Kanri Kyoku (Ministry of Justice Immigration Bureau). 2004. *Heisei 15 nen matsu genzai ni okeru gaikokujin torokusha toukei ni tsuite* (2003 statistics on registered foreigners). http://www.moj.go.jp/index .html. Accessed August 17, 2004.

Jichisho (Ministry of Home Affairs). 1988. *Chi-iki Kokusai Kouryuu Suishin Taikou no Sakutei ni kansuru Shirei ni suite* (Regarding the order on an outline for the promotion of local internationalization). Tokyo, February 14.

Joppke, Christian. 1999. *Immigration and the nation-state.* Oxford: Oxford University Press.

Kashiwazaki, Chikako. 2003. Local government and resident foreigners: A changing relationship. In *Japan's road to pluralism: Transforming local communities in the global era,* edited by S. F. a. T. Menju. Tokyo: Japan Center for International Exchange.

Kitayama, Toshiya. 2001. Local government policy initiatives. In *Program for the study of Japanese development management experience,* edited by F. Iqbal. Washington, DC: World Bank.

Kobe City. 2004. Home page. http://www.city.kobe.jp/. Accessed April 12, 2004.

Kobe kokusai kyouryoku kouryuu sentaa (Kobe International Center for Cooperation and Communication). 2001. Home page. http://www.kicc.jp/. Accessed August 1, 2004.

Kobe-shi bousai kaigi (Kobe City Natural Disaster Protection Council). 2003. Kobe-shi chiiki bousai keikaku: bousai taiou manyuaru (Kobe City local disaster protection plan: Response manual). Kobe.

Kobe-shi fukkou/kasseika suishin konwakai (Kobe City Restoration and Rejuvenation Promotion Council). 2004. Kobe-shi fukko/kasseika suishin konwakai kara no teigen. Kobe.

Kobe-shi jinken kyouiku/keihatsu konwakai. 2003. Jinken kyouiku oyobi jinken keihatsu no kihonteki arikata ni tsuite (teigen) (Declaration on basic methods of human rights education and enlightenment). Kobe.

Koff, Harlan. 2003. *Migration integration in European cities*. Rome: Ethnobarometer.

Komai, Hiroshi. 1997. Hajime ni–Uchinaru Kokusaika ni yoru Tabun Kyôsei Shakai no Kochiku (To begin: Building a multi-cooperative society through internal internationalization). In *Jichitai no Gaikokujin Seisaku: Uchinaru Kokusaika he no Torikumi* (Local governments foreigners' policy: Measures for internal internationalization), edited by H. Komai and I. Watadô. Tokyo: Akashi Shoten.

Kondo, Atsushi. 2001. *Gaikokujin no jinken to shiminken* (Human and civil rights of foreigners). Tokyo: Akashi Shoten.

Kosuge, Koichi. 2004. Nihon seifu/jichitai no taio: 'gaikokujin-cho' giron shite wa. *Asahi Shinbun*, February 11.

Kymlicka, Will. 1995. *The rights of minority cultures*. New York: Oxford University Press.

Kymlicka, Will, and Wayne Norman. 1994. Return of the citizen: A survey of recent work on citizenship theory. *Ethics* 104:352–81.

Kyoto City. 2004. Home page. http://www.city.kyoto.jp/koho/ind_h.htm. Accessed April 13, 2004.

Kyoto-shi kokusai kouryuu kyoukai (Kyoto City International Foundation). 2002. Home page. http://www.kcif.or.jp/. Accessed July 12, 2004.

Kyoto-shi kokusaika suishin shitsu. 1999. *Kyoto-shi kokusaika suishin shitsu.* http://www.city.kyoto.jp/somu/kokusai/index.html. Accessed April 13, 2004.

Laitin, David. 1998. *Identity in formation: The Russian-speaking populations in the near abroad*. Ithaca, NY: Cornell University Press.

Metropolis Project. 1998. Home page. http://canada.metropolis.net/. Accessed July 14, 2004.

Mindan. 2003. *Chiho Sanseiken: Chiho sanseiken shiryou: Ikensho saitaku chihou betsu toukei*. http://www.mindan.org/sidemenu/sm_sansei27.php. Accessed April 9, 2004.

———. 2004. *Chihou sanseiken: Chihou sanseiken undo no ayumi to tenbo (04.1.1)*. http://www.mindan.org/sidemenu/sm_sansei_view.php?newsid=2363&subpage=24. Accessed April 9, 2004.

Miyajima, Takashi. 2000. *Gaikokujin shim in to seiji sanka* (Foreigner citizens and political participation). Tokyo: Yushindo kobunsha.

Nagoya City. 2002. Nagoya jinken shisaku suishin puran (Plan to Promote human rights policy in Nagoya).

———. 2004. Home page. http://www.city.nagoya.jp/ Accessed April 12, 2004.

Nagoya Kokusai Sentaa (Nagoya International Center). 2002. Home page. http://www.nic-nagoya.or.jp/. Accessed July 7, 2004.

Nagoya-shi Shichou-shitsu Kokusai Kouryuu-ka (International Exchange Section, Mayor's Office, Nagoya City). 2003. Nagoya-shi kokusai kouryuu ji-gyou no aramashi (Overview of Nagoya City's international exchange operations). Nagoya.

Nagoya-shi Somukyoku Kikakubu Kikakuka (Nagoya City General Affairs Bureau Planning Section). 2001. Nagoya Shinseiki keikaku 2010 dai-ichiji jisshi keikaku (Operational plan for Nagoya's new century: 2010). Nagoya.

Osaka City. 2002. Osaka-shi kokusaika suishin kihon shishin (Osaka guiding principles for promotion of internationalization). Osaka.

———. 2004a. Osaka-shi gaikokuseki juumin shisaku kihon shishin (Guiding principles of Osaka policies toward foreign national residents). Osaka.

———. 2004b. Home page. http://www.city.osaka.jp/. Accessed April 16, 2004.

Osaka Kokusai Kouryuu Sentaa (International House Osaka Foundation). 2004. I-Koko 2004. http://www.ih-osaka.or.jp/i.house/. Accessed April 16, 2004.

Pateman, Carole. 1970. *Participation and democratic theory*. Cambridge: Cambridge University Press.

Prak, Maarten. 1999. Burghers into citizens: Urban and national citizenship in the Netherlands during the revolutionary era (c. 1800). In *Extending citizenship, reconfiguring states*, edited by M. Hanagan and C. Tilly. Lanham, MD: Rowman and Littlefield.

Putnam, Robert. 2000. *Bowling alone: The collapse and revival of American community*. New York: Simon and Schuster.

Putnam, Robert, Robert Leonardi, and Raffaella Nanetti. 1993. *Making democracy work: Civic traditions in modern Italy*. Princeton, NJ: Princeton University Press.

Rogers, Alisdair, and Jean Tillie. 2001. *Multicultural policies and modes of citizenship in European cities*, edited by A. a. J. T. Rogers. Alderson and Burlington, VT: Ashgate.

Rothschild, Teal. 1999. A bibliography of citizenship. In *Extending citizenship, rconfiguring states*, edited by M. Hanagan and C. Tilly. Lanham, MD: Rowman and Littlefield.

Saeki, Keishi. 1998. *Shimin to wa nani ka: Sengo minshuushuugi wo toinaosu* (What is the citizen?). Tokyo: PHP Shinsho.

Sapporo City. 2004. Home page. http://www.city.sapporo.jp/city/. Accessed April 12, 2004.

Sapporo Kokusai Puraza (Sapporo International Communication Plaza Foundation). 2003. Heisei 14 nendo jigyou houkokusho (2002 Operations report). Sapporo.

————. 2004. Home page. http://www.plaza-sapporo.or.jp/. Accessed July 13, 2004.

Sassen, Saskia. 1999. Whose city is it? Globalization and the formation of new claims. In *Cities and citizenship*, edited by J. Holston. Durham, NC: Duke University Press.

————. 2000. The global city: Strategic site/new frontier. In *Democracy, citizenship, and the global city*, edited by E. F. Isin. London: Routledge.

————. 2001. *The global city: New York, London, Tokyo*. 2d ed. Princeton, NJ: Princeton University Press.

Schuck, P. H. 2000. Citizenship in federal systems. *American Journal of Comparative Law* 48 (2):195–226.

Soysal, Yasemin Nuhoglu. 1995. *Limits of citizenship: Migrants and postnational membership in Europe*. Chicago: University of Chicago Press.

Statistics Bureau. 2002. *Current population estimates as of October 1, 2002*. http://www.stat.go.jp/english/data/jinsui/2002np/index.htm. Accessed April 7, 2004.

Tanaka, Hiroshi. 1996. *Q&A gaikokujin no chihou sanseiken* (Q & A on local suffrage for foreigners). Tokyo: Gogatsu Shobo.

Tarumoto, Hideki. 2003. State sovereignty vs. international human rights? In the case of the expansion in immigrant rights. Paper read at the conference Policy and Politics in a Globalizing World, Bristol, UK, July 24–26.

Tegtmeyer Pak, Katherine. 2000a. Foreigners are local citizens, too: Local governments respond to international migration in Japan. In *Japan and global migration: Foreign workers and the advent of a multicultural society*, edited by M. Douglass and G. S. Roberts. London: Routledge.

————. 2000b. Living in harmony: Prospects for cooperative local responses to foreign migrants. In *Local voices, national issues: The impact of local politics in Japanese policymaking*, edited by S. Smith. Ann Arbor, MI: Center for Japanese Studies, University of Michigan.

Toyota-shi shakai-bu jijishinkou-ka (Toyota City Municipal Community Development Division). 2004. *Kokusaika suishin jigyou* (Activities to promote internationalization). http://www.city.toyota.aichi.jp/. Accessed August 15, 2004.

Watadô, Ichirô. 1996. *Jichitai seisaku no tenkai to NGO*. Tokyo: Akashi Shoten.

Yamawaki, Keizo, Chikako Kashiwazaki, and Atsushi Kondo. 2001. Taminzoku Kokka Nihon no Koso (Constructing a multi-ethnic Japanese state). *Sekai*.

Yokohama City. 2004. Home page. http://www.city.yokohama.jp/front/welcome.html. Accessed April 12, 2004.

Yokohama-shi kaigai kouryuu kyoukai (Yokohama Association for International Communications and Exchanges). 2002. Youku 20 nen no ayumi: 1981–2000. Yokohama.

Yokohama-shi kokusai kouryuu kyoukai (Yokohama Association for International Communications and Exchanges). 1999. Tagengo joho sakusei manyuaru (Manual for drafting documents in multiple languages). Yokohama.

———. 2002. YOKE misshon suteitomento: youku no katsudo houshin. Yokohama.

———. 2003. Heisei 15 nendo jigyou keikakusho, heisei 15 nendo shuushi yosansho (2003 operations plan: 2003 budget report). Yokohama.

Yokohama-shi kyouiku iinkai (Yokohama City Board of Education). 1999. *Yume hama kyouiku puran* ("Dream Beach" [ideal Yokohama] education plan). http://www.city.yokohama.jp/me/kyoiku/eduplan/hajimeni_2.html. Accessed July 28, 2004.

Young, Iris Marion. 1990. *Justice and the politics of difference*. Princeton, NJ: Princeton University Press.

Zen nihon jichi dantai roudo kumiai (All Japan Prefectural and Municipal Workers Union). 2003. 2003–4 nendo jichirou chiiki jichitai seisaku-shu (Jichirou compilation of local and municipal policies, 2003–4).

CHAPTER **4**

Immigrant Incorporation and Women's Community Activities in Japan: Local NGOs and Public Education for Immigrant Children

KEIKO YAMANAKA

This chapter examines the politics of immigrant incorporation in Hamamatsu City, Japan. By focusing on community activities designed to assist immigrant children growing up in Japan, the study's aim is to understand the ways in which different parties are mobilized toward the common goal of bridging the gaps created by governmental neglect of immigrant social welfare. Its major conclusion is that, without a national policy of immigrant incorporation, efforts by local governments are insufficient and too fragmentary to meet immigrants' educational needs. The study also reveals the central role of women in grassroots activities to provide services to a variety of ethnic communities and to promote multicultural understanding. Their efforts, however, need to be understood in the context of their traditional gender roles and transnational experiences. The analysis begins with a brief overview of Japan's policy regarding new arrivals.

MIGRATION AND THE POLICY OF EXCLUSION

The large influx of global migrants to Japan beginning in the late 1980s has resulted in more than half a million "unskilled" foreign workers residing in

This study was funded in part by a grant from the Japan Foundation's Center for Global Partnership administered by the Center for Comparative Immigration Studies at the University of California, San Diego. Many individuals contributed to this research in Hamamatsu; I owe special thanks to Edvaldo Kondo, Ana Bortz, Miho Miike, and the Hamamatsu NPO Network Center.

the country.[1] Most of these newcomers are denied access to public services, including medical care, social welfare, social security, and participation in local politics (Takafuji 1991; Miyajima and Higuchi 1996). Castles (1997) aptly called such a policy "differential exclusion." The Japanese government maintains that Japan is not a country of immigration. Therefore, it has shown no interest in endorsing the International Convention on the Protection of the Rights of All Migrant Workers and Members of Their Families (Piper and Iredale 2003: 14–17). Nor has the government enacted domestic legislation to eliminate racial discrimination, as required by the International Convention on the Elimination of All Forms of Racial Discrimination, to which it became a signatory in 1995 (Yamanaka 2003a). After decades of vehement protests, "oldcomer" Koreans and Chinese in Japan have achieved equality in the areas of health care, social security, and social welfare, but they remain without the right to participate in local politics (Kondo 2002: 420). Even legally resident unskilled newcomer workers, such as Brazilians and Peruvians of Japanese descent, and their families have been denied rights to inexpensive health and medical care (Yamanaka n.d.). In addition, many of their children are denied education equal to that of Japanese children because legal, institutional, and cultural barriers hinder them from learning effectively in Japanese schools (Ota 1996).

Since the 1960s, local governments have been more responsive than the national government in implementing innovative policies on environmental and social welfare issues. The state's neglect of social rights for recent immigrants has prompted some local governments to take progressive actions to meet their needs. With the arrival of massive numbers of foreign workers since the late 1980s, local governments have become independent policymakers to meet demands from the "internal internationalization" process that is rapidly progressing throughout Japan (Tegtmeyer Pak 2000). For example, in order to counteract a 1990 Ministry of Health and Welfare request to local governments not to apply social welfare programs to sick foreign residents with short-term visas, the Tokyo metropolitan and Kanagawa prefectural governments have revived operation of a 1901 law aimed at assisting travelers who had fallen ill. Similarly, since the early 1990s Gunma and a few other prefectures have launched the public medical emergency fund by which hospitals are guaranteed compensation

---

[1] For Japan's immigration policy and immigrant populations, see Kondo 2002; Tsuda and Cornelius 2004.

for medical costs incurred in treating uninsured foreign patients (Ikegami 2001a: 233–34). In 1992 the Board of Education of Hamamatsu City introduced Japanese language classes for foreign children enrolled in public elementary schools. Moreover, the recent literature is replete with examples of experimental educational programs in which teachers and schools have initiated efforts to reduce the linguistic and instructional barriers that confront non-Japanese-speaking children (Ota 1996; Ikegami 2001b; Onai et al. 2001; Miyajima and Suzuki 2000). Despite these efforts, the challenges of meeting the basic needs of newcomers and their families are overwhelming local governments constrained by inexperience and limited budgets.

MIGRATION AND COMMUNITY ACTIVISM

Japanese citizens' spontaneous responses to mounting immigrant problems are in sharp contrast to the prevailing neglect on the part of the national government and many industries that depend heavily on immigrant labor. Since the early 1990s, a few committed citizens—often members of labor unions, professional associations, and religious organizations—have assisted immigrants in meeting their basic needs in law, employment, health, housing, education, welfare, and human rights (Shipper 2002). They have also advocated for the rights of immigrants as residents, workers, and human beings, in public debates, publications, campaigns, and lobbying efforts with elected officials and government offices (Gurowitz 1999; Tegtmeyer Pak 2000). In many industrial cities where immigrants have settled, often with their families, citizen activists have responded to the immigrant population's lack of access to inexpensive health and medical care as an urgent and alarming community problem (Hamamatsu NPO Network Center 2001; Yamanaka n.d.). Citizens, many of them women, have organized to teach Japanese to immigrants and to help their children in their school studies (Hamamatsu NPO Network Center 2003; Yamanaka 2003b), demonstrating that recent global immigration has energized Japan's civil society and motivated concerned citizens to fill the gap between obsolete governmental policies and the social problems they have imposed upon immigrants.

The inequalities and injustices that migrant workers experience have also motivated them to take collective actions themselves to overcome legal and institutional barriers that block their rights (see Naples 1998; Naples and Desai 2002). Their migrant organizations are often formed on the basis of common interests and shared religious and ethnic affiliations, and they are frequently associated with citizen activists' community and civil rights organizations. Though severely constrained by lack of time, resources, and official visas, migrant workers and foreign residents have engaged in community and civil activism. For example, Filipino women, many of them married to Japanese husbands, have developed extensive networks throughout Japan, aimed at sharing information and enhancing their ability to adapt to Japanese culture and institutions.[2] In Tokyo, with assistance from Japanese activists, a small but determined number of migrant workers, many of them undocumented, have organized a labor union to press employers for the rights guaranteed to them under the Labor Standards Law (Roberts 2000). In the Tokai region, some five hundred Nepalese visa overstayers have organized a variety of community and leisure activities to enhance their national and ethnic solidarity and to counteract problems arising from their illegal status (Yamanaka 2003c). In the northern Kanto region, where large numbers of Pakistani and Bangladeshi migrants have worked since the late 1980s, several mosques have been built with donations from the migrants and their associations. Muslim workers and their families gather regularly in the mosques to pray and socialize with their co-religionists, thus demonstrating their strong will to maintain their religion and culture in an alien environment (Sakurai 2003).

Among the more than 250,000 Brazilians of Japanese descent (the nationality group comprising the largest number of newcomers in Japan), collective actions to enhance their rights as residents are yet to develop.[3] According to Koga (2000), this is explained in part by their temporary employee status in the manufacturing industry, which discourages them from engaging in intense labor and civil rights activism. It may also be attributable to the lack of political consciousness among Brazilian immigrants, most of whom intend to return to Brazil after a short period of employment in Japan. However, the absence of political activism does not suggest that Brazilians have never attempted to organize their social activities in Japan. Within a few years after their arrival, many Brazilians who had been intent only on accumulating savings and returning to Brazil as soon as

[2] Carmen Yamashita's July 2002 interview on activities of Nagaisa no Kai, a group of Filipino women in Hamamatsu.
[3] The massive influx of Brazilian migration began in 1990 when Japan implemented the Revised Immigration and Refugee Control Law, which provided a long-term visa category to people of Japanese ancestry up to the third generation (and their family members), regardless of their occupational skill level and without restriction. For Brazilian labor migration to Japan, see Linger 2001; Roth 2002; Tsuda 2003.

possible began to turn to religion, hobbies, arts, and sports to enrich their lives. As a result, since the early 1990s several community and social organizations have emerged around specific interests in the Brazilian population. These include Catholic churches, Brazilian schools, and Brazilian stores and restaurants where immigrants gather to socialize. Roth (2002: 92–117) describes a popular but short-lived Brazilian cultural center that a young Brazilian man launched in downtown Hamamatsu.[4] This center was a manifestation of the shift in goals and identities as Brazilians made the transition from short-term migrants to long-term residents.

INCREASING NUMBERS OF UNSCHOOLED IMMIGRANT CHILDREN

By the mid-1990s, the presence of a large legal Brazilian resident population in Japan spurred a new type of civil response among Japanese citizens. From the beginning of the immigrants' arrival in the late 1980s and early 1990s, their access to health and medical services was the focus of contentious policy debates among policymakers, medical professionals, and civil activists (Yamanaka n.d.). In contrast, since the mid-to-late 1990s, the emerging social problem of immigrant children's education has attracted public attention from diverse segments of Japanese society—including policymakers, educators, and activists, as well as Japanese parents, ordinary citizens, and the immigrants themselves. Among the many problems concerning immigrant children's education, the greatest attention has gone to the increasing number of unschooled children and their daily unsupervised activities.

Brazilian children in Japan who are of school age (between six and fourteen years of age) have three educational options. They can enroll in Japanese public schools, in Brazilian private schools, or in neither. Because instruction in the public schools is provided only in Japanese, most Brazilian children, especially those ten years and older, are linguistically and culturally unprepared to benefit from this option. Moreover, as noncitizens, they are not required to attend school. Consequently, most municipal boards of education do not recruit foreign children to the public schools. By 2002 many cities had private Brazilian schools, where classes are taught in Portuguese and credits can be transferred to schools in Brazil upon return. However, most immigrant parents cannot afford the tuition at these private schools, which receive little financial support from either the Bra-

---

[4] The center failed primarily because of weak leadership and a resulting financial crisis.

zilian or the Japanese government. As a result, many children remain un-schooled. Some work in factories while others roam the streets, giving local citizens the impression that Brazilian teenagers are truants and delin-quents.

HAMAMATSU: A CASE STUDY OF A CITY WITH A TRANSNATIONAL POPULATION

Hamamatsu, with a population of half a million, is located 257 km south-west of Tokyo. It is one of many industrial cities that received significant shares of the approximately 250,000 Japanese Brazilian immigrants that arrived in Japan between 1990 and 1995. Together with its satellite cities, Kosai and Iwata, it serves as headquarters for several major automobile and motorcycle companies, including Suzuki, Yamaha, and Honda. The city also hosts the two major makers of musical instrument, Yamaha and Kawai Piano, prompting Hamamatsu to label itself the "music capital." Each of these multinational corporations commands thousands of large and small subcontractors that supply parts for assembly into cars and mu-sical instruments by the parent company. Contiguous and to the west, in the eastern part of adjacent Aichi Prefecture, lie the cities of Toyohashi, Toyokawa, Toyota, and others. Collectively, they host another giant auto-maker, Toyota, with its thousands of subcontractors. Both documented and undocumented immigrant workers are drawn to this area because of the chronic labor shortage among its small-scale employers (Kuwahara 2001). By 2001, 12,000 Brazilian nationals and their families had registered as alien residents in Hamamatsu. They accounted for two-thirds of the city's foreign residents, which was 3.5 percent of its total population. Women composed 44 percent of the city's Brazilian population, and children fifteen years old and younger accounted for 21 percent.

Beginning in the 1960s, Hamamatsu's major manufacturing companies were among the trailblazers for Japan's globalizing economy. These firms launched factories in several developing countries in Asia and Latin Amer-ica, where costs for labor and materials were far lower than in Japan and markets for the companies' products were expanding rapidly. Soon these multinational corporations had established branch operations throughout the world, with factories in many regions and with retail markets virtually everywhere. Such a global expansion of business operations entailed mas-sive transfers of capital, technology, and the skills of company managers, engineers, and specialized personnel. Frequently the Japanese employees assigned overseas brought along their families (see, for example, White

1988), who spent between two to ten years as residents in the host society. As they had done in Japan, the wives cared for their households and children while their husbands worked. School-age children were enrolled in local schools or in the Japanese schools available in major cities. Upon coming home to Japan, these "returning children" faced enormous difficulties adjusting to Japanese schools. Their unprecedented situation has attracted much popular and academic attention (Cunningham 1988).

Over the past four decades, Hamamatsu has received thousands of company men and their wives and children who have lived overseas. In addition, the global operations of the city's many multinational corporations have required significant numbers of skilled foreign workers, businessmen, and industrial trainees to work and live in the city for extended periods. The sudden and massive influx of unskilled foreign workers from Brazil (and, in much smaller numbers, from Peru) and their families further expanded the number of foreigners, and the city's total foreign population tripled (from 7,000 to 22, 700) between 1990 and 2003. The 2003 foreign population comprised 13,000 Brazilians, 2,300 Filipinos, 1,600 Koreans, 1,600 Chinese, 1,500 Peruvians, 700 Vietnamese, 600 Indonesians, and 1,200 individuals from seventy other countries (*HICE News* 2004: 6). The extraordinarily diverse composition of the Hamamatsu population now provides a valuable political resource to the city administration, promoting the city's participation in and contribution to the global economy. Mayor Yasuyuki Kitawaki has celebrated Hamamatsu's emergence as a multicultural city unique among Japan's midsize cities. In his words:

> Hamamatsu offers many things universal to the rest of the world. It has many native global corporations. Naturally, its population includes those citizens who have worked overseas and those children who have grown up abroad. They are human resources that provide links to the world.... Hamamatsu also has many foreign residents. It is true that there are problems associated with different cultures and customs. However, these foreigners contribute to the economy and pay taxes for community development. I accept the fact that they live in Hamamatsu, and I want to consider them as partners with citizens in building the city together.... For this goal, I consider it important that we, foreigners and citizens alike, create the ground upon which both parties are able to understand and appreciate each other (Hamamatsu City 2002a).

GENDER AND COMMUNITY ACTIVISM IN A GLOBAL CITY

In July 2001 Hamamatsu celebrated its ninetieth anniversary. In September of that auspicious year, the mayor and his planners laid out their vision of the city's future in a colorful book entitled *Global City Vision: Hamamatsu as a Global City of Technology and Culture* (Hamamatsu City 2001). Presented in three languages—Japanese, English, and Portuguese—*Global City Vision* emphasized a diverse population, cutting-edge technology, and cultural accomplishments (especially in music) as the city's unique universal (or global) characteristics. In this grand plan, a global city is defined as one capable of sending a wide range of technological and cultural activities to the world (Hamamatsu City 2001: 8–9). Such a city, according to this publication, would strive to promote global interaction by making efforts to develop international cooperation and collaboration among cities. As a city with global corporations and a multiethnic population, Hamamatsu also encourages its Japanese citizens and foreign residents to establish mutual understanding and common rules for the construction of a multicultural city with social cohesion, a key element in Hamamatsu's "global vision."

The city has proposed five major "policies and projects" directed toward achieving this goal (Hamamatsu City 2001: 40–43). First, the city will attempt to provide foreign citizens with equal access to government services and will support activities by citizens and nongovernmental organizations aimed at building a socially cohesive multicultural city. Second, the city will make efforts to provide an opportunity wherein citizens and foreign residents can discuss community rules; this goal may be achieved by establishing a Committee for Social Cohesion (*kyosei kaigi*). Third, the city will help foreign residents develop a Foreign Citizens' Assembly to voice their opinions and participate in local governance. Fourth, to create a safe and pleasant living environment for foreign residents, the city will strive to address such urgent community issues as health and medical services, disaster prevention measures, and emotional counseling services. Fifth, to meet the needs of foreign residents, the city will make special organizational and cultural efforts to reach out to foreign communities; these measures include the use of foreign languages at service counters in city hall and visits by officials to foreign communities for discussion and counseling.

The "Global Vision" does not, however, include any proposals to establish a task force or organization within the city administration that would be responsible for carrying out multicultural projects. Nor does it mention how the city would finance such projects under its authority. The only specific proposal was that the city's civil society, comprising volunteers and nongovernmental organizations, would be called upon to bridge the gaps between different cultures and languages in order to deepen mutual understanding. This absence of a concrete blueprint implies that, instead of taking responsibility by launching its own initiatives, the local administration leaves it to citizen volunteers, foreign volunteers, and volunteer organizations to liaise with foreign communities in order to "bridge the gap" between immigrant communities and the city administration. This suggests that the local government is willing to delegate its authority to grassroots groups in carrying out multicultural projects. It will not, however, financially reward volunteers who would dedicate their ideas and energy to the projects.

Over the course of the 1990s, Hamamatsu witnessed rapid growth of a wide range of voluntary services and activities among its citizenry. Underlying this surge of community organizing is a growing emphasis throughout Japan on self-governance at the grassroots. Rising from the ashes of the 1995 Kobe earthquake, and endorsed by the passage of the 1998 Law to Promote Specified Non-Profit Activities, this new civil society movement has energized all segments of Japanese society in the practice of participatory democracy. In contrast to traditional community activism, which serves the interests of specific neighborhoods, the new community activism stresses public interest, voluntarism, nonprofit objectives, and nongovernmental organization (Tajiri 2001: 19). It addresses a broad range of societal concerns, including education, health, aging, disability, environment, immigration, human rights, and so on. Under increasing budgetary constraints, coupled with rapidly aging populations, local governments are inclined to delegate policy projects to nongovernmental organizations (Sakuma 2001: 147–48). In an era of decentralization of state power, the partnership between local governments and nongovernmental organizations has been consistent with the interests of the national government, at the expense of local governments and nongovernmental agencies.

Women volunteers constitute a substantial majority of the new community activists (Japanese Economic Planning Agency 2000, in Tajiri 2001: 24). Japanese women have been active in social and community services throughout the postwar era. These activities are often segregated according to the existing gender division. Women concentrate, for example, in the parent-teacher associations of local schools, local women's groups, and branches of township neighborhood associations (Imamura 1987). During the mid-1960s, a new form of community activism arose: a movement among suburban housewives who established consumers' cooperatives as a means of obtaining safe and inexpensive food (Amano 1996: 186–87). According to LeBlanc (1999), the ideology of a cooperative movement appeals to Japanese women's self-identity as housewives and mothers, enabling it to survive as a viable basis for political reform. In the context of today's global migration, new demands for community services have emerged that match women's traditional roles. In response to the lack of educational programs for immigrants, such services as teaching Japanese and helping children learn effectively in Japanese schools, appeal to socially conscious women. As will be discussed below, the demands for such services have attracted a small but dedicated number of Hamamatsu women, who have responded spontaneously, enthusiastically, and with determination.

UNSCHOOLED IMMIGRANT CHILDREN IN HAMAMATSU

According to statistics from the Hamamatsu Board of Education, 1,556 foreign children from six to fourteen years old were registered as city residents in spring 2002. Of these, 66 percent were enrolled in schools—816 in the city's public elementary and junior high schools, and 210 in Brazilian schools (Hamamatsu City Board of Education 2002). The remaining third (530 children) were not recorded as attending school. However, these statistics refer to only one point in time. Because of the frequent relocation of their parents, the enrollment figures on foreign children fluctuate widely over short periods. Moreover, they provide no information on how foreign children fare in Japanese schools. Recent studies by Japanese scholars report serious challenges for these children, including language handicaps that hinder their understanding of instructions and materials, misunderstanding and prejudice on the part of teachers and school administrators, and social isolation and rampant bullying by their peers (Ota 1996; Ikegami 2001b; Onai et al. 2001; Kobe Gaikokujin Shien Network 2001).

A high percentage of foreign youths who remain unschooled would pose an embarrassment to Hamamatsu's "global vision" and its goal of being seen as progressive and characterized by multicultural harmony. In 1997 a report that a group of Brazilian teens in Japan had purchased drugs from underground gang members generated substantial concern among educators, school administrators, and the general public. The following year the city was a focus of national—and international—media attention when a Brazilian customer sued a Hamamatsu jewelry shop owner for racial discrimination after he attempted to evict the customer from his store (French 1999; Yamanaka 2003a).

The political significance of the unschooled foreign children is clearly evident in the city administration's special attention to this issue in the policy projects of the "Global City Vision": "Hamamatsu will endeavor to support *volunteers* who teach the foreign resident community the benefits of attending school and learning Japanese, and we will continue to support diverse education opportunities such as schooling in foreign languages" (Hamamatsu City 2001: 44–45; emphasis added). Accordingly, in 2002 the city's newly formed Foreign Citizens' Assembly recommended to the mayor that the city respond with urgency to the emerging issue of unschooled foreign children.[5] Their proposal cautioned that "this issue is not only a major problem for the children and their future but also a major problem for all Hamamatsu citizens and communities" (Hamamatsu Foreign Citizens' Assembly 2002: 1). The time was ripe for both the city administration and the city's civil society to take action.

IMMIGRANT WOMEN'S ACTIVITIES: ALA BRASIL

In 1996, in response to the mounting problems facing their children, some fifty Brazilian parents and their sympathizers established an informal support network in Takaoka township in northwestern Hamamatsu.[6] Takaoka and adjacent towns are home to many companies and factories that subcontract to Honda Motor Corporation. These subcontracting firms have attracted many Brazilian workers and their families, with a concomitant influx of Brazilian children into the town's public Azusa Elementary School.

Activities to Assist Education of Children

To compensate somewhat for their unfamiliarity with the Japanese language and Japan's school system, immigrant parents began gathering to exchange information about school customs and also to collect used textbooks, backpacks, and clothing for new arrivals. Because most of the parents worked, they had only a few hours in the evenings and on weekends

---

[5] The Hamamatsu Foreign Citizens' Assembly began in April 2000. Ten members representing several national groups are appointed for one-year terms. They meet regularly and at the end of the year propose policy solutions to the mayor.

[6] This is a shortened version of a discussion included in Yamanaka 2003b.

during which to participate in the parents' network. Marisa Tanaka,[7] the group's leader and a mother of two, was the only full-time staff member, responsible for planning, managing, and coordinating school and community activities. She also taught private Portuguese classes after school to children whose Brazilian parents were concerned that their children would lose fluency in their mother tongue. To increase the Brazilian children's awareness of their heritage, Tanaka and other network members also organized cultural and national activities common in Brazil such as Easter celebrations, Carnival, Children's Day, and Christmas.

Many mothers in the network also participated in activities organized by Japanese mothers in the school's parent-teacher association (PTA). In 1998 Tanaka became a member of the PTA's Board of Directors and in that role was able to participate in planning events hosted jointly by Japanese and foreign parents. By 2000 the foreigners had established their own branch PTA, which soon became formally integrated into the Azusa PTA, now called "the Rainbow Society" in recognition of its ethnic diversity. Most PTA activities were held on weekend mornings at the school. In accord with traditional gender roles among both Japanese and Brazilians, it was the mothers who usually represented the family. These activities, which began in 1996, included twice-yearly get-togethers at which mothers of different nationalities cooked and shared their nation's foods. Immigrant children and parents, together with Japanese children and parents, participated in traditional Japanese celebrations. Mothers of different nationalities exchanged cultural customs. Brazilian mothers organized a Samba class at which they and their children taught Japanese mothers and children to dance to the Samba beat. In return, Japanese mothers taught immigrant mothers to wear a kimono and to understand the complex customs of Japanese weddings and funerals.

Collaboration with the City Administration

By the time that Marisa Tanaka's term as a board member of the Azusa PTA ended, she was fully convinced of the importance of her group's role in bridging the gap between the Brazilian and Japanese cultures. In January 2000, she founded the Associação Latin America, Brasil (ALA Brasil), expanding its membership beyond Takaoka to all Hamamatsu townships. ALA Brasil's ability to reach out to Brazilian families beyond a single

---

[7] This and other names presented throughout the chapter are pseudonyms.

township suggested to officials at the Office of International Affairs (OIA) that this organization could be a useful link to the city's Brazilian community. Soon, ALA Brasil became an official channel through which Hamamatsu officials disseminated information about garbage disposal, recycling, disaster management plans, and so on. Barriers of language and culture had stymied the dissemination of such information to Brazilian residents in the past, often leading to friction between them and their native neighbors.

ALA Brasil's value to the city's policymakers was also demonstrated in 2001 when the Office of International Affairs turned to the issue of unschooled foreign children, which by now was also a serious concern within the Brazilian community, though for somewhat different reasons. The members of ALA Brasil were witnessing a rapid "Japanization" of their children who attended Japanese schools, many of whom were born in Japan or came at an early age. The erosion of their Brazilian identity, along with their loss of the Portuguese language, was viewed as serious by Brazilian parents, most of whom intended to return to Brazil in the near term. In response, Tanaka and other ALA Brasil members requested OIA support for an after-school class for Brazilian children in which Portuguese would be taught three days a week and Japanese one day a week.

The OIA's director proposed an alternative. Concerned about the looming issue of unschooled children in the city, he suggested that Japanese classes be given three times a week to currently unenrolled Brazilian children. He reasoned that if they could better understand Japanese, they would be more willing to attend Japanese public schools. His office would appoint Japanese volunteer teachers, locate a venue for the class, and subsidize a weekly Portuguese class for these children. By reversing the proportion of time devoted to Portuguese and Japanese classes, the director underscored his belief that, because these children were in Japan, they should be learning Japanese rather than Portuguese.

The director's proposal offered both a gain and a loss to Tanaka and the other parents. On one hand, they were discouraged by the strong emphasis on Japanese, to the relative neglect of their native Portuguese. On the other hand, the director's proposal was a significant step toward institutional support for Brazilian children who were not in school. Tanaka reluctantly accepted the proposal for the benefit of those children and helped OIA recruit ten Brazilian children for the Japanese class. In return, the OIA appointed a voluntary, all-female group of Japanese language instructors, known as the Blue Sky Society, to teach the class. It opened in May 2001 in an unused classroom of the Azusa Elementary School.[8]

Collaborations with Citizens' Organizations

As ALA Brasil's reputation grew, Japanese citizens' groups interested in cultural exchange and multicultural education began to invite Tanaka and other ALA representatives to participate in seminars and symposiums on multicultural society building. Soon, these collaborations led Japanese groups to expand the scope of their activities to include Brazilian children. For example, in a Street Performance Festival held in downtown Hamamatsu in April 2001, children of ALA Brasil families enacted a drama by a Mexican artist. And in November 2001, fifty university students from Hamamatsu and adjacent areas formed the College Student Network to provide learning support programs for Brazilian children enrolled in Azusa and two other local elementary schools. With the support of the city's OIA, the group began a weekly tutoring program in February 2001 in a community center in Takaoka.

Changes and Transition

By 2002, ALA Brasil had grown from a small network of families with children attending the same elementary school to a citywide organization that provided a channel through which city policies could be communicated and implemented. In the absence of public programs to assist their children, immigrant mothers took responsibility for improving their educational opportunities, thereby assuming a role that should have been filled by the municipal government. At the same time, they did what they could to preserve the Brazilian identity and Portuguese fluency of children who were rapidly becoming "Japanese" as a result of their Japanese schooling. Through their activities in the PTA and the community more generally, Brazilian mothers were able to build rapport with local citizen volunteers and aid the city government in bridging the distance between Hamamatsu's Brazilian and Japanese populations.

In the meantime, however, ALA had undergone many changes that undermined its vitality as an organization. Substantial numbers of children

---

[8] According to the leader of the Blue Sky Society, the group's name implies equality; as the sky is open to all, so is the class. The same program is offered by volunteers in two other venues in the city.

had graduated from Azusa, leaving few Azusa families remaining. Other families had attained their goal of accumulating savings and had returned with their children to Brazil.

This latter group included Marisa Tanaka, who left Japan for Brazil in 2002. She was followed in the ALA Brasil presidency by former ALA vice president Misa Nomura. The bilingual Nomura had been assisting Tanaka in her communications with the city administration and citizens' organizations, including the ALA's support in disseminating OIA policy information and implementing new educational programs for Brazilian children.[9] However, this collaborative work with the city had drawn sharp criticism from ALA members who felt it was not in keeping with the organization's core purpose of assisting children in education. This criticism intensified when the OIA director declined ALA Brasil's request for support for a Portuguese language class. After Tanaka left Japan, Nomura's continued collaboration with city officials led some members to say that the ALA was being "used" by the city (author interview with ALA member, February 2003).

Another factor that damaged ALA Brasil was the rapidly increasing cultural assimilation of Brazilian immigrants into Japanese ways of life. Among twenty-five member families of ALA Brasil surveyed and interviewed by this author in 2002 and 2003, over 80 percent had migrated to Japan between the late 1980s and mid-1990s and had lived in Hamamatsu for over five years.[10] This suggests that many ALA members had acquired considerable familiarity with Japanese language and culture and that they enjoyed relatively stable employment and satisfying community lives. By 2002, Hamamatsu's Brazilian population had become increasingly fragmented by individualism and consumerism (author interview with Misa Nomura, July 2002). Nomura observed that as Brazilians became accustomed to Japanese society, they no longer sought out other Brazilians for socialization or assistance.

In combination, these demographic, organizational, and community changes—children's graduations, immigrants' return home, internal frictions, and cultural assimilation—have brought a major restructuring in

---

[9] In May 2002, OIA launched the Canalinho Class in which unschooled Brazilian children are taught in both Japanese and Portuguese in four subjects: Japanese, math, science, and social science (Hamamatsu City 2002b). The class is offered in three venues, including the Azusa Elementary School. ALA Brasil assisted OIA by recruiting students to enroll in the class.

[10] For descriptions of interviews, see Yamanaka 2003b.

ALA Brasil. They have also meant a redefinition of the organization's goals and relationships with its Japanese collaborators.

ACTIVITIES OF JAPANESE CITIZEN WOMEN: THE BLUE SKY SOCIETY

The Blue Sky Society began in 2001 when the Office of International Affairs launched the new Japanese language class in Azusa Elementary School in an effort to reduce the numbers of unschooled foreign children. The eight women who composed the Blue Sky Society in February 2003 had responded to a call for teachers of Japanese circulated in a newsletter distributed to all households (author interviews). These Japanese citizens, ranging in age from their twenties to their fifties, volunteered to teach the Japanese language to unschooled Brazilian children three times a week at the Azusa Elementary School. Some had taught Japanese prior to coming to Blue Sky; others had no prior teaching experience and had to gain the requisite teaching skills through self-teaching or coursework. When asked about their reasons for volunteering, each of the eight discussed details of their personal and family background that had led them to volunteer services (group interview with the author).

Transnational Experience

The women's narratives reveal that their personal experiences had been intimately connected to the characteristics of Hamamatsu as home to many global corporations. Five of the eight reported that they had spent at least a few years living abroad—in Toronto, Amsterdam, Los Angeles, Sydney, Shanghai, Manila, or Mexico City—with husbands posted overseas by their companies. The remaining three members also referred to direct international contact. One had been a university student in California for a year. Another had hosted an American foreign student in her parents' home for a year while she was in high school. The third had taught Japanese to foreign children for ten years in a class that the Hamamatsu City Board of Education established in 1992.

Among the five women who had lived abroad, a few referred to the experience of sending their children to the local schools in the foreign country as the factor that triggered their decision to volunteer. For example, Yoshiko Takahashi spent seven years in Toronto, during which her son completed the third through ninth grades at a local school. Recounting her overseas experience, Takahashi described how she had decided to join the Blue Sky Society to teach Japanese to foreign children:

In Toronto, I witnessed my son suffering psychologically in an alien environment with a foreign language. Upon return to Hamamatsu after his seven years, he found himself again struggling in an alien culture. This time his own culture was alien to him. I have learned from this experience that mastering the language of the society where we live is crucial because only through the language can we be connected to the society. I wished to do something for foreign children in Hamamatsu who could not even receive education in Japan.

Mieko Nakamura recalled her similar experience more than twenty years ago when she sent her daughter to a kindergarten in Amsterdam:

When I sent my daughter to a local kindergarten in Amsterdam, she had no problem adjusting to its environment. There were diverse groups of children there, including Japanese children. There I witnessed a society that accepts everyone. After we returned to Hamamatsu, when my other child was in an elementary school, Brazilian children began to show up. The school's response was to enroll them in the "Class of Friends," a class then intended for retarded children. I was shocked to see that this was all they would do for foreign children. Japanese children were treated so well in other countries, but Japan does so little for foreign children. I thought that I should help them.

Voluntarism and Multicultural Policy

While their transnational experiences motivated these Japanese women to undertake community action and they derived personal gratification from doing so, they were nonetheless well aware of the heavy responsibility they bore in being commissioned by the city administration to socialize these children into Japanese society. In interviews and in unstructured discussions that followed the interviews, the eight Blue Sky teachers did not hide their feelings of inadequacy in assuming responsibility for filling the gap between governmental neglect and the needs of immigrant children. They also expressed skepticism about a city administration that would rely solely on volunteers to implement the complex matter of language policy and practice among young foreigners. Vacillating between personal satisfaction and social cynicism, Yasuyo Sawada, a Japanese language teacher with ten years' experience, shared this political insight:

> I think it strange that ordinary citizens like us do this kind of important work. This should be done by the state. I wish to help children within my ability. But I am aware that the state is making good use of us well-educated women. I personally resist the notion that I am being used. Instead, I try to convince myself that I am doing this because I want to do it.

Yoshiko Takahashi, whose experience in the multicultural environment of Toronto had taught her the importance of education, also raised questions about the void between immigration policy and multicultural policy:

> Japan lacks a long-term vision for what kind of multicultural society it wants to become. The presence of many foreigners in the country poses a question of how we are going to interact with others. Without good educational opportunities, immigrant children can become a reserve army of juvenile delinquents. The administration wants to contain them before this happens. The policy we are part of is not aimed at helping foreigners, but at controlling them. What is most important, I think, is to be clear on what we want to do with Japanese society in the future.

CONCLUSION

In her analysis of the discourse on multiculturalism in Japan, Morris-Suzuki (2002: 154–55) warns that narrow nationalism underlies the increasingly popular use of the term in the media and in government publications. In her view, "culture," as in "cultural diversity," refers primarily to an "esthetic framework" separated from politics and ordinary people's everyday lives. Cultural diversity, so defined, is manifested in well-organized activities and other symbolic expressions in tightly controlled spaces and contexts, such as the opening ceremonies of the 2000 G-8 Kyushu-Okinawa Summit or the 1998 Nagano Winter Olympics. This implies to Morris-Suzuki that multiculturalism is acceptable in contemporary Japan only when it does not challenge the status quo and remains merely "cosmetic," without substance. One result of this superficial nature of Japanese multiculturalism is that it applies social pressure on non-Japanese residents to be loyal to Japan as a nation and to its symbolic culture, rather than enabling them to celebrate their own diverse origins and traditions. According to Morris-Suzuki, "cosmetic multiculturalism" aims to achieve two interrelated goals of the nation-state: to standardize diversity by eliminating substantial cultural differences, and to integrate its diverse populations into the ideology and practice of a single homogeneous nation-state.

This study of Hamamatsu City offers an example of Japan's local responses to the global phenomenon of increasing cross-border migration and its resulting multiculturalism. Until recently, Japan assertively identified itself as ethnically homogeneous—although vigorously pursuing integration into the global economy at the same time. A massive influx of foreign workers from Asia and Latin America during the 1990s exposed the growing contradiction between Japan's narrow nationalism and its globalized economy (Lie 2001).

Hamamatsu's many multinational corporations have attracted a substantial influx of global migrants, and the city is now confronting its new multiethnic character. Having defined its ethnic diversity as a valuable resource, the city government has launched an innovative multicultural project to convert itself into a global city of ethnic harmony. Grassroots groups have been responsive to the city's requests for their participation in such a grand plan. With little guidance or support from the national government, however, the local administration and grassroots forces are left to struggle within their limited jurisdictions and with limited resources to address such issues of national scope as immigrant education and language policy. As a result, grassroots groups are overwhelmed by the enormous task of bridging the gap between the local administration and the needs of ethnic communities.

This case study also demonstrates the centrality of women in the process of incorporating immigrants into local institutions. As a result of existing gender roles, it is they who take responsibility for homemaking, including children's education and community participation. Women's groups have been drawn into community action because of their concerns for the welfare of immigrant children growing up in Japan. This points to the emergence of a new avenue for collective mobilization, one that combines women's traditional gender roles with their increasingly transmigrant experience. In the context of their own transnational experience, the women in ALA Brasil and the Blue Sky Society have been able to empathize with the situation of the foreign children and are therefore motivated to participate in community service. The women volunteers who are thus mobilized comprise a convenient pool of inexpensive labor for the local administration because they provide high-quality, high-value service but ask for few financial rewards.

This study also underscores the narrow nationalism embedded in the local administration's vision of a multicultural society. This is apparent in the administration's keen interest in keeping foreign children in school and teaching them Japanese. Amidst the sweeping social transformation under way in the city, the municipal government is trying to maintain social control. In so doing, it tolerates a form of multiculturalism that does not challenge the supremacy of Japanese culture and national identity. By forcing foreign children to learn Japan's language and culture, the local government is attempting to diminish the impacts of ethnic diversity and to meet the nation-state's goal of cultural homogeneity. And by mobilizing women's volunteerism to achieve the city's multicultural goals, the city is drawing on Japan's traditional division of labor and family norms that dictate that it is women who, without payment, attend to children's needs.

Japan has never been mono-ethnic. There have always been ethnic minorities within Japanese society: Koreans, Chinese, Ainu, Okinawan, Burakumin, and so on (Lie 2001). But now the list has grown to include foreign workers of many nationalities and ethnicities scattered throughout the country. Japan's path to an acknowledged multicultural society is being paved, therefore, in local politics. In this process, grassroots forces are as important as policymakers; only they can assert the diversity of needs and viewpoints that must go into the construction of a truly multicultural society. The time is ripe for the Japanese state to accept the multiethnic, multilingual reality of the country and to redefine its nationhood accordingly.

References

Amano, Masako. 1996. *Seikatsusha toha Dareka*. Chuko Shinsho 1323. Tokyo: Chuo Koronsha.

Castles, Stephen. 1997. Multicultural citizenship: The Australian experience. In *Citizenship and exclusion*, edited by Veit Bader. New York: St. Martin's Press.

Cunningham, Hisako. 1988. *Kaigai Shijo Kyoiku Jijo*. Shincho Sensho. Tokyo: Shinchosha.

French, Howard W. 1999. "Japanese only" policy takes body blow in court. *New York Times* (international edition). November 15.

Gurowitz, Amy. 1999. Mobilizing international norms: Domestic actors, immigrants, and the Japanese state. *World Politics* 51 (3):413–45.

Hamamatsu City. 2001. *Hamamatsu City global city vision*. Hamamatsu: Office of International Affairs.

———. 2002a. *Gijutsu to Bunka no Sekai Toshi, Hamamatsu*. http://www.city .hamamatsu.shizuoka.jp/intro/bijon.htm. Accessed September 14, 2002.

———. 2002b. *Gaikokujin no Kodomotachi heno Gakushu Shien.* Hamamatsu City: Office of International Affairs.

Hamamatsu City Board of Education. 2002. Hamamatsu-shi ni okeru Gaikokujin Jidou Seito Kyoiku. Hamamatsu: Hamamatsu City Board of Education.

Hamamatsu Foreign Citizens' Assembly. 2002. 2001 nendo Hamamatsu-shi Gaikokujin Shimin Kaigi Teigen. Hamamatsu City: Hamamatsu Foreign Citizens' Assembly.

Hamamatsu NPO Network Center. 2001. *Daremoga Kenko ni Kuraser Shakai wo Mezashite.* Hamamatsu: The Center.

———. 2003. *Gaikokujin Kyouiku Shien Zenkoku Kyoryukai.* Hamamatsu City: The Center.

HICE News. 2004. *Hamamatsu foreign resident population (December 26, 2003).* HICE News No. 203. Hamamatsu City: Hamamatsu Foundation for International Communications and Exchanges.

Ikegami, Shigehiro. 2001a. Gaikokuseki Teijusha to Iryo Hosho. In *Brajiru-jin to Kokusai-ka suru Chiiki Shakai: Kyoju, Kyoiku, Iryo,* edited by Ikegami Shigehiro. Tokyo: Akashi Shoten.

———. 2001b. Shizuoka-ken Ogasa-gun no Chugakko niokeru Burajirujin Seito Kyouiku no Genkyo to Kadai. In *Brajiru-jin to Kokusai-ka suru Chiiki Shakai: Kyoju, Kyoiku, Iryo,* edited by Ikegami Shigehiro. Tokyo: Akashi Shoten.

Imamura, Anne E. 1987. *Urban Japanese housewives: At home and in the community.* Honolulu: University of Hawaii Press.

Kobe Gaikokujin Shien Network, ed. 2001. *Nikkei Nanbeijin no Kodomo no Bogo Kyoiku.* Kobe: Kobe Teiju Gaikokujin Shien Center.

Koga, Eunice A. Ishikawa. 2000. "Dekasegi Taizaisha" to "Jumin" no Aida de: Nikkei Nanbeijin no Chiiki Shakai Sanka. In *Gaikokujin Shimin to Seiji Sanka,* edited by Miyajima Takashi. Tokyo: Yushindo.

Kondo, Atsushi. 2002. The development of immigration policy in Japan. *Asian and Pacific Migration Journal* 11 (4):415–36.

Kuwahara, Yasuo, ed. 2001. *Global Jidai no Gaikokujin Roudousha: Dokokara Kite Dokohe.* Tokyo: Tokyo Keizai Shinposah.

LeBlanc, Robin M. 1999. *Bicycle citizens: The political world of the Japanese housewife.* Berkeley: University of California Press.

Lie, John. 2001. *Multiethnic Japan.* Cambridge, MA: Harvard University Press.

Linger, Daniel Touro. 2001. *No one home: Brazilian selves remade in Japan.* Stanford, CA: Stanford University Press.

Miyajima, Takashi, and Higuchi Naoto. 1996. Iryo, Shakai Hosho: Seizonken no Kanten kara. In *Gaikokujin Rodousha kara Shiminn he,* edited by Kajita Takamichi and Miyajima Takashi. Tokyo: Yuhikaku.

Miyajima, Takashi, and Suzuki Minako. 2000. *Newcomer no Kodomo no kyouiku to Chiiki Network.* In *Gaikokujin Shimin to Seiji Sanka,* edited by Miyajima Takashi. Tokyo: Yushindo.

Morris-Suzuki, Tessa. 2002. *Hihan-teki sôzôryoku no tame ni: gubôbaru-ka jidai no Nihon.* Tokyo: Heibonsha.

Naples, Nancy A., ed. 1998. *Community activism and feminist politics: Organizing across race, class, and gender.* New York: Routledge.

Naples, Nancy A., and Manisha Desai, eds. 2002. *Women's activism and globalization: Linking local struggle and transnational politics.* London: Routledge.

Onai, Tooru, et al. 2001. Kodomo no Kyoiku to Gakko Seikatsu. In *Nikkei Burajirujin no Teijuka to Chiiki Shakai,* edited by Tooru Onai and Sakai Eshin. Tokyo: Ochanomizu Shobo.

Ota, Haruo. 1996. Nihongo Kyoiku to Bokokugo Kyoiku. In *Gaikokujin Rodousha kara Shiminn he,* edited by Kajita Takamichi and Miyajima Takashi. Tokyo: Yuhikaku.

Piper, Nicola, and Robyn Iredale. 2003. *Identification of the obstacles to the signing and ratification of the UN Convention on the Protection of All Migrant Workers 1990: The Asia perspective.* Paris: UNESCO.

Roberts, Glenda S. 2000. NGO support for migrant labor in Japan. In *Japan and global migration: Foreign workers and the advent of a multicultural society,* edited by Mike Douglass and Glenda S. Roberts. London: Routledge.

Roth, Joshua Hotaka. 2002. *Brokered homeland: Japanese Brazilian migrants in Japan.* Ithaca, NY: Cornell University Press.

Sakuma, Tomoko. 2001. Global jidai no borantia katsudo wo kangaeru. In *Volunteer Hakusho 2001,* edited by The Editorial Committee. Tokyo: Nihon Seinen Hoshi Kyokai.

Sakurai, Keiko. 2003. *Nihon no Musulimu Shakai.* Chikuma Shinsho 288. Tokyo: Chikumka Shobo.

Shipper, Apichai W. 2002. Pragmatism in activism: Organizing support for illegal foreign workers in Japan. Civil Society in the Asia-Pacific Monograph Series. Cambridge, MA: Harvard University Program on U.S.-Japan Relations.

Tajiri, Keishi. 2001. Kininaru "borantia" to "NPO" no kannkei. In *Volunteera Hakusho 2001,* edited by The Editorial Committee. Tokyo: Nihon Seinen Hoshi Kyokai.

Takafuji, Akira. 1991. Gaikokujin Rodousha to Wagakuni no Shakai Hoshou Housei. In *Gaikokujin Rodousha to Shakai Hoshou,* edited by Shakai Hoshou Kenkyujo. Tokyo: Tokyou Daigaku Shappankai.

Tegtmeyer Pak, Katherine. 2000. Foreigners are local citizens, too: Local governments respond to international migration in Japan. In *Japan and global migration: Foreign workers and the advent of a multicultural society,* edited by Mike Douglass and Glenda S. Roberts. London: Routledge.

Tsuda, Takeyuki. 2003. *Strangers in the ethnic homeland: Japanese Brazilian return migration in transnational perspective.* New York: Columbia University Press.

Tsuda, Takeyuki, and Wayne Cornelius. 2004. Immigration to Japan: Myths and realities. In *Controlling immigration*, edited by Wayne A. Cornelius et al. 2d ed. Stanford, CA: Stanford University Press.

White, Merry. 1998. *The Japanese overseas: Can they go home again?* Princeton, NJ: Princeton University Press.

Yamanaka, Keiko. 2003a. A breakthrough for ethnic minority rights in Japan: Ana Bortz's courageous challenge. In *Gender and migration: Crossing borders and shifting boundaries*, edited by Mirjana Morokvasic Muller, Umut Erel, and Kyoko Shinozaki. International Women's University Series. Opladen, Germany: Verlag Leske+Budrich.

———. 2003b. Feminized migration, community activism and grassroots transnationalization in Japan. *Asian and Pacific Migration Journal* 12 (1–2):155–87.

———. 2003c. Transnational activities for local survival: A community of Nepalese visa-overstayers in Japan. Kroeber Anthropological Society Papers, no. 89/90.

———. n.d. Migration, differential access to health services and civil society's responses in Japan. In *Migration and health in Asia*, edited by Santosh Jatrana, Mika Toyota, and Brenda S. A. Yeoh. London: Routledge. In press.

Part III

ACTIVISM FOR IMMIGRANTS IN JAPAN: LOCAL, NATIONAL, AND
INTERNATIONAL CONTEXTS

CHAPTER 5

Policy Advocacy for Foreign Residents in Japan

DEBORAH J. MILLY

What impact have Japanese citizens had through policy advocacy on behalf of foreign residents? What is the significance of their efforts? For years,
groups of Japanese citizens have worked in support of foreign residents in
ways that have changed policies and their implementation. Advocacy on
behalf of foreign residents in Japan over the past two decades has produced pervasive, dispersed, and at times barely perceptible changes in
public policies, in how they are implemented, and in policy discussion. The
policy impacts are distinctive in two respects. First, substantive impacts,
which range widely across many policies, are often characterized by a
linking of specific problems of implementation at the local level with efforts to change formal policy provisions. Support groups' efforts to influence policies range from pushing for change in formal central government
laws and regulations to changes in central agencies' handling of specific
cases and street-level practices of implementation. Second, in the process of
these efforts, advocates' informal interactions with public officials have in
many cases resulted in mediating across different parts of the state. These
citizens have established a policy role for themselves that frequently includes filling a vacuum in communications and coordination among public
agencies. To demonstrate this role for advocates, this chapter situates advocacy in terms of the needs posed by the pattern of immigration and the
policy context. I then outline the development of political advocacy vis-à-

This essay draws on research for which I have received support over the years
from the Abe Fellowship Program, the Japan Society for the Promotion of Science, the Northeast Asia Council of the Association for Asian Studies, and the
former College of Arts and Sciences of Virginia Polytechnic Institute and State
University.

vis central officials and the methods adopted. Three brief examples illustrate advocates' efforts to change policy and their impact. Finally, I conclude with comments on the impact of advocacy in terms of policy and process.

THE PATTERN OF IMMIGRATION

Between 1980 and 2004, the profile of the "foreign resident" in Japan changed dramatically. With this shifting profile, new needs arose that have been the basis for emergency responses as well as modification of a range of Japanese domestic policies. This shift involved a weakening of the predominance of the "special permanent residents," primarily Koreans, whose families were in Japan at the end of World War II, and a growing presence of new entrants from a number of Asian countries and from South America (table 5.1). The foreign residents discussed here are those who entered Japan sometime in the 1980s or later and who have posed particular kinds of policy challenges to Japanese society and its state. At the end of 2003, there were 1,915,030 registered foreigners residing in Japan, who constituted 1.5 percent of the total population. Of those, 74.3 percent were from Asia, 17.9 percent from South America, 3.3 percent from North America, 3 percent from Europe, 0.8 percent from Oceania, and 0.5 percent from Africa. About one-quarter (24.9 percent) of registered foreigners at the time were permanent residents whose families were in Japan at the end of World War II. Aside from this group, almost all other registered foreigners were from Asia or South America (Hômushô nyûkoku kanrikyoku 2004a, tables 2, 3, 4, and 9).

The internationalization agenda and the bubble economy of the late 1980s have had a lasting impact on the groups that have tended to migrate to Japan; developments in other parts of Asia certainly contributed as well. In the late 1980s, the strong yen and the bubble economy encouraged the in-migration of workers from many countries, especially Asian countries; these workers found employment even though there was no legal framework that provided for this. After the lengthy and intense debate over revising the Immigration Control and Refugee Recognition Act (ICRRA, passed in 1951 and revised periodically thereafter), two innovations in the early 1990s further contributed to the current profile of foreign residents in Japan. The category of family relatives who could obtain residence visas was expanded, and through this, many ethnic-Japanese families from Brazil and Peru were able to enter and find work in the manufacturing sector. This accounts for the large portion of foreign residents from these countries (table 5.1). In addition, expansion of possibilities for industrial trainees from developing countries, discussed later in this chapter, also accounts for a large number of especially Asian residents in agriculture and manufacturing. Although these trainees are not legally considered workers, they have an option to remain for an additional specified time as skilled labor if they meet the necessary skills tests. There were approximately 55,000 such trainees and skilled laborers registered as residents at the end of 2003 (Hômushô nyûkoku kanrikyoku 2004a: tables 14 and 15). In addition, consistent with the internationalization initiative, the number of students in Japan from other countries has steadily increased, and by the end of 2003 approximately 176,000 residents, the vast majority of them Chinese, held visas for study at the college or pre-college level (Hômushô nyûkoku kanrikyoku 2004a: tables 12 and 13).

One reality that underlay the policy debates of the late 1980s was the high demand for manual laborers and the resulting large numbers of foreign residents working in violation of immigration regulations. Since the changes of 1990, periodic revisions of the ICRRA have strengthened penalties intended to support enforcement of regulations, and arrests are made on a regular basis. Government estimates of those who are in Japan illegally have fallen somewhat since the peak of 1993, when about 299,000 persons were estimated to be residing without documentation. As of the beginning of 2004, the official estimate of illegally resident foreigners stood at 219,418 (Hômushô nyûkoku kanrikyoku 2004b). When considered as a portion of the total of registered foreigners and estimated illegally resident population together, this comes to about 10 percent—a fairly low portion cross-nationally and particularly low when compared to South Korea.[1]

Some but not all of the issues that Japanese advocates take up involve problems related to irregularities in visa status. At times, regulations have seemed to make foreign visitors susceptible to becoming undocumented. Because advocates have addressed problems affecting groups with and without proper visas, both types of cases are considered here.

---

[1] At the end of 2002, prior to passage of the new Employment Permit System in Korea and the regularization associated with it, the percentage of unauthorized workers as a percent of foreign migrants was approximately 86 percent, based on data from the Republic of Korea, Ministry of Justice, published in Lee 2003: table 2.

Table 5.1. Trends in Numbers of Registered Foreigners, by Nationality[a]

Country of Nationality	1980	1985	1990	1995	1997	2001	2003
North and South Korea	84.9%	80.3%	64.0%	48.9%	43.5%	35.6%	32.1%
China	6.8	8.8	14.0	16.4	17.0	21.4	24.1
Brazil	0.2	0.2	5.2	13.0	15.7	15.0	14.3
Philippines	0.7	1.4	4.6	5.5	6.3	8.8	9.7
Peru	0.0	0.1	1.0	2.7	2.7	2.8	2.8
United States	2.9	3.4	3.6	3.2	3.0	2.6	2.5
Others	4.6	5.7	7.7	10.5	11.8	13.8	14.5
Total	100.0%	100.0%	100.0%	100.0%	100.0%	100.0%	100.0%
Total Number of Persons	782,910	850,612	1,075,317	1,362,371	1,482,707	1,778,462	1,915,030

Sources: Hōmushō nyūkoku kanrikyoku 2004a; Japan Statistical Yearbook, 1993.
[a] As of December 31 of each year.

THE INSTITUTIONAL CONTEXT OF POLICIES AFFECTING FOREIGN RESIDENTS

Key Features

Advocates confront a set of policies and institutions specific to Japan, and their efforts both respond to and take advantage of these frameworks to pursue policy improvements. Key features of the institutional and policy environments have influenced the policy problems that advocates confront and the avenues they have used for trying to improve conditions: the dominance of relevant policy decisions by administrative decision makers; the fragmented and uncoordinated character of the system of policies that have a bearing on resident foreigners' lives; a correspondingly weak level of interagency coordination over policies; and a system of courts that at times has taken an activist position vis-à-vis government and that is the next resort after administrative appeals are exhausted.

A large role for administrative decision makers is hardly specific to Japan when it comes to the general area of immigration and immigrant-related policies (Freeman 1995), but given the lack of political leadership on behalf of immigrants in the legislature in Japan, bureaucratic officials wield a great deal of power. The implication for advocates who seek to influence policy as it is practiced is that the officials who make the regulations—namely, central ministry officials—are also those responsible for giving instructions as to their implementation. In concrete terms, this means that the central officials to whom advocates may plea for better guidance to local offices are the same ones who are responsible for crafting and changing the regulations at issue.

Outside of basic immigration provisions for entry and residence status, the policy system in Japan for the most part fits foreign residents into a system designed for Japanese citizens. There is no comprehensive piece of legislation in Japan that specifies all of the rights and policy entitlements of foreign residents, nor does a single coordinating agency exist for policies affecting foreign residents. Instead, policies designed for Japanese citizens have produced policy-by-policy revisions, reinterpretations, or clarifications as needed when their applicability to foreign residents has been questioned. This means that advocates need to target a plethora of agencies and offices to work for policy change, and also that no institutional organ has an agency mission to oversee the inclusion of immigrants in domestic society and policies.

In connection with the fragmented and segmented character of policies that affect foreign residents, weak interagency coordination across policies poses problems for two reasons. Not only does this lack of coordination result in contradictions among policies and how they are applied, but the lack of communication across agencies also means that the policy contradictions easily go unrecognized and that it is difficult to achieve amelioration unless external political leadership is brought to bear. For this reason, in attempting to make policy improvements, advocates end up bridging different parts of the state and compensating for the gaps in communication. Their impact is one of process as much as one of policy outcome.

Finally, a system of courts is a resource for efforts both to reverse administrative approaches or clarify policy and to set limits on public officials' discretion. While rulings have gone in both directions, the courts have become an important authoritative mechanism for reviewing a wide range of questions related to the treatment of foreigners by public and private actors.

The Specific Policy Context

For the above reasons, Japan's policy regime toward foreign residents has evolved in an ad hoc and piecemeal fashion, and still awaits a reform effort to bring these pieces into better alignment. The relevant policies that affect foreign residents in the country—whether immigration policies or those one might term immigrant policies—remain uncoordinated across ministries. To the extent that coordinated action has been taken, it was mainly as a result of Japan's signing of international human rights conventions in the 1970s rather than reforms in response to the pattern of immigration since the 1980s. After Japan's ratification of international covenants on human rights (1979) and concurrent with appeals by Korean residents to the United Nations Commission on Human Rights, exclusionary clauses toward non-Japanese residents were eliminated from many policies (Yamamoto 1995; Iwasawa 1986: 1–3). Such formal policy changes, important as they were, only went so far and did not purge discriminatory treatment from all policies, nor did passage ensure that these would be implemented fully.

Because the range of policies relevant to the well-being of recent immigrants is broad, several governmental actors share responsibility for them, and the administrative character of the Japanese state ensures that many policy changes are handled without ever being considered by the legislature. As a result, not only do foreign residents and their advocates have to interact with a diverse set of public officials over specific problems, advocates also target these officials in trying to change policies. The Ministry of Justice (MOJ), particularly its Immigration Control Bureau, acts as a leader to coordinate with certain agencies over criteria for entry and immigration control enforcement, but it has demonstrated little leadership in attempting to coordinate policy responses of other agencies related to the life of foreign residents in Japan. MOJ's jurisdiction includes such things as basic immigration control planning, specifics of regulations and their implementation, supervision of the work-trainee program, and detention centers. Other agencies with a strong interest in certain facets of immigration include the Ministry of Foreign Affairs—which has a special connection to the work-trainee program, asylum policy, and immigration controls as they relate to the establishment of an Asian Free Trade Area—and the Ministry of Economy, Trade, and Industry, which tends to be responsive to industry's pressures for changes in immigration law.

But the range of agencies that have had to confront questions about the treatment of foreign residents goes well beyond those agencies whose jurisdiction would cause them to have a stake in decisions about encouraging or discouraging immigration of certain types. Many agencies face the question: how should we treat foreign residents in our particular policy arena? The Ministry of Health, Labor, and Welfare (MHLW; previously the Ministry of Health and Welfare and the Ministry of Labor) is responsible for access to health care and for labor protections; the Ministry of Education, Culture, Sports, Science, and Technology is responsible for international students in Japan as well as extra educational supports for non-native-speaking children in the schools. Local governments engage in independent initiatives; and they, local welfare offices, local labor standards offices, and local schools all have a hand in applying national policies locally and determining what they will mean for individual foreign residents. Further, the police and prosecutors' offices face questions related to due process and language, and the courts likewise face questions related to the scope of procedures for which linguistic interpretation is required and procedural questions as to the treatment of defendants and witnesses who are scheduled to be deported. From this litany, it should be clear that policies for foreign residents, though related to immigration policy and what groups of immigrants are welcome in a country, encompass a much broader and more diverse set of policies and considerations. For advocates, choices regarding which actors to target, coordination among advocates over different types of issues, and specialization of activities by certain professionals are important considerations for making an impact.

Absent a concerted government effort to develop comprehensive and consistent reforms to address relevant policies, much of advocates' effort to improve policy conditions has focused on engaging or protesting the specific agencies involved. When that route has been unsatisfactory, the courts have provided another avenue, particularly once administrative appeals have been exhausted.[2] The courts have found the MOJ at fault in the handling of certain immigration and asylum decisions, and at times have ruled with clear statements that MOJ had acted beyond the discretion allowed (see, for example, Tôkyô chihô saibansho 1995; Saikô saibansho 1996). Beyond handling administrative and criminal challenges aimed at public officials, the courts have played a role in clarifying the rights of foreigners in civil suits involving compensation in relation to work injuries, traffic accidents, and divorce settlements; these rulings have been important in setting standards for calculating compensation and the extent to which Japanese standards or the wage and living standards in one's home country should be the guide (see, for example, Bo-bii Makkusuto vs. Yûgengaisha Kaishinsha 1997).

By the late 1980s, the need for new policies or changes in existing local and national policies or their local or national implementation had become apparent, but the nature of those needs has evolved. Initially advocates became involved with policy by attempting to have established state protections applied to foreign residents in emergency circumstances. Frequently their intervention had to do with employment conditions, such as unpaid wages and workplace injuries; the need for emergency health care; and the problems of women who had been trafficked as sex workers. The character of problems changed, however, from emergency circumstances that were often related to a foreigner's lack of familiarity with Japanese language and customs to problems associated with day-to-day realities of relatively settled foreigners and policies that failed to respond to them.

Advocates' policy concerns range widely. Relevant policies include any that affect an ordinary person's life in Japan, and some of the major areas of advocacy have included immigration control policy, asylum decisions, labor protections, access to health care, children's education, due process in

---

[2] In its 2003 report on border control administration, the Immigration Control Bureau devotes several pages to data and discussion of administrative lawsuits, which have increased dramatically and steadily in recent years (Hômushô nyûkoku kanrikyoku 2003).

administrative proceedings and before the courts, and social discrimination. Table 5.2 provides a sampling of the sorts of problem issues that non-governmental advocates have tried to address. Some of those issues undeniably are tied to problems of visa violations, but others are a product of the inconsistencies of Japanese law or a failure to protect the rights of foreign residents as already provided by law. Officials' responses have been uneven across localities and decisions, and the problematic issues have often involved very specific central policy provisions in given regulations or their implementation.

Advocacy Activities

To address this plethora of concerns, the organization, methods, and national-level impacts of advocates over the past fifteen to twenty years began from efforts to deal concretely with immediate local-level problems and evolved into coordinated efforts to change policies. As responses became more routine and as local governments became better equipped to handle many such problems, advocates continued to expand the range of their intervention and expertise to address problems of relatively settled immigrants.

Since the mid-1980s, advocacy in support of recently arrived foreign residents has evolved into a vast network of organizations that brings together groups and individuals with a wide range of policy expertise and experience. Some advocacy groups identify with the general issues of foreigners, including undocumented residents; these are likely to be church groups, lawyers' groups and bar associations, local labor activists, and other social relief–oriented groups. Some groups are focused specifically on the issues of migrant workers but have expanded their attention to a broad range of immigrant concerns. Other groups, such as those supporting asylum seekers, overlap in concerns because many in this category are undocumented; but their primary objective is the rights of refugees. At the community level, various groups are engaged in volunteer activities such as providing English instruction; however, they frequently do not engage in policy advocacy or forge ties with groups that assist undocumented foreigners or aim to change policy. The discussion here concerns primarily a loose network of organizations that have both provided supports to migrants and pursued a political agenda of policy change through lobbying and other activities. They are groups that have focused on the more vulnerable among resident foreigners, who sometimes are undocumented and who are often from economically disadvantaged countries.

Table 5.2. Sampling of Problem Issues Taken Up by Nongovernmental Advocates

	Visas
	• Handling of spouse visa renewals
	• Residence visas for parents supporting a Japanese child
	• Residence visa exceptions for undocumented families
	• Monitoring of organizations accepting "trainees" and enforcing contracts
	Asylum
	• Refusal of entry at airport
	• The 60-day limit for application
	• System of appeals for refusals
Immigration	• Inadequate personnel assigned
control	• Placing of asylum applicants in detention
system	• Biases against certain nationalities
	Detention Centers
	• Violence and abuse by detention center staff
	• Conditions of detention center facilities
	• Transparency of regulations and guidelines for detention center staff
	• Abuses by private "detention centers" at airports for those refused entry
	• Access to legal counsel for those in detention
	• Access to linguistic interpretation with police and prosecutors
Legal and	• Question of when and to what degree charges need to be explained to persons in their own languages
procedural rights	• Development of a system of trained interpreters for the courts
and protections	• How much of court proceedings must be interpreted for defendants
	• Improprieties and biases against foreigners by judges in criminal trials
	• Reincarceration after acquittals when cases are being appealed by prosecutors
	• Ensuring that employers observe contracts and minimum labor standards
Labor protections	• Detecting the covering up of work injuries by employers
and employee-related	• Calculation of compensation amounts for foreign residents with work injuries
policies	• Enforcing enrollments of foreign employees in the Employees Social Insurance system
	• Protections for work-trainees
Social	• Eligibility for public assistance

The discussion here involves activities of organizations that have participated in or cooperated with the National Network in Solidarity with Migrant Workers (hereafter, Migrants' Network), a major coordinating network organization that grew out of a previous, much looser network of information exchange. Besides support groups of volunteers and an occasional paid staff member, groups of professionals such as lawyers often focus on the issues through their own professional networks' activities, but they may also maintain a connection and provide professional expertise to the Migrants' Network.[3] Another major organization whose membership is dominated by foreign residents (Asian People's Friendship Society, or APFS) shares many similar goals but is not formally a member, even though the Migrants' Network and APFS have a mutually supportive relationship, as seen below. For the kinds of policy efforts discussed here, immigrants' organizations in general have played a secondary role, except for efforts to challenge immigration officials in 1999 and 2000 concerning the treatment of undocumented families.

The evolution of cooperation among support groups paralleled the changing needs for assistance, and eventually resulted in national coordination to facilitate a proactive approach to lobbying the central government. When church and labor groups began responding to emergency needs in the mid-1980s, their lack of familiarity with the issues and their paucity of resources produced virtually immediate cooperation. The urgent need for basic resources for new residents (such as multilingual handbooks with key medical terms and basic information about access to public services) put pressure on groups and local governments to pool their knowledge. Informal communications networks were actively formed and drew on some preexisting networks—for instance, those among churches, women's shelters, and labor unions targeting workers in small firms or day laborers (Shipper 2002; Tegtmeyer Pak 1998). Networks of support organizations set up in specific localities facilitated regular sharing of information, bureaucratic processes, and potential sources of assistance. From the standpoint of policy, the local governments became the primary targets of advocacy and intervention, and regional immigration offices were the place

---

[3] For instance, numerous of the local bar associations have established committees whose concerns include the rights of foreign residents. In addition, examples of other organizations include the now-disbanded Lawyers for Foreign Laborers' Rights, Zenkoku nanmin bengodan renraku kaigi, and Nyûkan mondai chôsakai.

where advocacy in the processing of individual visa applications took place. In 1987 a loose network of support organizations formed the Asian Workers' Problems Discussion Network (hereafter, Ajikon) with the encouragement of the Asia-Pacific Research Center, and founding members decided on a moderate approach that would attract a broad spectrum of advocates (Kimoto 1997). Over the years, more organizations emerged, needs changed, and the network continued to grow, but their experience in dealing with public officials remained primarily local.

This locally rooted advocacy and a loose network of communications formed the basis for national coordination in responding to crises but not for systematic lobbying efforts. With the exposure in 1994–1995 of abuses at detention centers, advocates mobilized nationally and made effective use of the media to bring very public challenges to practices that came under the jurisdiction of the Immigration Control Bureau (Nyûkan mondai chôsakai 1996). Other examples include periodic mobilizing to protest revisions of the Immigration Control Act being considered in the Diet, and the efforts made to engage central government officials after the Hanshin earthquake hit the Kobe area in 1995, when many organizations mobilized to support victims.

The major organizational shift in support of national policy initiatives occurred in 1997, when the previous network was folded into the new National Network in Support of Migrant Workers. This new network aimed for greater national coordination of activities and better information exchange that would take advantage of electronic communications to support a proactive policy agenda. Along with establishing a skeletal leadership structure and system of regional representation, project teams were established to focus on specific policy domains to develop policy proposals, lobby politicians, and engage agency officials in discussion (*Ijû rôdôsha tsûshin*, May 1997: 3–4). To pursue this central policy agenda, affiliated networks and member organizations brought together policy-specific expertise and knowledge of local implementation practices that enabled advocates to enter into discussions with central agencies with a grounding in policy knowledge.

Advocacy efforts have employed a mix of adversarial and cooperative approaches in calling on public officials to make improvements in policies, and it is not unusual to see the two combined over a single issue. In the late 1980s and early 1990s, demonstrations, litigation, and direct intervention with local employers and authorities dominated the methods used. More recently, such methods have expanded to include regular informal meetings with central ministry officials over policy problems, having questions raised by sympathetic Diet members in Diet proceedings, and, minimally, providing expert testimony for standing committees in the Diet considering legislative changes. At certain crucial junctures, the ability to mobilize as a traditional protest movement—with demonstrations, effective media attention, and petitions—has had a place, as is seen in one of the cases below. But as advocates have grown in policy expertise and sophistication, they have also made inroads through informal discussions with central officials, even though they maintain an independent and often adversarial stance. The cases discussed here highlight this form of policy advocacy, how local experience has provided a basis for that advocacy, and how that advocacy has involved intermediating between different parts of the state.

THREE CASES

The following brief discussions of visa decisions, access to health care, and abuses in the trainee system illustrate some of the ways that advocates have influenced the direction of policy. The impacts of advocates can be seen in street-level practices of implementation, in central agencies' handling of specific kinds of cases, and in gradual changes in specific government regulations. The cases also illustrate the mediating role of advocates among state officials in ways that address coordination problems.

Visa Decisions and the Ministry of Justice

With the Immigration Control Bureau of the Ministry of Justice, advocates have acted as representatives for foreign residents, sometimes handling visa applications and appeals, but also mobilizing at times to press for changes in immigration regulations. A pattern of incremental change in the handling of certain types of cases is directly tied to the character of immigration law, which gives the minister of justice extensive discretion over immigration decisions. For this reason, change in policy has often involved a progression from specific visa decisions to general practices for handling certain types of decisions; this progression has also included a gradual formalization of previous practices and apparent, but not publicized, criteria. Likewise, the efforts of advocates have merged assistance with individual cases and pressures for appropriate and clear criteria. Advocates' efforts include the full range of methods discussed earlier and, in this sense, combine visibly adversarial approaches with professional low-key interactions over individual cases and use of the courts. At one point, advocates even inserted themselves into the formal legislative process by being included in Diet committee hearings.

Advocacy groups have played an important role by speaking for undocumented persons who seek a special permission for a residence visa or persons appealing asylum decisions, and by pressing for transparency concerning the criteria used in visa decisions. Over time, the criteria for granting such permissions have been broadened. In this process, interactions have generally remained between advocates representing individual foreign residents (either attorneys or other advocates who have helped to prepare their documentation) and regional immigration bureau officials (Nyûkan jitsumu kenkyûkai 2000: 36–39). Although Japan has never had a general amnesty program, over the years authorities have developed a system that amounts to "individualized amnesties" in that the minister of justice reserves the right to grant long-term residence visas "in consideration of special circumstances" (ICRRA, annexed table II). As decisions on similar types of visa cases have accrued, the bureau has appeared to follow internal guidelines that have not been made public. This lack of explicit standards has been a chronic complaint of support groups and even attorneys attempting to advise foreign residents on their visa cases. As a result, changes in policy often have to be inferred from the results of individual decisions, but sometimes official directives are issued that specify criteria (Nyûkan jitsumu kenkyûkai 2000).

This pattern played out over the 1990s in a sequence of expansions in the granting of residence visas. By 1992, authorities already had developed procedures for handling the applications of undocumented spouses of Japanese citizens (Nyûkan jitsumu kenkyûkai 2000: 66–67). Over the next several years, as increasing numbers of Japanese citizens were born to foreign parents, special permissions for a residence visa were granted in many cases to women who had lost their visa eligibility as a spouse because their Japanese husbands had died or divorced them. The role of advocacy groups was important to the degree that they assisted with completing necessary paperwork, dealing with immigration officials, and providing social support throughout the process. During those years, what outwardly were individual cases weighed "case-by-case" came to be decided according to predictable—but nontransparent—criteria. Finally, a central directive of July 30, 1996, spelled out the conditions and criteria for granting these visas and extended eligibility to persons who were already living as undocumented residents. While advocacy groups had often become involved in assisting individual applicants with paperwork, making sense of the pattern of decisions being rendered, and dealing with officials on individual cases, it is also true that this directive was a means of dealing with the heavy load of requests with which immigration officials contended. The new guidelines were particularly significant in that the needs of children with one Japanese parent (in most cases, the father) were viewed as a basis for overriding the undocumented status of the second parent, even if there had not been a formal marriage (Hômushô nyûkoku kanrikyoku 1996).

Although the granting of residence visas to undocumented family members of Japanese citizens had become routine over the 1990s, entire families of undocumented residents who had settled in Japan lacked visas and remained at risk. Revisions of the ICRRA that were passed in 1999 were expected to make such families significantly more vulnerable legally and subject to criminal prosecution when revisions took effect in 2000. A set of challenges from immigrant families supported by a very strong mobilization effort on the part of advocacy groups and scholars led to MOJ decisions in 2000 that reflected a major shift from previous criteria used in granting exemptions for residence visas. Until then, having Japanese family relations was a key criterion for obtaining residence visas in such circumstances.

In September 1999, a group of undocumented families (five families and two individuals totaling twenty-one persons) presented themselves to the Ministry of Justice; a second group (five families and seventeen persons) did the same in December. The role of advocates in this case was to combine support mobilization through petitions and media coverage, highly symbolic protest activities, and necessary legal supports. Academics and advocates for foreign residents speak with pride about their effective mobilization through an international petition drive among academics and through intensive media, education, and petition campaigns at home (Komai et al. 2000). The case is also distinctive in that it was immigrants themselves who initiated a public and direct challenge to the Ministry of Justice over their status.

In the resulting decisions, sixteen people in the first group and three (one of the five families) in the second received residence (*Migrant Network News* 2000a, 2000b). Other families have since sought and received permissions. Among the families who were refused visas, some have taken their cases to the court system, though with little success. The one case in which the family received a positive verdict at the district level was subsequently overturned by the Tokyo High Court (Asian People's Friendship Society

2003, 2004). These decisions on undocumented families, while major steps in opening up residence to a new category of undocumented persons with a stable life in Japan, fit into the longer-term pattern of policy change concerning the granting of residence visas to certain undocumented residents. As with the previous pattern of Ministry of Justice changes, the granting of visas expanded incrementally and internal guidelines initially were not made explicit.

Although the Ministry of Justice has encountered advocates in the above sorts of confrontational circumstances and at the regional level over individual decisions, it has now begun to interact with them in the context of lobbying and legislative hearings. Overall, the regular visits by Migrants' Network representatives to Ministry and Immigration Bureau officials generally appear to be unproductive (except in the case of the trainees network discussed later). However, the advocates' activity concerning legislation became visible in the debate over revisions to the ICRRA that began in spring 1999. The debate was prolonged, and members of the Migrants' Network were able to mobilize better than they had before the network's 1997 reorganization. In the spring, members of the House of Councilors, where the bill was first introduced, appended a resolution calling for humanitarian consideration, especially for families. In August, network representatives testified before the Justice Committee of the House of Representatives on the problems of families (Kokkai shūgiin gijiroku 1999).[4] In such contexts, the availability of sympathetic Diet members willing to raise questions and intercede with administrative officials has also been important, as seen in the next case as well.

Access to Medical Insurance and Other Medical Programs

Advocacy to ensure access to medical care goes beyond the plight of foreigners without legal status and has called attention to problems of foreign persons residing legally in Japan. Problematic issues have included unpaid medical bills resulting from lack of health insurance coverage, development of alternative services for those without health insurance, access to public health–related welfare programs besides insurance, and inconsis-

---

[4] Watanabe Hidetoshi, founder of Kalabaw-no-kai and part of the collective leadership of the current Migrants' Network, testified on August 3, 1999, as did a longtime volunteer for foreigners' counseling assistance (Kokkai shūgiin gijiroku 1999).

tencies in the administration of employees' health insurance, in which many foreign residents are supposed to be enrolled.[5] Because local governments are responsible for implementing national medical care programs, advocates' activities over medical needs have been far more dispersed and conditions more varied than in the case of visa problems. The discussion below emphasizes efforts since the Ministry of Health and Welfare made key policy decisions concerning foreign migrants in 1994 and 1995. Advocates have intervened locally to pressure local governments to follow central guidelines, but they have also lobbied central officials to improve oversight of implementation practices and to change certain formal regulations and policy interpretations. In conjunction with these efforts, they have taken advantage of a legislative practice whereby individual Diet members can submit written questions and receive written responses that become part of the official record. In this case, the response has constituted an official clarification of eligibility to several programs. The discussion here highlights this process of engaging central officials and advocates' efforts to overcome administrative failures of communications and inconsistencies in implementation.

Advocacy over medical care for recent immigrants falls into two phases, before and after 1995, when an Ad Hoc Council on Medical Care of Foreigners (*gaikokujin ni kakaru iryō ni kansuru kondankai*) established by the Health Ministry issued its recommendations (Gaikokujin ni kakaru iryô ni kansuru kondankai 1995). In the late 1980s and early 1990s, nongovernmental advocacy and volunteer support services complemented initiatives taken by numerous prefectures and municipalities, but as these became inadequate, pressure built for a national government response. The resulting Ad Hoc Council's 1995 recommendations became the basis for national policy and shaped the direction of subsequent activism. The Ministry's immediate response to the Council's proposals was to establish a fund to cover (under a very limited set of circumstances) a portion of foreigners' unpaid medical fees at approximately 130 emergency hospitals (*Asahi Shinbun* 1995).

Other Council recommendations became the basis for advocates' lobbying efforts that continued throughout the 1990s. The Health Ministry adopted the Council's recommendation that medical welfare programs with no specific nationality exclusion should also be applicable to foreign

---

[5] The campaign for undocumented residents' access to national health insurance has been conducted largely through the courts and is not discussed here.

residents, regardless of visa status, but failures to implement that policy locally have been a major target of advocates' interactions at local offices and with central officials. Another relevant problem raised in the report was that of foreign employees eligible for but not enrolled in social insurance.

Since 1995, advocates have focused primarily on the application of existing programs to all foreign residents, documented or not, in their interactions with central officials. The Hanshin earthquake in 1995 made direct dealings with the Ministry of Health necessary because the number of registered foreigners in the areas most affected by the earthquake was about 80,000, with an estimated additional 4,000 to 5,000 unregistered foreigners. Even in the context of disaster, the Health Ministry's consistent position in meetings with advocates was that foreigners who lacked registration as foreign residents were ineligible for any form of relief (*Ijû rôdôsha tsûshin* 1995a, 1995b).[6]

Apart from raising the earthquake relief problems, advocates have met repeatedly with the Health Ministry over the application of health and welfare laws. As early as October 1995, representatives from one medical care network asked the Ministry to allow undocumented residents access to assistance provided by the Children's Welfare Law and the Mother-Child Health Law. According to the advocates present, Ministry officials claimed to have no knowledge of the problematic practices that prevailed at local welfare offices (*Ijû rôdôsha tsûshin* 1995c). Disparities in implementation of policies nationally have continued to be a central part of advocates' message to the Ministry of Health.

Although advocates' efforts to engage central officials predated the formation of a medical project team under the Migrants' Network, the organization of the latter produced intensified efforts to lobby the central government, to engage prefectural and municipal governments, and to create a broad network of medical professionals. The medical project team in the Migrants' Network has encouraged formation of a broader medical network that would include organizations that had already been working on behalf of foreigners' medical issues, involve regional health-care providers and international exchange organizations, and become more of a consultative network (*Ijû rôdôsha tsûshin*, July 2000: 3–4; Gaikokujin iryô-seikatsu nettowaaku 2004: 40–42).

---

[6] Some of these costs were later defrayed through local government and support groups' contributions (Tamura 1996).

Using tactics to improve access to medical care provided through a range of welfare laws for children, pregnant women, and the disabled, advocates have engaged officials at all levels. At the central level, in meetings with Health Ministry officials in October 1999, February 2000, and March 2000, advocates sought clarification of the Ministry's position on the Children's Welfare Law and similar laws, for which local practice has varied greatly. Much of the discussion again involved explanation of the intricacies of the laws and the extent to which local governments could exercise discretion. In those meetings, although the Ministry officials clarified their position, the tenor of the discussion, as summarized by advocates who attended, was that the Ministry would explain this position if consulted by local governments but would not actively check up on local practices (*Ijû rôdôsha tsûshin*, November–December 1999, February 2000, July 2000). Moreover, such meetings, as productive as they were, did not produce official statements or documents that could be used in interacting with local officials.

Staff members of Councilor Owaki Masako (Social Democratic Party of Japan), who had intermediated in arranging the meetings with the Health Ministry, suggested the alternative of a formal written question (*shitsumon shuisho*) that Diet members can submit to the speaker of the house. That response has the status of a cabinet decision in the name of the prime minister. In this case, such a written response has become the basis for advocates' negotiations with local government officials. The question, submitted by Owaki Masako on April 26, and its response of May 26, 2000, signed by Prime Minister Mori, put into writing the extent to which access to various medical welfare provisions depends on one's visa status. Advocates began to use this as a basis for engaging prefectural and municipal governments to insist on implementation (Gaikokujin iryô-seikatsu nettowaaku 2004: 44–57; *Ijû rôdôsha tsûshin*, July 2000). In this regard, not only have advocates played the role of informing central officials of the realities of how individuals have been treated at local offices, but they have also become the communicators and enforcers of policy.

Although many of the implementation problems reflect failures in vertical communication and oversight in the Health Ministry, others have been linked to horizontal failures to coordinate among ministries. Earlier advocate challenges to the Health Ministry's refusal to grant medical public assistance to foreigners highlighted contradictions between the policy approaches of the Ministries of Justice and Health. Members of the newly formed medical care network in 1998 arranged a three-way meeting with representatives of both agencies to discuss the extent of discretion local governments could exercise in granting medical assistance to undocumented foreigners awaiting processing of applications for residence visas they were very likely to receive. Advocates considered the Health Ministry's stringent stand to be in conflict with a Justice Ministry directive of July 1996 regarding residence visas. At a meeting arranged by Owaki Masako of the House of Councilors in May 1998, at which representatives of support groups spoke with officials from both ministries, the discrepancies became manifest. The Ministry of Justice expressed more flexibility than the Health Ministry in interpreting the eligibility of such foreigners for assistance while their visa decisions were pending. Tangentially, however, it became clear that the Justice Ministry was out of touch with how its policies were being implemented by regional immigration offices and the lack of uniformity that existed (*Ijû rôdôsha tsûshin*, March 1998, June 1998).

The above examples highlight how advocates have engaged officials in ways that have affected policy implementation and bridged segments of government both horizontally and vertically; but there are other problems of health care access that advocates have tried to ameliorate with little success. For many legally resident foreign employees, employers' failure to enroll them in the employees' insurance system has left them unprotected, given that the Health Ministry maintains they are not eligible for national health insurance coverage. Although the report of the Ad Hoc Council of 1995 raised this problem, it did not directly recommend that they should be covered by national health insurance, and instead stressed the importance of making sure that employers fulfill their responsibility of enrolling them in employees' social insurance. However, the report *does* emphasize that legally resident foreigners should be treated as equal members, whether that be in a geographic or an occupational community (Gaikokujin ni kakaru iryô ni kansuru kondankai 1995). The Health Ministry continues to insist that the solution resides in properly implementing the insurance system made available through employers. Local governments, advocates, certain Diet members, and even the Brazilian consul have pressured for changes, with no results to date (*Asahi Shinbun* 1997a, 1997b). Nevertheless, many communities choose to enroll such foreign residents anyway, a practice that advocates contend is inherently discriminatory (Gaikokujin iryô-seikatsu nettowaaku 2004: 62–63).[7]

---

[7] This is for two reasons. First, they claim that, in practice, Japanese in a similar position are allowed to enroll in national health insurance. Second, because of

Overall, the image that emerges of advocates' impact on health care access is mixed. It is true that the policy impact has occurred primarily at the level of local implementation, and for this very reason the impact has been uneven. However, the pattern of interactions recounted here suggests three points relevant to the broader impact of advocates. First, the persons negotiating with the Health Ministry have the professional skills to engage in quite technical discussion of regulations and practices. Second, advocates have a significant degree of information concerning implementation that Health Ministry officials do not always have, and in this sense they serve as a mediating force and alternative communications conduit for vertical relations within the Ministry. Third, advocates have developed skills in using legislators and legislative mechanisms so as to bring about very specific but concrete results in policy adjustment.

The Work-Trainee Program and Advocacy Organizations' Mediating Role

In relation to the work-trainee (*kenshūsei*) program, advocates have played an active role locally in intermediating among relevant government and private parties when problems have come to their attention, but they have also engaged in apparently productive informal interactions with central officials. The receptivity of central officials to the overtures of advocates undoubtedly is because of the chronic and pervasive implementation problems in a program over which the Ministry of Justice has jurisdiction. In addition, the timing of the formation of the work-trainee network and its lobbying initiative coincided with two circumstances that probably predisposed Ministry officials to welcome groups with firsthand knowledge of trainees' conditions. While local support organizations had been actively involved in specific cases earlier in the 1990s, when the national work-trainees' network affiliated with the Migrants' Network began to meet with Justice Ministry officials in 1999, Japan had recently promised increased support to Asian countries still trying to get their economies on a solid

---

the differential in calculating health care costs for insured and noninsured patients, one could argue that refusing admission of such foreign residents to national health insurance is inherently discriminatory, as hospitals' fees for medical services for those without health insurance are often set at a much higher rate.

course after the currency crisis of 1997 and 1998. An expansion of the trainee program was one element of that support (Murayama 1998a, 1998b).

In addition, throughout 1998 a major investigation was under way
involving the embezzlement of the stipends of a large group of Chinese
trainees, and by February 1999 approximately eighty Chinese trainees had
filed suit against the association involved (*Japan Economic Newswire* 1999).
Against such a backdrop, in February 1999 the Justice Ministry's Immigration Bureau issued a lengthy and specific directive concerning the implementation of the trainee program, the activities that constituted violations
and the penalties to be imposed, and methods for increased supervision of
the program (Hômushô nyûkoku kanrikyoku 1999). For such reasons,
initiatives of the advocates to engage officials in discussion in 1999 dove-
tailed with the Ministry's agenda.

As with questions of access to medical care, grassroots involvement
with problems of implementation produced calculated and sustained efforts to engage central officials in a policy discussion over fundamental
policy inadequacies. Advocates' accounts of the interactions by 2002 were
so distinctly positive, compared to such chronicles of meetings with central
officials of other ministries, that they suggested a rapport that had the
potential for producing concrete improvements (Hatade 2002). By June
2004, however, the earlier energy had given way to a sense of stalemate
(Hatade 2004).

Although the Immigration Control and Refugee Recognition Act had
long provided for the possibility of a trainee visa for foreign employees of
Japanese firms overseas or for trainees sponsored by public programs such
as the Japan International Cooperation Agency, revisions of the act in 1990
were soon followed by an expansion of this provision such that small and
medium-sized firms could become hosts to foreign trainees through collective sponsorship of organizations like local trade associations or chambers
of commerce (see Shimada 1994: 59–75, on the origins of the program).
Even though this trainee arrangement was to be facilitated by either local
governments or a quasi-public body set up for this purpose (primarily the
Japan International Training Cooperation Organization, or JITCO), the
program has attracted much criticism because of the difficulties of enforc-
ing the provisions that host associations and enterprises are to meet. The
difficulty of enforcement is consistent with the general difficulty of enforc-
ing labor protections in small firms, but it also reflects ambiguities of jurisdiction related to the ambiguity of status—legally trainees are not workers
and generally are not protected by labor laws, except for certain limited

circumstances. Primary enforcement authority lies with the Ministry of Justice, which can issue and revoke visas as well as the permission for small business associations to host trainees, but the Ministry lacks the personnel to directly monitor compliance; the Ministry of Labor and its successor have had only marginal jurisdiction specifically for trainees. Since 1993, an additional status of technical training intern (*ginō jisshūsei*), subsequent to being a trainee, has been treated as a worker status protected by law, and it gives trainees a chance to remain longer in Japan to work.

Given their "nonemployed" status, trainees have little legal recourse concerning basic labor standards protections, even though they engage in many of the same activities that employees do. As a result, problems have arisen that include payment of an allowance much lower than that contracted for, "overtime" work whose payment does not meet minimum labor standards, sponsors' failure to provide the degree of classroom training required for this type of visa (one-third of hours are supposed to be for classroom instruction), and the withholding by the receiving farm or firm of all sorts of "costs" from the trainees' stipends. When such abuses occur, the trainees' predicament worsens. If they flee the firm, they may end up without passports, which the host society may be holding, or at minimum they will have violated the terms of their visas and end up vulnerable to deportation by the Immigration Bureau. But even if the Ministry of Justice is proactive and attempts to enforce its rules on delinquent businesses, the trainees most likely will be sent home.

In this overall context, support groups have ended up as advocates and mediators at a local level, but they have also been bearers of crucial knowledge of practices and have been policy advocates vis-à-vis central officials. At the local level, the constellation of individuals and groups involved can be complex. Focusing on "proper implementation" can entail bringing together the various local and central officials responsible for oversight of at least two different economic actors – the sponsoring cooperative and the specific receiving enterprise. For instance, in Kumamoto in 1993 and 1997, advocates intervened to bring in Fukuoka regional immigration authorities, who imposed restrictions on a cooperative that dispatched trainees to member farms. Prefectural authorities, because of their role in conferring corporate status to the cooperative, were also in a position to potentially intervene if immigration authorities relaxed restrictions (*Asahi Shinbun* 1993a, 1993b, 1993c, 1997a; *Ijû rôdôsha tsûshin*, May 1997: 3–4). In Gifu prefecture, when advocacy groups intervened on behalf of Chinese trainees and technical training interns at a cooperative of clothing manufacturers, they found themselves enmeshed in a complicated mediation process that involved the prefectural branch of the Japanese Trade Union Confederation (Rengō) and local labor unions; the Nagoya regional immigration authorities; the Division of Commerce, Industry, and Labor of Gifu Prefecture; the local labor standards office; JITCO; the Center for International Exchange of Gifu Prefecture; and relevant city international centers. Ultimately, the advocates succeeded in working out a settlement between the cooperative and the trainees (Abe 1997).

Obviously, the above examples involved horizontal intermediation at the local level, but advocates have also played a role in communicating vertically between the grassroots and central authorities. The formation of an advocacy network specifically devoted to the trainees' issue (*Gaikokujin kenshūsei mondai nettowaaku*) in July 1999 under the auspices of the Migrants' Network took advocates a major step further toward achieving influence with the central government. Over subsequent years, network representatives developed ongoing talks with the Ministry of Justice with a tone that is distinctive among network efforts to engage central officials. The network's initial agenda included exchanging, pooling, and disseminating information on conditions of trainees, along with discussions with the Ministries of Justice and Labor. A network participant's report of the discussion between network representatives and Justice officials in January 2000 provides a systematic and detailed account of the questions, answers, and exchanges of opinion at the meeting. The general tone indicates that officials saw this as a meeting from which they had something to gain, and were receiving information they clearly did not have. The published summary also expressed the network representatives' satisfaction with the meeting (Hatade 2000).

Typically, in preparation for meetings with any central officials, advocates are expected to submit written questions in advance. After the initial meeting between representatives for the trainee network and Justice Ministry officials, however, the representatives were no longer required to do this, indicating the two sides' shared interests and the officials' willingness to meet informally. Meetings were held with the Ministry of Justice in March, July, and November 2000 and with the Ministry of Labor in March, July, and September of that year (Hatade 2001, 2002).

Since that time, informal talks between network representatives and officials from the Ministries of Justice, Labor, and Health have continued, but the kind of policy revisions for which advocates had hoped have failed to materialize (Hatade 2001, 2000; Kawakami 2001). On one hand, more scandals—such as that revolving around the chairman of KSD, the insurer foundation for smaller business owners—have brought public scrutiny to the program, and JITCO has gradually extended its mechanisms for monitoring firms as called for by the Immigration Bureau's directive of 1999 (Kokusai kenshû kyôryoku kikô 2003). However, a June 2004 issue of *Ijû rôdôsha tsûshin* reviews the directions and events of the previous two years, with mixed appraisal. On the negative side, it highlights the Immigration Bureau's failure to pursue the agenda outlined in its *Second Basic Plan for Immigration Control Administration* and the fact that serious problems continue to surround certain associations recruiting and receiving trainees. In a meeting with representatives of five ministries in July 2003, advocates requested and subsequently received data gathered since 2000 on the administration of the trainee system from the regional offices of the Administrative Assessment Bureau of the Ministry of Public Management, Home Affairs, Posts, and Telecommunications. Although the list of recurring problems remains long, an outsider might at least see the existence of data as a positive thing. Furthermore, Hatade Akira, advocate-author of the retrospective, does evaluate positively the increased discussion of the question of foreign workers in various parts of government and in the private sector (Hatade 2004).

Overall, however, the advocates' impacts regarding the trainee system have remained at the informal level. Although officials may share their concerns, advocates are one voice among many. They are important at times in bringing abuses to light, yet it is difficult for them to learn of abuses that trainees are reluctant or unable to disclose. Yet locally, advocates have played a mediating and monitoring role by appealing to and bringing together the different groups with direct or indirect responsibility for overseeing the trainee program: regional immigration authorities, local labor standards offices, and prefectural offices. They have negotiated directly with the intermediary organization (such as a local agricultural or industrial cooperative) that has assigned trainees to specific enterprises. They have also developed credibility with central officials and have continued to meet with them periodically.

CONCLUSION

The above examples allow us to consider both the substantive policy impact of advocates as well as the role they play in mediating within and across agencies. Clearly, the net impact on policy writ large has been small, yet in some cases advocates have seen some desired changes in formal regulations, even if their impact has been indirect. Instead, their role has been relatively informal and more visible in the area of implementation practices.

Where there has been a convergence of interests with the agency with jurisdiction for a given policy, advocates have been able to engage officials in a reasonably positive manner. Where this has not been the case, they have employed additional tactics to put pressure on officials. Among the three cases discussed here, central officials have been most receptive to advocates working on behalf of trainees who have entered the country legally under a program for which the Ministry of Justice is responsible. Compared to their efforts to intervene over visas and health care, advocates have been most effective in establishing constructive dialogue based on their direct experience with the trainee program at the local level, but only to the extent that their concerns mesh with the Justice Ministry's agenda. On the other hand, a combination of adversarial protest and media tactics, combined with informal interactions with officials, was more effective for visa issues. In the health care area, advocates have been relatively unsuccessful in generating formal policy changes, but they have used informal negotiations and formal mechanisms to promote implementation of official policy.

Taken together, the cases illustrate how advocates contend with and compensate for failures of organizational communication and coordination that are linked to failures in implementation. These groups end up being mediators across state agencies. Yet the process remains invisible and informal. To the extent that it remains informal, the process is inherently unstable and vulnerable to changes in personnel and in agency agendas.

Beyond that, the escalation of official rhetoric on "criminal foreigners," particularly since fall 2003, accentuates the uncertain prospects for even the changes that advocates have had a hand in bringing about.[8] Just as we have witnessed the scaling back of protections for resident foreigners in a

---

[8] The central theme of Japan's 2003 *Police White Paper* (*Keisatsu hakusho*) was "organized crime" — primarily foreigners' organized crime (Keisatsu-chô 2003). In conjunction with this, a joint declaration by the Immigration Bureau of the Ministry of Justice, the Tokyo Regional Immigration Bureau, the Tokyo Metropolitan Government, and the Tokyo Police articulated the goal of reducing by half the number of foreign residents illegally in Tokyo in the next five years, and drew a direct link between illegal residence in Japan and serious crime (Hômushô nyûkoku kanrikyoku 2003).

number of countries in the past several years, policies—legislated or not—
are always vulnerable to reversals.

References

Abe, Kiji. 1997. Chügokujin kenshüsei mondai kara miete kita koto. *Migrants'*
Netto 1:6–8.

Asahi Shinbun. 1993a. Gaikokujin nôgyô kenshûsei no tairyô kikoku. September 2.

———. 1993b. Mekishikojin no 11-nin mo kikoku e. December 3.

———. 1993c. Nôgyô kenshû naiyô hidoi. August 3.

———. 1995. Zainichi gaikokujin no miharai iryôhi kyûmei senta—ni hijo.
September 10.

———. 1997a. Zainichi nikkeijin no kakaeru mondai o meguri kôenkai. March 7.

———. 1997b. Muhoken no burajirujin no kokuho ka'nyû mitomete. June 25.

Asian People's Friendship Society. 2004a. *1-gatsu 20-nichi zaitoku tokubetsu kyôka*
o motomeru amine kariru-san saiban kôsoshin ga hajimarimasu. January 20.
http://www.jca.apc.org/apfs/event/event20040120.htm. Accessed September 19, 2004.

———. 2004b. *Tôkyô kôsai ga amine-san kazoku ni futô hanketsu*.
http://www.jca.apc.org/apfs/event/event20040330-2.htm. Accessed September 19, 2004.

Bo-bii Makkusuto vs. Yûgengaisha Kaishinsha. 1997. Saikô saibansho, 2d. Petty
Bench.

Freeman, Gary P. 1995. Modes of immigration politics in liberal democratic
states. *International Migration Review* 29 (4):881–902.

Gaikokujin iryô-seikatsu nettowaaku, ed. 2004. *Maruwakari gaikokujin iryô: kore*
de anata mo roppô irazu. Tokyo: Gendai jinbunsha.

Gaikokujin ni kakaru iryô ni kansuru kondankai. 1995. Gaikokujin ni kakaru
iryô ni kansuru kondankai hôkokusho.

Hatade, Akira. 2000. Gaikokujin kenshüsei-gaikokujin ginô jisshüsei mondai—
hômushô kôshô. *Migrants' Netto* 24:6–8.

———. 2001. Gaikokujin kenshûsei o meguru ugoki. *Migrants' Netto*, January.

———. 2002. Gaikokujin kenshû, jisshû seido no genjô to mirai. *Migrants' Netto*,
July.

———. 2004. Kaizen susumanu gaikokujin kenshû seido. *Ijû rôdôsha tsûshin*,
June, pp. 2–6.

Hômushô nyûkoku kanrikyoku. 1996. Nihonjin no jisshi o fuyô suru gaikokujin
oya no toriatsukai ni tsuite.

———. 1999. Kenshûsei oyobi ginô jisshûsei no nyûkoku-zairyû kanri ni kansuru shishin. In *Reprinted in Kokusai Jinryû (March 1999)*. Tokyo.

———. 2003. Shutsunyûkoku kanri: Shinjidai ni okeru shutsunyûkoku kanri
gyôsei no tai-ô. Tokyo.

———. 2004a. *Heisei 15-nenmatsu genzai ni okeru gaikokujin tôrokusha tôkei ni*
tsuite. http://www.moj.go.jp. Accessed September 7, 2004.

————. 2004b. *Honpô ni okeru fuhô zanryûsha ni tsuite (Heisei 16-nen 1-gatsu tsuitachi genzai)*. Accessed September 7, 2004.

Hômushô nyûkoku kanrikyoku, tôkyô nyûkokukanrikyoku, and tôkyô-to keishi-chô. 2003. *Shutô tôkyô ni okeru fuhô taizai gaikokujin taisaku no kyôka ni kansuru kyôdô seimei*. Tokyo: hômushô nyûkoku kanrikyoku.

Ijû rôdôsha tsûshin. 1995a. 3.20 Gaikokujin hisaisha ni kansuru kôseishô kôshô. April.

————. 1995b. Gaikokujin hisai jôkyô chûkan hôkoku, April.

————. 1995c. Gaikokujin iryô mondai: 10.30 kôseishô kôshô, December.

————. 1998. Kumamoto no nôgyô kenshüsei mondai 5:6.

Iwasawa, Yuji. 1986. Legal treatment of Koreans in Japan: The impact of international human rights law on Japanese law. Washington, DC: International Human Rights Law Group.

Japan Economic Newswire. 1999. New cooperative urges review of foreign trainee system. February 28.

Kawakami, Sonoko. 2001. KSD giwaku de fujô shita aimu-japan mondai. *Migrants' Netto*, January.

Keisatsu-chô. 2003. Keisatsu hakusho: soshiki hanzai to no tatakai: Keisatsu-chô.

Kimoto, Shigeo. 1997. Zainichi gaikokujin no shiminken kakuritsu no tame ni. *Migrants' Netto*, October, pp. 8–9.

Kokkai shûgiin gijiroku. 1999. In *Hômu iinkai*, 145th Diet, August 3. Tokyo.

Kokusai kenshû kyôryoku kikô. 2003. *Gaikokujin kenshû-ginô jisshû jigyô jisshi jôkyô hôkoku JITCO hakusho*. Tokyo.

Komai, Hiroshi, Ichirô Watado, and Keizô Yamawaki, eds. 2000. *Chôka taizai gaikokujin to zairyû tokubetsu kyôka*: Akashi shoten.

Kumamoto no nôgyô kenshûsei no bisa enchô fukyôka. 1997. *Asahi Shinbun*, November 11.

Lee, Hyekyung. 2003. Gender, migration and civil activism in South Korea. *Asian and Pacific Migration Journal* 12 (1–2):127–53.

Migrant Network News. 2000a. 16 People obtained special permission for residence. February.

————. 2000b. The simultaneous movement for special permission for residence. August.

Murayama, Kohei. 1998a. Gov't raises FY 1999 ODA budget to help Asia. *Japan Economic Newswire*, December 25. In Lexis-Nexis Universe, September 3, 2004.

————. 1998b. Smaller FY 1999 draft ODA budget focuses on Asia aid. *Japan Economic Newswire*, December 21, 1998. In Lexis-Nexis Universe, September 4, 2004.

Nakashima, Shin'ichirô. 1997. Kumamoto-ken no nôgyô kenshûsei no jittai. *Ijû rôdôsha tsûshin* (1):4–5.

Nyûkan jitsumu kenkyûkai, ed. 2000. *Nyûkan jitsumu manyuaru*. 2d ed. Tokyo: Gendai jinbunsha.

Nyûkan mondai chôsakai, ed. 1996. *Misshitsu no jinken shingai: Nyûkan kanri shûyô shisetsu no jittai*. Tokyo: Gendai jinbunsha.

Saikô saibansho. 1996. Supreme Court, 3rd Petty Bench, July 2. In *Hanrei Times* 920 (December):126–29.

Shimada, Haruo. 1994. *Japan's "guest workers": Issues and public policies*. Trans. R. Northridge. Tokyo: University of Tokyo Press.

Shipper, Apichai. 2002. Pragmatism in activism: Organizing support for illegal foreign workers in Japan. Monograph Series on Civil Society in the Asia-Pacific. Cambridge, MA: Harvard University Program on U.S.-Japan Relations.

Tamura, Tarô. 1996. Hanshin daishinsai to gaikokujin no sono go. *Ijû rôdôsha tsûshin*, June.

Tegtmeyer Pak, Katherine. 1998. Outsiders moving in: Identity and institutions in Japanese responses to international migration. PhD dissertation, University of Chicago.

Tôkyô chihô saibansho. 1995. Tokyo District Court, 3rd Civil Matters Division. October 11. In *Hanrei Times* 896 (March 1996): 62–68.

Yamamoto, Fuyuhiko. 1995. Sengo no zainichi gaikokujin to shakai hoshô o meguru kihon mondai. In *Zainichi gaikokujin to shakai hoshô*, edited by M. Yoshioka. Tokyo: Shakai hyôronsha.

CHAPTER 6

Looking Outward: International Legal Norms and Foreigner Rights in Japan

AMY GUROWITZ

Despite Japan's lag behind other major developed countries in integrating long-term foreigners, it has made important changes toward greater rights for noncitizens. Foreigners in Japan, both long-term Korean residents and more recent migrant workers, have historically received few legal protections under domestic law. Without domestic resources to draw on in fighting discrimination, foreigners and their advocates have extensively, and successfully, employed a wide range of international human rights standards, including social norms about the modern state and standards codified as law. The influence of international norms and law on Japan's policy toward noncitizens has received little attention in the literature, especially in contrast to studies of European countries. The influence of ideas about the modern state has been especially noteworthy at the local level, where local bureaucracies have brought together the ideas of internationalization and integration of foreigners in very progressive ways. The impact of codified international laws has also been noteworthy in that courts have drawn not only on laws applicable to Japan (that is, international treaties to which Japan is a party) but also on laws by which Japan need not abide, such as treaty law found in European regional organizations.

This chapter is reprinted from *The Politics of International Law* (Reus-Smit 2004). The original project research was conducted with the support of an SSRC-MacArthur Peace and Security in a Changing World fellowship, with additional travel support from the Cornell University Graduate School and Peace Studies Program, and while visiting at the Institute of Social Sciences at Tokyo University. I would like to thank CCIS workshop participants and Takeyuki Tsuda for helpful comments on this version.

These international standards have been crucial in extending rights to two groups of foreigners in Japan: Koreans and other migrant workers. Most of the Koreans now living in Japan immigrated, or were forced to immigrate, after the 1910 Japanese annexation of Korea. Koreans were then made citizens, but after World War II were classified as aliens and stripped of their Japanese citizenship. Until the 1965 peace treaty between Korea and Japan, Koreans lived in a state of limbo, with no official status and with few remedies for the discrimination directed against them. For most, even the 1965 treaty did little to change their situation despite granting many of them permanent residency.

Since World War II, Japan's general approach to foreign residents has been to avoid them if possible, and to maintain a policy of nonintegration when exclusion is impossible. Immigration and integration, it is thought, will compromise the ideal of Japan as a homogeneous nation. Nonetheless, in addition to a significant population of ethnic Koreans, Japan has experienced nearly a quarter-century of migration. After getting a late start in the importation of labor, Japan's first stage of postwar labor in-migration began in the late 1970s and lasted until around 1986. This phase was characterized by the migration of large numbers of female workers from Thailand, the Philippines, South Korea, and Taiwan. The second stage, beginning in the mid-1980s, saw a shift toward male undocumented labor from South and Southeast Asia, China, South Korea, and Iran. The third stage is marked by the 1990 reform of Japan's immigration laws, which opened a number of "side doors" to low-skilled labor under the guise of reuniting ethnic Japanese from Latin America (*nikkeijin*) with their country of origin, bringing in trainees, and allowing foreign students to work 20 or more hours per week.

In this chapter I first place the study of migrants in Japan in the context of debates over internationalization. I argue that the impact of international standards has to be understood in this larger context, briefly discussing the first type of international norm—diffuse, noncodified social norms about what it means to be a modern, developed state—and then turning to my main argument: that the impact of international law on noncitizen rights in Japan has been significant.

IMMIGRATION AND THE MODERN STATE

Japan is not thought of as a state eager to accept international standards, particularly those relating to foreigners. It is important, therefore, to recognize that the importance of international standards in Japan cannot be understood outside of the general context and historical significance of "the perennial theme" of internationalization (Passin 1983: 16). One purpose of this section is to lay the groundwork for my argument regarding the importance of international law by showing that sensitivity to international standards dates back to 1853. My second purpose here is to show that diffuse, noncodified norms about what it means to be a modern state—or, put differently, what it means to internationalize—have been important for making arguments on behalf of noncitizens in Japan.

The theme of internationalization began in 1853 when U.S. Commodore Matthew Perry, at the behest of the Western powers, arrived in Japan with the mission to open and civilize the country. Between 1853 and 1858, treaties were negotiated between Japan and Western nations and Western consuls were sent to Japan. As with other states that the West deemed uncivilized, the treaties were unequal and were forced on Japan to the benefit of the Western states.

When the Tokugawa Empire fell in 1868, the Meiji government announced "that the goal of the whole nation should be to restore the glory of Japan in the eyes of all nations, that the iniquitous aspects of the treaties the Bakufu had concluded with the West would be revised, but that foreign relations should be conducted in accordance with the law of nations" (Suganami 1984: 191; see also Gong 1984: 181). Japanese intellectuals adopted the distinction between East and West from Europeans whose authority derived from their imperialist power and, according to Victor Koschmann (1997: 84), began to narrate their own history in terms of European assumptions.[1]

Yasuaki Onuma argues that after Japan was forced to enter into international society, it tried to master modern international law, seeking survival and equal status among the European powers (Onuma 1986: 23). After the Meiji restoration, maintaining independence was the foremost concern of the government because of the fear that, if Japan was not sufficiently strong militarily and economically, it might be colonized. During the negotiation of Japan's unequal treaties with the Western states, these latter powers had argued that extraterritoriality was necessary in order to protect Westerners from the "primitive" Japanese legal system, and now international law was seen as a mechanism for overturning the treaties (Port 1991: 146). Adoption of international law, quite explicitly the law of *civilized* nations, was also seen as a way to demonstrate that Japan was itself civilized (Onuma 1986: 29; Suganami 1984: 192).

---

[1] Gong (1984) points out that Japan modeled the unequal treaty it imposed on Korea after the unequal treaties the West had imposed on Japan.

The use of international law in this period was part of a larger move to "internationalize," meaning essentially to modernize and Westernize.[2] Passin (1983: 20) argues that today internationalization can be seen on at least four levels: nationally in Japan's participation in international society; organizationally in adjustment of Japanese organizations; culturally in the adaptation of Japanese culture to international interdependence; and individually at the level of popular culture.[3] He argues that internationalization involves "being in step with the world" (*sekai nami*) where "the world" refers to the Western industrialized states (1983: 21n48).[4] The term internationalization (*kokusaika*), which became widespread in the 1970s and 1980s, is used to refer to such diverse things as learning English, traveling internationally, keeping up with other advanced industrial states and the latest high technology, and fully participating in international institutions (Weiner 1998: 9).[5] Although Japan has a long history of questioning its role in the world and its position vis-à-vis the major powers and the West, this debate reignited around the late 1970s and early 1980s, especially once Japan's role as a major economic power became clear. Hook and Weiner (1992b: 1) argue that the salience of the theme of internationalization in this period can be seen from former Prime Minister Nakasone's 1980 pledge to transform Japan into an international state. Whereas historical debates about internationalization involved catching up, contemporary debates have more to do with the idea that economic power brings with it new responsibilities that extend beyond the purely economic realm (Ogata 1992: 64n49). In short, internationalization has evolved from meaning modernize/Westernize/catch up, to taking on a more subtle implication that Japan should look more like its Euro-American counterparts, not only in its in-

---

[2] Gong (1984: 164) notes that the terms modernization, Westernization, and civilization were all used during the Meiji era.

[3] On internationalization, see also Hook and Weiner 1992a; Mannari and Befu 1983.

[4] See also Ogata 1992: 64. It should be noted though that internationalization does not only mean Westernization. There have historically been strong counterarguments in Japan for Asianization, and today Japan is trying to become more integrated in the Asian region. I am grateful to Saori Katada for stressing this point.

[5] Weiner argues that internationalization did not mean the incorporation of foreigners into Japanese society. While this was clearly not the intent, I argue that the idea of a closed, ethnically homogeneous society has been called into question by the idea of internationalization, and that the two issues are now intimately linked in domestic debates.

ternational dealings but also domestically. It is important to note though that one consistent thread in the meaning of internationalization has been the importance of adopting international standards.

The government has pursued a number of diverse policies to meet the demands of internationalization. These include developing closer links with European states and regional institutions (Yasutomo 1993: 330) and, more recently, becoming increasingly involved in aid to Eastern Europe. Ezra Vogel (1986: 756) points out that internationally minded Japanese have begun to envision their country taking a leadership role by assisting developing countries and championing their causes at international meetings, an idea reflected within the Ministry of Foreign Affairs.[6] The government has also increased its role in the Asian region. One of the clearest shifts in Japan's international involvement, and one with direct bearing on issues of immigrants, is its participation in United Nations human rights machinery and with the UN in general.[7] Yasuhiro Ueki (1993: 347) argues that Japan's attitude toward the United Nations has been ambivalent and pragmatic, but that economic success is undermining this and creating expectations in and out of Japan for more global responsibility.

This intense pressure to internationalize—coming from the outside largely in the form of demands on Japan's economy but translating within Japan into a much more general call to be open and socially and culturally modern—has had crucial implications for immigrants and for the use of international standards in Japan.[8] Activists within and outside of the government have linked the issue of immigration and migrant rights to this larger debate over internationalization, and they have used this linkage to set the terms of the discussion over foreigners. There is a widespread feeling in Japan that it is against international norms for Japan to remain closed to immigrants. While it is true that Japan lags behind other industrialized states in both its numbers of foreigners and its treatment of them, there are no written, codified norms indicating that states should admit immigrants and become more accepting of them (although there are codi-

---

[6] Author interview with Haruka Okumura, Human Rights Division, Ministry of Foreign Affairs, February 1997.

[7] Japan has also been actively seeking a seat on the UN Security Council and has been engaged in much debate over participation in international peacekeeping missions.

[8] This section sets the stage for discussing the impact of legal norms in Japan. For a more extensive treatment of the relationship between internationalization and debates about foreigners, see Gurowitz 2003.

fied norms specifying more narrow treatment of them). Rather, there is a more diffuse sense that being a normal modern state entails a degree of openness. Interestingly, while pressure to open economically has come largely from outside Japan, pressure to open to foreigners (and foreign-ness) has come largely from within Japan. While transnational nongov-ernmental organizations (NGOs) and United Nations agencies may com-ment on Japanese policies toward foreigners, the more extensive campaigns on foreigners' behalf have been domestic.

The debate over immigration has largely taken place along the lines of "to internationalize or not to internationalize" and has occurred in the context of increased international and domestic pressure on the Japanese government to do so. In general, supporters of immigrant rights and more extensive migrant worker programs make three related arguments that as one of the most advance industrialized countries, Japan has a responsibility to accept immigrants, that Japan should become more internationalized, and accepting immigrants and refugees will express a commitment to in-ternationalization, and that Japan must shed its image as an ethnocentric society.[9] Opponents, on the other hand, tend to argue that diversity is a cause of social disintegration; that the economic benefits of migrant worker programs in Europe have been outweighed by the enormous social costs and that technological innovation can continue to absorb demand for labor; and that Japan should increase aid to improve living standards in devel-oped states, not import labor, thereby creating a dual labor market (Sekine 1991: 60).[10]

Acceptance of at least some immigration and respect for the rights of immigrants in Japan is seen as one of the key symbols of internationaliza-tion, and the problem of discrimination in Japan—which previously fo-cused on Burakumin, Ainu, and Koreans—is becoming more internation-ally visible as it expands to encompass migrant workers (Hook and Weiner 1992b: 2). Shimada, a leading economist and specialist on immigration to Japan, argues that the foreign worker issue is:

---

[9] The issues of admitting migrants and increasing rights for foreigners in Japan, while separate issues, are often discussed together when proponents and op-ponents are speaking in general terms.

[10] Interestingly, the two sides of the debate use the terms *sakoku* (keep them out at all costs) and *kaikoku* (open the doors, at least to some degree). Both words are taken from the mid-nineteenth-century debates over whether Japan should remain in feudal isolation or open its borders in order to catch up with the West (Oka 1994: 4).

likely to call into question Japan's position in the world community. It is undeniable that Japan has forged ahead of the world, and even of the other industrialized countries, in terms of economic and income opportunities, and yet it still protects its homogeneity on the human level, and plainly gives the outside world the impression that it is a closed society (Shimada 1994: 202).

Shimada goes so far as to say:

[T]he future of the Japanese economy and society, the nation's position in the world, and its international reputation will very largely depend on whether or not it adopts [policies for accepting foreign workers] and how effectively it is able to implement them. In this sense Japan's response to the foreign worker problem is a litmus test of the kind of nation it seeks to become (1994: viii).[11]

Similarly, while the position of business leaders and trade unions seem to ebb and flow, one 1988 proposal offered by a business organization called opening Japan's labor markets "an important responsibility of the state as a member of international society." That same year, the General Council of Trade Unions stated that "in order to become an advanced country, it is necessary for Japan to reform itself because it is regarded as being by nature a 'closed society,' to broaden its views, and to create the conditions to become a multiracial state in the distant future" (cited in Hanami 1991: 16). Hanami argues that these statements represent the popular opinion that Japan is closed and not international and that the country should open up to international society.

The connection between debates over internationalization and over immigration issues can be seen most directly at the level of local government. Tegtmeyer Pak, in an extensive study of the differences between national and local responses to foreigners in Japan, argues that local actors commonly invoke an ideal of internationalization that envisions a transformation of domestic social relations and reconciliation of Japan with Asia. She argues that a number of local governments "are filling the gap left by the national government's unwillingness to consider what is to be done with the migrants already living in Japan." Local governments are directly responsible for managing the impact of foreign populations within

---

[11] Sellek and Weiner (1992: 205) also refer to this as a "litmus test."

their midst, and this gives them a different perspective. Furthermore, the idea of local independent policy making gained legitimacy after a period of local governance movements in the 1960s and 1970s. Most interesting in this context are the rising number of international sections in local governments and the way in which local governments have redefined the national project of internationalization (Tegtmeyer Pak 2001: 3–4). According to Tegtmeyer Pak, a nationally sponsored local internationalization project opened up the space for local governments to pursue their own approach to integrating foreigners. Local governments, in the spirit of internationalization, began offering classes for foreigners and finding other ways to integrate them as local "citizens" (14–16). According to the Japanese press, many municipalities have begun to treat foreigners like other residents, even ignoring the question of legal status (*Migrant News*, December 1996), and Tegtmeyer Pak (1995: 21) finds that position papers in Kawasaki and Hamamatsu are "laden with radical language which promises to protect [foreign nationals'] human rights."

THE IMPACT OF INTERNATIONAL LAW

The foregoing discussion highlighted how activists in Japan have linked ideas of internationalization and the modern state with immigrant issues to shape the debate over foreigner integration. The broader context of internationalization is also directly related to the impact of international standards codified as law on foreigners in Japan. As noted earlier, with little domestic recourse for discrimination and rights abuses, international standards became potentially crucial for foreigners in Japan. But prior to 1979, Japan had ratified only two international human rights agreements. In 1973, on the twenty-fifth anniversary of the Universal Declaration of Human Rights, seventeen NGOs launched an appeal to the Japanese government to take immediate action on ratification of international human rights conventions. They made further appeals in 1974, 1976, and 1977, each on International Human Rights Day (Yasuhiko 1981: 88–90). NGOs like the Japanese Civil Liberties Union lobbied vociferously for ratification of the International Covenant on Civil and Political Rights (ICCPR),[12] and groups like the National Women's Committee of the United Nations, Amnesty International, the Tokyo Bar Association, and the Asian Human Rights Center protested

---

[12] Article 27 of the ICCPR is one of the most important for minorities in any international covenant. Though it applies to national minorities (who generally are citizens), it is often used in court cases involving immigrants.

by attempting to embarrass the government through comparisons of its ratification record to that of other states and through arguments that failure to ratify would "seriously damage the Japanese image as a peace-seeking nation that pledges to give first priority in her policy and diplomacy to the high ideals enshrined in the United Nations Charter" (quoted in Yasuhiko 1981: 89–91). During major debates about ratification in the Diet, Minister of Foreign Affairs Sunao Sonoda spoke about the developing international environment in which the human rights issue was gaining salience, and he stressed the need to ratify the covenants in order to pursue diplomacy on an equal basis with other states (Yasuhiko 1981: 94).

Under this pressure to internationalize, the Japanese government ratified both the International Covenant on Civil and Political Rights and the International Covenant on Economic, Social, and Cultural Rights in 1979, the Refugee Convention in 1982, the Convention on the Elimination of All Forms of Discrimination Against Women in 1985, and the Convention on the Elimination of All Forms of Racial Discrimination in 1995.[13]

Japanese lawyers, activists, and government officials attribute much of the improvement in policy toward Korean Japanese and other minorities in Japan to these ratifications. Treaties have the force of law in Japan and are generally regarded as taking precedence over statutory law, though they are subordinate to Article 98 (2) of the Japanese Constitution (Iwasawa 1996a: 2). Therefore, the ratification of treaties requires, and has resulted in, extensive change in domestic law. These changes occurred largely through the legislature, although the courts have also enforced Japan's treaty commitments. Japanese courts tend to be conservative and reluctant to deal with arguments based on international law, in part because they are relatively unfamiliar with it and in part because of the relationship between the universal nature of international law and the view within Japan that the country is unique in the international system.[14] While international law is rarely *directly* successful in Japanese courts (that is, the courts do not tend to find that a domestic practice is illegal based on international law), international

---

[13] The Convention on the Elimination of All Forms of Racial Discrimination is one of the most widely ratified human rights conventions in the world. Japan ratified it only after the United States did so, a fact not lost on human rights observers in Japan (author interviews at the International Movement Against All Forms of Discrimination and Racism, Tokyo, February 1997).

[14] Author interviews with Professor Yuji Iwasawa, University of Tokyo, and Yasushi Higashisawa, February 1997. On universalism versus uniqueness, see Katzenstein 1996: 177; Katzenstein and Tsujinaka 1991.

organizations have found a number of other routes to be very effective in achieving judicial change in many human rights–related issues. These include treaties not ratified, treaties to which the Japanese state cannot be a party (for example, a European treaty), United Nations declarations, and so on.[15]

The impact of Japan's international legal obligations is due in part to an "internationalization" among Japan's legal professionals—that is, an increasing awareness of, and education about, international law among Japanese lawyers. One prominent international law professor noted that student interest in international law has increased dramatically over the last fifteen years.[16] This interest began and is strongest in the area of human rights. The Japanese Federation Bar Association began extensive research into international norms around 1984–1985 and now has a practical manual for lawyers on the International Convention on Civil and Political Rights and other covenants which interprets the covenants and discusses cases from around the world that have made use of them (including cases from other countries and UN Human Rights Committee decisions).[17] In addition, the Japanese Federation Bar Association has begun organizing symposiums on human rights during their regular meetings, attended by six hundred lawyers in 1996.[18] Government ministries have also begun consulting with international lawyers in the last few years.[19]

The results of this recent turn to international law have been significant. The most important changes for foreigners in Japan have occurred as a result of either the direct impact of international law through the legislature or courts or its indirect impact in the courts. Before 1982, Koreans were excluded from the national pension plan, but in 1982, in connection with Japan's ratification of the Convention Relating to the Status of Refugees, the plan's nationality restrictions were eliminated. Prior to this revi-

---

[15] Information on the role of law in Japan, and on current trends, was gathered from author interviews in February 1997 with attorney Yuichi Kaido, Yasushi Higashizawa, Susumu Yamagami (director of Adjudication Division, Immigration Bureau, Ministry of Justice), Yuji Iwasawa, and personnel of the International Movement Against All Forms of Discrimination and Racism, as well as from the writings cited by Yuji Iwasawa.

[16] Author interview with Tadashi Hanami, Sophia University, February 1997.

[17] This resource is entitled *Utilizing International Human Rights Covenants in the Courtroom* (Hotei ni ikaso kokusai jinken kinyuko).

[18] Author interview with Yasushi Higashizawa.

[19] Author interview with Yuichi Kaido.

sion, a Korean who had been persuaded to join the plan, even though it was known that he was Korean, had brought suit against the Social Insurance Agency, demanding payment of his pension. The plaintiff argued that the agency's refusal to pay him contravened both the Constitution and Article 9 of the Covenant on Economic, Social, and Cultural Rights. A district court rejected the suit, arguing that Article 9 was not self-executing, but the High Court reversed the decision in 1983 and used human rights treaties in its interpretation. The government now recognizes that the "everyone" in Article 25 refers to aliens as well as to nationals.[20]

In 1985 Japan ratified the Women's Convention and as a result revised its nationality law so that now not only children born to Japanese fathers but also those born to Japanese mothers are considered Japanese nationals. All children previously born to Japanese mothers can acquire Japanese nationality simply by declaring their intention to do so before their twentieth birthday.

The requirement that permanent foreign residents in Japan carry documentation has been a continual source of conflict. In 1993 the UN Human Rights Committee determined that making it a penal offense for aliens to fail to carry documentation with them at all times—a requirement that does not apply to Japanese nationals—violates the ICCPR. While the government did not fully comply with this finding, it did reduce the documentation to the size of a credit card, and the Diet adopted a resolution urging police not to abuse their power to demand presentation of the document (Iwasawa 1998: 158–59).

In 1982 Japan revised its law regarding deportation of aliens to conform with requirements of the international covenants and, in order to comply with the refugee convention, made some improvements to its reentry system for immigrants. Prior to 1982, permission was required for each reentry, and the permission expired in under a year. This was revised in 1982 to allow Koreans multiple reentry permits and to extend their stays for up to two years. Yet many still faced hardship if they wished to study abroad or work overseas. In 1991 the law was amended again to extend the time allowed outside of Japan (Iwasawa 1998: 144, 149).

In 1979, upon ratification of the covenants, the Japanese government acknowledged that it would need to modify its national health insurance laws to cover aliens. It made changes in 1982, in conjunction with ratification of the refugee convention, to include refugees; and finally in 1986 it

---

[20] Certain protections, such as livelihood protection, apply to Koreans but not to short-term migrants or illegal aliens. See Iwasawa 1996b: 156.

eliminated the nationality requirement from the health insurance scheme (Iwasawa 1998: 170). Similarly, to conform to its obligations under the refugee convention, in 1982 Japan removed nationality requirements from the Child Dependency Allowance Law, the Special Child Dependency Allowance Law, and the Child Allowance Law (Iwasawa 1998: 174). In an additional smaller change, the Tokyo Appeals Court has concluded that the requirement that defendants pay the expense of interpreters in court is in violation of the ICCPR.[21]

In a case that the *New York Times* noted could one day be seen as Japan's Rosa Parks, Ana Bortz, a Brazilian journalist living in Japan, brought a discrimination suit against the owner of a jewelry store who refused her service because of her nationality. Bortz won her case based on the Convention on the Elimination of Racial Discrimination (French 1999). In October 1999 a district court judge ruled that Bortz has suffered discrimination and ordered compensation. The court found that although the government was obligated by its 1996 ratification of the Convention on the Elimination of All Forms of Racial Discrimination to legislate against all forms of racial discrimination, it had failed to do so. In the absence of such legislation, the court argued, the Convention would serve as a standard for judging discrimination. This was the first case in Japanese history that ruled on discrimination between two private individuals (Yamanaka 2000: 9).

Finally, additional changes to social policies have occurred following, or in conjunction with, the changes noted above, though they cannot be directly linked to international legal norms. For example, before 1994, an individual had to have been affiliated with the national pension plan for twenty-five years in order to receive a pension, yet foreign workers still had to pay into the system though they could rarely expect to complete the extended eligibility period. In 1994 the law was amended to enable foreign workers to receive a lump-sum payment upon request within two months of leaving Japan. There have also been improvements in housing. In June 1994 the Osaka district court reached a key decision when it ordered a landlord to pay damages to a Korean resident against whom he had discriminated on the basis of nationality (Hanami 1998: 233). Finally, in 1991 the Ministry of Health and Welfare ruled that foreigners with a visa status of a year or more could join the national health plan. This has since been further expanded to include visa overstayers and short-term migrants.[22]

---

[21] Author interview with Yasushi Higashizawa.

[22] Author interview with Yasushi Higashizawa.

As noted previously, in addition to the direct impacts of international standards—legislative changes to make national law conform with the Japanese government's obligations and court findings that certain practices are inconsistent with Japan's legal obligations—international standards have a less direct impact when lawyers and judges use unratified conventions, declarations, and acts of international organizations to interpret domestic law in favor of migrants. Interestingly, in interpreting domestic law, lawyers and judges have used international norms and rules to which Japan is not directly subject, either because they are specific to Europe or because Japan is not a signatory to a particular convention. These may be considered codified norms that are laws applicable to some countries but not to Japan. This form of legal argumentation, relatively new in Japan and due largely to the internationalization of the legal profession, has resulted in a number of key changes for foreigners.

Article 900 of Japan's civil code states that illegitimate children receive half as much in inheritance as children born to married parents. In 1990 a child born out of wedlock brought suit, arguing that this policy was unconstitutional and invoking the Women's Convention, the Universal Declaration of Human Rights, the UN Convention on the Rights of the Child, the ICCPR, and a 1972 Economic and Social Council resolution on the status of the unmarried mother. The Tokyo High Court dismissed the claim without reason in 1991. But in 1993, in "an epoch-making decision" in which "the Tokyo High Court took an initiative to change society with the support of international human rights law" (Iwasawa 1996a: 13), another challenge to Article 900 invoked the preceding conventions as well as an additional provision of the Children's Convention and a general comment of the Human Rights Committee (with the latter offered as the authoritative interpretation of the ICCPR). The court held that Article 900 was unconstitutional on the grounds of unreasonable discrimination and used international human rights law as an aid in interpreting the Constitution.

The naturalization process is not overly difficult in Japan (though it is highly discretionary), but in the past most Korean Japanese did not try to naturalize because of government policy requiring applicants to assimilate into Japanese society and "recommending" that they take Japanese names.[23] The name requirement has been very controversial and is clearly not in the spirit of international trends.[24] In 1982, when a Vietnamese individual who

---

[23] Annual naturalization rates are extremely low, less than 1 percent of the Korean population. See Iwasawa 1996b: 128.

[24] Most specifically, the recommendation runs counter to Article 27 of the ICCPR.

had become a naturalized citizen of Japan wanted to legally recover his Vietnamese name in court, the judges allowed it, arguing that "in view of the present reality that the society increasingly has become mobile and internationalized ... this Court believes that the selection of one's name ... should be allowed" (in Iwasawa 1996b: 130). In 1985 the law was changed so that Japanese nationals married to foreigners could take the foreign spouse's name. This was a profound change in the sense that being Japanese is no longer necessarily equated with having a Japanese name (Iwasawa 1996b: 129).

While the courts have generally rejected arguments based on the Universal Declaration of Human Rights, arguing that it is not legally binding, the Supreme Court has used the Declaration as an aid in interpreting the Constitution. Under constitutional Article 14, "all nationals [*kokumin*] are equal under the law, and there shall be no discrimination in political, economic, or social relations because of race, creed, sex, social status, or family origins." The term *kokumin* is a source of historical dispute. After World War II, the supreme commander for the Allied Powers wrote a draft constitution that used the term "all natural persons," not "all nationals." The final Japanese version changed the wording to *kokumin*, literally "all of the people" but understood to mean all Japanese nationals (Shoichi 1988). In the early postwar period the courts interpreted the human rights provisions of the Constitution as applying to nationals, not aliens. But in 1964, much earlier than most of the other changes affecting aliens, the Supreme Court found that while Article 14 is technically directed at nationals, it must apply in spirit to foreigners in light of the fact that Article 7 of the Universal Declaration provides that all are equal before the law (Iwasawa 1998: 85).

Fingerprinting of aliens is one of the most criticized practices in Japan's treatment of foreigners. Since 1980 many resident aliens have refused to be fingerprinted, claiming that the practice violates their human rights as stated in the Constitution and in the ICCPR's clauses on degrading treatment, discrimination, and due process. The Tokyo District Court in principle acknowledged arguments about the ICCPR but held that fingerprinting did not violate the Constitution because there was sufficient cause for the practice and it is not clear from the *travaux preparatoires* of the ICCPR what is meant by degrading treatment.[25] Nonetheless, in 1982 the Alien Registra-

---

25 *Travaux preparatoires* refers to the legal process of tracing the proceedings leading up to a law, treaty, or convention when the meaning is unclear from the text of the law. The process is intended to identify the spirit or intent of a law.

tion Law was revised, raising the age limit for fingerprinting to sixteen and increasing the interval between fingerprintings (but also raising the fine for noncompliance). In 1985 the law was changed yet again when, in the face of international and domestic protests, the method for fingerprinting was modified. Finally, after countless adjustments in response to international, Korean, and domestic pressure, fingerprinting was eliminated for permanent residents in 1993, removing one of the Japanese government's most despised immigration control procedures (Iwasawa 1996b: 144). Following this change, an Osaka High Court, in ordering compensation for a plaintiff who was arrested for refusing to be fingerprinted and then forced to comply, cited international covenants on degrading treatment and the Vienna Convention on the Law of Treaties. To interpret the covenants, the court referred to general comments of the Human Rights Committee, a decision of the European Commission on Human Rights, and a judgment of the European Court of Human Rights.[26]

Yasushi Higashizawa, a lawyer working on foreigners' rights in Japan, mentions a number of cases in which lawyers cited international covenants to back up their cases and interpret international law but where the impact of these references is unclear. Higashizawa argues that many lawyers cite them but without details, thus making it easy for courts to reject them. He and the Japanese Federation Bar Association are pushing lawyers to make better use of international resources. For example, in one case a Filipina overstayer had a child with a Japanese national. They planned to marry but the man died. The woman and child stayed in Japan, but they were not allowed to join the insurance plan because of the Ministry of Health and Welfare ruling that only foreigners legally in Japan for a year or more were eligible for the national health plan. In late 1995 the Tokyo District Court rejected the woman's claim, saying it is up to government discretion whether to include foreigners in the plan. Higashizawa argues that the attorneys for the case did not place sufficient emphasis on the two international human rights conventions. Since 1996 the government has addressed the problem of foreign undocumented women having children with Japanese men who do not marry them. The Immigration Bureau has now said that, generally speaking, these women should get special permission to remain in Japan legally.[27]

---

[26] Author interviews with Yasushi Higashizawa and Yuji Iwasawa, February 1997.

[27] Author interview with Yasushi Higashizawa.

CONCLUSION

From the late 1970s and into the mid-1990s, Japan underwent important changes—at the level of local government policy, through legislative changes, and through the courts—that affected its openness to and treatment of foreign residents and migrant workers. This shift cannot be understood without examining the impact of international human rights norms and laws. First, Japan has a history of sensitivity to global and/or Western ideals of what it means to be a modern state. These sensitivities were most clearly visible in late-nineteenth-century debates over Westernization, and during the 1980s and 1990s in discussions about internationalization. In the more recent phase of debate, internationalization has been equated with openness, and advocates for greater immigration and greater rights for immigrants have, sometimes successfully, linked openness to "openness to foreigners."

Second, as part of the push for internationalization, Japan signed a number of important international human rights treaties in the late 1970s and the 1980s that stimulated important changes through the legislature and courts. In addition, courts have used international or regional laws not binding on Japan to interpret domestic law in ways that have been significant for foreigners living in Japan. This push to internationalize came as Japan's economic power was on the upswing. It is clear that outside pressure to internationalize has now diminished. What is less clear is whether there is enough momentum domestically to keep the movement for greater rights for foreigners alive even in the phase of long-term economic downturn, when activists can no longer easily link their calls for internationalization to outside calls for economic openness.

References

French, Howard W. 1999. "Japanese only" policy takes body blow in court. *New York Times*, November 15.

Gong, Gerrit. 1984. *The standard of civilization in international society*. Oxford: Clarendon Press.

Gurowitz, Amy. 1999. Mobilizing international norms: Domestic actors, immigrants, and the Japanese state. *World Politics*, April, pp. 413–45.

———. 2003. Mobilizing international norms: Domestic actors, immigrants, and the state. Manuscript.

Hanami, Tadashi. 1991. Discrimination in the US and Japan: From a legal viewpoint. *Journal of American and Canadian Studies* 8 (Autumn): 1–31.

————. 1998. Japanese policies on the rights and benefits granted to foreign workers, residents, refugees and illegals. In *Temporary workers or future citizens*, edited by Myron Weiner and Tadashi Hanami. New York: New York University Press.

Hook, Glenn D., and Michael A. Weiner. 1992a. Introduction. In *The internationalization of Japan*, edited by Glenn D. Hook and Michael A. Weiner. London: Routledge.

————, eds. 1992b. *The internationalization of Japan*. London: Routledge.

Iwasawa, Yuji. 1996a. The domestic impact of acts of international organizations relating to human rights. Paper presented at the Second Trilateral Symposium, Atlanta, March 24–26.

————. 1996b. The impact of international law on Japanese law: Revolution or accommodation. SJD dissertation, University of Virginia.

————. 1998. *International law and human rights in Japanese law*. Oxford: Clarendon Press.

Katzenstein, Peter J. 1996. *Cultural norms and national security: Police and military in postwar Japan*. Ithaca, NY: Cornell University Press.

Katzenstein, Peter J., and Yutaka Tsujinaka. 1991. *Defending the Japanese state: Structures, norms and the political responses to terrorism and violent social protest in the 1970s and 1980s*. Ithaca, NY: East Asia Program, Cornell University.

Koschmann, Victor J. 1997. Asianism's ambivalent legacy. In *Network power: Japan and Asia*, edited by Peter J. Katzenstein and Takashi Shiraish. Ithaca, NY: Cornell University Press.

Mannari, Hiroshi, and Harumi Befu, eds. 1983. *The challenge of Japan's internationalization*. Hyogo, Japan: Kwansei Gakuin University.

Ogata, Sadako. 1992. Interdependence and internationalization. In *The internationalization of Japan*, edited by Glenn D. Hook and Michael A. Weiner. London: Routledge.

Oka, Takashi. 1994. *Prying open the door: Foreign workers in Japan*. Washington, DC: Carnegie Endowment for International Peace.

Onuma, Yasuaki. 1986. "Japanese international law" in the prewar period: Perspectives on the teaching and research of international law in prewar Japan. *The Japanese Annual of International Law* 29.

Passin, Herbert. 1983. Overview: The internationalization of Japan: Some reflections. In *The challenge of Japan's internationalization*, edited by Hiroshi Mannari and Harumi Befu. Hyogo, Japan: Kwansei Gakuin University.

Port, Kenneth L. 1991. The Japanese international law "revolution": International human rights law and its impact in Japan. *Stanford Journal of International Law* 28.

Reus-Smit, Christian, ed. 2004. *The politics of international law*. Cambridge: Cambridge University Press.

Sekine, Masami. 1991. Guest worker policies in Japan. *Migration*.

Sellek, Yoko, and Michael A. Weiner. 1992. Migrant workers: The Japanese case in international perspective. In *The internationalization of Japan*, edited by Glenn D. Hook and Michael A. Weiner. London: Routledge.

Shimada, Haruo. 1994. *Japan's "guest workers."* Tokyo: University of Tokyo Press.

Shoichi, Koseki. 1988. Japanizing the constitution. *Japan Quarterly* 35 (3):234–40.

Suganami, Hidemi. 1984. Japan's entry into international society. In *The expansion of international society*, edited by Hedley Bull and Adam Watson. Oxford: Clarendon Press.

Tegtmeyer Pak, Katherine. 1995. Immigration politics in Japan: Differences in issue articulation across levels of government and society. Paper presented at the meeting of the American Political Science Association, Chicago.

———. 2001. Towards local citizenship: Japanese cities respond to international migration. CCIS Working Paper No. 30. La Jolla: Center for Comparative Immigration Studies, University of California, San Diego.

Ueki, Yasuhiro. 1993. Japan's UN diplomacy: Sources of passivism and activism. In *Japan's foreign policy after the Cold War*, edited by Gerald L. Curtis. New York: M. E. Sharpe.

Vogel, Ezra F. 1986. Pax nipponica. *Foreign Affairs* 64 (Spring).

Weiner, Myron. 1998. Opposing visions: Migration and citizenship policies in Japan and the United States. In *Temporary workers or future citizens?* edited by Myron Weiner and Tadashi Hanami. New York: New York University Press.

Yamanaka, Keiko. 2000. Contesting immigrant rights in Japan. *World On the Move* 6 (2).

Yasuhiko, Saito. 1981. Japan and human rights covenants. *Human Rights Law Journal* 2.

Yasutomo, Dennis T. 1993. The politicization of Japan's post–Cold War multilateral diplomacy. In *Japan's foreign policy after the Cold War*, edited by Gerald L. Curtis. New York: M. E. Sharpe.

Part IV

COMPARATIVE PERSPECTIVES: IMMIGRANT RIGHTS AND INTEGRATION
POLICIES IN ITALY, SPAIN, AND SOUTH KOREA

CHAPTER **7**

Does Hospitality Translate into Integration? Subnational Variations of Italian Responses to Immigration

HARLAN KOFF

Many stereotypes persist regarding Italian culture and society. Some, such as bureaucratic inefficiency or mafia *omertà*, are less than flattering. Others, however, not only portray Italy in a positive light, they contribute to national pride and are actively perpetuated by many Italians. One such stereotype is that "Italians are very hospitable." Visitors to Italy are often impressed by the warmth of the welcome they receive and the size of the meals they are served. This view of Italians is in many ways directly opposed to the stereotype that pervades foreigners' views of Japanese society. Unlike Italians, the Japanese are often accused of being inhospitable. Japan's colonial history, business culture, and net ethnic differentiation between nationals and *gaijin* or "foreigners" contribute to this stereotype.

Obviously, such generalizations do not accurately reflect the realities of either Italian or Japanese society. However, within the context of international migration, Italians have the reputation of being more hospitable or welcoming to immigrants. This is especially true in Italy's southern regions, where citizens have been praised for their "open" attitudes toward migrants, relative tolerance of illegal migration, and relative absence of overt racism. This chapter analyzes immigration politics in Italy's regions and discusses the subnational variations that exist both in integration policies and in public reactions to migrants. It argues that levels of integration do not necessarily reflect public opinion on immigration in determined geographic areas, but rather are determined by structural factors related to political institutions and economic markets.

The remainder of the chapter is divided into four sections. The first discusses national immigration strategies in Italy and Japan and explains why certain reactions to immigration in Italy can provide valuable lessons for the Japanese case. The second defines the notion of "hospitality," which is a major focus of this chapter, and examines it in Italy. This regional discussion is continued in section three through analysis of subnational integration policies. Finally, the fourth section presents some conclusions.

BACKGROUND: COMPARING NATIONAL CONTEXTS

Despite the supposed differences that exist between cultural reactions to migration in Italy and Japan, many historical, political, and demographic similarities make these two nations comparable cases. It is important to note that this essay is not a truly comparative study. Instead, it simply outlines the similarities that exist between Italy and Japan and indicates why the Italian case could provide useful lessons regarding Japanese immigration politics.

Both of these states are considered "recent immigration countries." Migration's demographic pressures have increased in both countries due to similar economic and population trends. As Japan advanced technologically and became a world economic power, it needed new sources of labor power. Japan's women had already been absorbed into the labor force to meet the needs of the industrializing nation and to replace male workers during World War II. Moreover, falling reproduction rates and the aging of the native population further limited the native labor supply. By the 1980s, the only available pool for the country's extensive labor needs was foreign labor, and it was in this decade that the country received its first significant immigration flows.

Italian industry had also opened its doors to women workers during its postwar "economic miracle." And, as in Japan, declining birthrates exacerbated the labor shortage. As the Italian economy continued to expand — to become Europe's third economic power, after Germany and France — the country was forced to depend on foreign labor, and non–European Union (EU) immigration to Italy became significant in the 1980s.

Today, legal foreign residents in Japan and Italy number approximately the same — about two million in each country, which represents small percentages of these countries' overall populations (about 1 percent in Japan and 2 percent in Italy). Moreover, the foreigners' presence is not uniformly distributed in either state. In Japan, a disproportionate number of migrants reside in the major metropolitan areas of Tokyo-Yokohama, Osaka, and Nagoya. The plurality of non-EU immigrants in Italy are found in the urban centers of Rome, Milan, Florence, Turin, and Naples.

In addition to their parallel immigration histories and demographic characteristics, Italy and Japan share comparable political backgrounds. Fascist allies in World War II, both countries embarked on processes of democratization following the war. In each, the newly defined democratic systems were heavily influenced and protected by external U.S. involvement and the context of the Cold War. Fearing further extension of Soviet influence in both Asia and Western Europe, the United States heavily supported single-party regimes (the Christian Democrats in Italy and the Liberal Democrats in Japan), which often manipulated government to serve party interests rather than those of the people. In fact, by the early 1990s, when the Cold War ended and Communism no longer posed a significant political threat to U.S. security and prestige, the ruling parties in both Italy and Japan were embroiled in major corruption scandals (the Tangentopoli scandal in Italy and the Recruit scandal in Japan). These scandals led to widespread institutional changes in both political systems, including processes of decentralization that increased the significance of subnational actors and organizations. It is within this dynamic context that both states became immigration regimes, and it is within this same framework that both states created their contemporary legal-institutional strategies regarding immigration-related questions.

It should come as no surprise that, due to these comparable economic and political contexts, immigration policies in Italy and Japan followed very similar strategies. We can identify three significant similarities. First, in both countries, due to the lack of immigration throughout much of the twentieth century, legislative responses remained flat and inadequate for decades. Before Italy passed its first immigration law in 1986, regulation of migration was based not on national legislation, but on international treaties, such as the 1951 Geneva Convention, 1966 International Treaty on Human Rights, and other European Community conventions and treaties (1950, 1957, 1961). Moreover, until 1986, immigration legislation focused solely on public security, ignoring all other socioeconomic aspects of the migration phenomenon. In Japan, the Immigration Control and Refugee Recognition Act of 1951, which regulated migration until the 1980s, concentrated strongly on tourism and temporary migration, neglecting aspects of immigration politics linked to more permanent flows.

Second, both Italy and Japan began developing more coherent, if incomplete, legislative responses to migration in the mid-1980s. After Italy's 1986 immigration law created an initial legal response to the migration phenomenon, the so-called Martelli law of 1990 introduced labor quotas and included some reference to the rights of foreign workers (to be implemented by local governments). However, the main objective of this law was to harmonize Italy's immigration policies with other European Community member states in view of the upcoming negotiations for the Maastricht Treaty and Schengen Accords. Thus the quotas were utilized to close Italian borders to unskilled labor as "Fortress Europe" was being created. Similarly, under the revised 1989 Immigration Control and Refugee Recognition Act, the Japanese government followed a strategy in which it has left responsibility for integration policies to local government, while the national administration focused on border controls. This legislation essentially closed Japan's borders to unskilled migration and outlined a set of employer sanctions for hiring undocumented labor. Moreover, the law perpetuated a significant norm in Japanese immigration politics: immigration must be limited by temporary visas.

Third, immigration policies in Italy and Japan have suffered from a lack of coordination among the various institutions responsible for different aspects of government migration strategies. According to Tsuda and Cornelius:

> During the immigration policy debate of the late 1980s, a grand total of seventeen [Japanese] government ministries and agencies were involved in immigration policymaking, each responding to different pressures and possessing different, if not conflicting, viewpoints and agendas, including those that strongly advocated more open immigration policies (Tsuda and Cornelius 2004: 452).

Specifically, Tsuda and Cornelius identify the debate that pitted Japan's Ministries of Construction, Agriculture, Transportation, and Forest and Fisheries against the Ministries of Foreign Affairs, Labor, and Justice. In Italy, similar debates have created the institutional chaos that has characterized Italian responses to migration. On one hand, the Ministries of Education, Housing and Social Services, and Economy and Finance, as well as the Bank of Italy, have favored more open immigration policies, while the Ministries of Foreign Affairs and Justice have opposed them.

These frictions can be explained by two characteristics of the Italian and Japanese public administrations. First, due to the hegemony created by single-party democratic systems in both countries, information became a source of power within the public administration as intra-party competition created factions. Through intra-party bargaining, these factions controlled specific ministries with specific interests. Thus public administra-

tion had as much to do with power struggles as with the provision of public goods and services. Second, due to the above-mentioned corruption
scandals, reform created instability. A result was competition for power
within new bureaucratic structures as leaders tried to position themselves
to maximize their personal power and prestige as the "rules of the game"
were changing. In both countries, the result of this institutional competition has been that governments in power since the late 1980s have focused
on immigration policy narrowly defined as border control, while integration strategies have often been implemented by the nongovernmental sector due to government inactivity and gridlock.

At this point it is important to mention one major formal difference
between the Italian and Japanese immigration cases. Since 1990 the immigration laws of these countries have begun to diverge due to the presence
or absence of external pressures. In Japan, where external pressures to
open migration policies have been minimal, successive governments have
made migration laws more restrictive since the early 1990s. Until now, the
Japanese government has refused to be influenced by the economic trends
mentioned above, or by global humanitarian emergencies; it has only facilitated high-skilled legal migration and has only admitted foreigners on a
temporary basis. Moreover, it has strengthened employer sanctions and
other measures aimed at punishing those caught facilitating illegal migration. This response has also perpetuated the myth that Japan is an ethnically homogeneous country—one of the main reasons the Japanese are
viewed as "inhospitable."

Conversely, Italian responses to migration have been strongly influenced by European strategies since the early 1990s. On one hand, the
Treaty on European Union and the Schengen Accords forced the EU member states to adopt restrictive third-country migration laws. On the other
hand, the Dublin Convention, the Treaty of Amsterdam, and even the EU's
Convention on Fundamental Rights all created a two-track immigration
strategy in Europe. While the EU has kept its doors closed to unskilled
labor and reinforced its commitment to communitarian protection of the
European Union's external borders (especially in view of enlargement),
member states have also been forced to open access to social and political
citizenship (including education, housing, and social services) and to implement measures to combat racism and xenophobia. In Italy, where two
major pieces of immigration legislation were passed in 1998 and 2002, border controls have been reinforced, but at the same time, social and political
rights—such as access to the state's health care and public housing sys-

tems and naturalization—have been explicitly guaranteed to legal migrants. Moreover, the government included nondiscrimination clauses in these acts.

While Italian responses to migration may seem more comprehensive than those passed in Japan, it is important to examine how Italy's 1998 and 2002 laws have been implemented. In both cases, responsibility for the provision of integration programs and socioeconomic services was given to regional and local governments. Conversely, the national government increasingly focused its efforts in the arena of border control and the fight against human smuggling and human trafficking. In addition, both of these laws strengthened the judicial penalties for illegal migrants and streamlined deportation procedures. Thus, while the laws include integration strategies, the application of these strategies has not been uniform due to prominent regional differences present in Italian politics and society. These differences are, in fact, the focus of this chapter, because they influence both "Italian hospitality" and the socioeconomic integration of immigrants.

ITALIAN "HOSPITALITY": THE POLITICAL GEOGRAPHY OF RACISM

The contradictions that mark Italian politics have fascinated scholars since the beginning of the Republic at the end of World War II. Seeming paradoxes exist in most arenas of Italian politics and society, often reflecting social, cultural, and economic cleavages that date back many centuries. Sondra and Stephen Koff write:

> Because of its many dualities, Italy has frequently been described as a study in contradictions. Youth versus antiquity, continuity versus sharp change, the North versus the South, competition versus co-operation, persistent economic cycle crises versus outstanding long-term performance, regionalism versus centralization, clericalism versus secularism, and democracy versus authoritarianism are just a few of the dichotomies (Koff and Koff 2000: 1).

Italian immigration politics have followed this pattern. Scholars of immigration have correctly noted that Italy, in its short history as an immigration state (since the early 1980s), has been characterized by neither a tradition of intolerance nor one of integration. Even though most Italians condemn xenophobia and racism, tension between citizens and immigrants clearly marks Italian society. Moreover, immigration has evidenced many of the above-mentioned problems that characterize the Italian political system, such as bureaucratic inefficiency and lack of trust in the government, the North-South divide, and the fragmentation of the nongovernmental sector.

Much has been written on anti-immigrant reactions in Italy. Most of these works focus on the cultural and structural changes caused by Italy's shift from an emigration to an immigration state in the 1980s. These studies examine public attitudes (Bonifazi 1992; Balbo and Manconi 1990), government reactions (Calavita 1994; Papademetriou and Hamilton 1996), political parties, and social movements (Watts 2002; Della Porta 2000) at the national level. However, scholars of immigration to Italy, and of Italian politics in general, have accurately noted that regional differences are fundamental in Italian society. Differences in local cultures and levels of economic development have created substantial subnational variance in Italian responses to immigration (Koff 2001; Pugliese 2000; Ambrosini 2001).

This section analyzes the distribution of anti-immigrant responses in contemporary Italy at the subnational level. True to form, the Italian response to immigration does not follow the usual trends present in advanced industrial states. Unlike in most European countries, xenophobic reactions in Italy have often been linked to regional identities rather than nationalism. This is reflected in the positions taken by the political parties of the right on the immigration issue. Whereas the nationalist Alleanza Nazionale, whose support is concentrated in the poorer South, has backed away from xenophobic, anti-immigrant platforms at the national level, the North-based, ethno-regionalist Lega Nord has made immigration a central aspect of its political activity. Declarations against immigrants by the Lega's populist leader, Umberto Bossi, have been so strong that his right-wing coalition partners—most notably Silvio Berlusconi, leader of Forza Italia and the current prime minister—have reproached him for "going too far."

Anti-immigrant activity in the Italian party system reflects two paradoxes that have created friction within the right-wing coalition that currently governs. First, unlike anti-immigrant reactions in many other advanced industrial states, nativist positions in Italy cannot be explained by socioeconomic factors. The success of the Lega Nord, due in part to the presence of elevated anti-immigrant sentiments, is concentrated in Italy's northeastern regions, where the local economies are strong and most in need of immigrant labor. Even though many small industrial factories would close without the influx of migrant workers, many independent businessmen have supported the Lega Nord and its xenophobic rhetoric and actions. This has alienated Forza Italia to a certain extent, due to its position as a centrist party that represents many business interests.

Second, religion has been a prominent aspect of the immigration debate, and the Lega Nord has vociferously attacked Islam. In an August 2000 special issue of *Quaderni Padani*, a Lega-affiliated journal, an editorial condemned Islam as one of the "three worst diseases in history," along with Communism and Imperialism. Statements such as these have created much friction within the Catholic Church and led to official criticism of the Lega from Italy's center-right Catholic parties (the Cristiani Democratici Uniti and Centro Cristiano Democratico), which are also members of the ruling coalition. The presence of these seeming contradictions—elevated nativist positions in regions most in need of immigrant labor, and the alienation of the Lega from the Catholic Church due to the former's virulent anti-Islam, pro-Catholic positions—would suggest that cultural, not structural, variables best explain Italian nativist responses to immigration.

Defining "Hospitality"

According to award-winning novelist Tahar Ben Jalloun:

> The industrialized countries, obedient to a cold rationality, have had to unlearn hospitality.... There's a shortage of accessibility, or in other words of generosity and freedom, because everything is calculated and measured. Doors are shut, and so are hearts. What is left is the individual and his privacy, a withdrawn universe generating egoism and loneliness (Ben Jalloun 1999: 37).

Ben Jalloun's discussion focuses on the pervasive nature of racism in France. Specifically, he is contemplating the relationship between French culture and society and nationals of formerly colonized countries. He argues that there is a need in France for openness in both public discourse and legal reactions to migration. The crux of this criticism is that France, much as other advanced industrial states, is "inhospitable" due to the economic rationality of its current migration laws and the prejudice and racism that dominate public discussions.

Even though Ben Jalloun's book focuses on France, one must question the generalizations that he makes concerning advanced industrial states. Are the citizens of advanced industrial states inhospitable? Ben Jalloun provides an acceptable definition of the term "hospitality" as "the act of taking somebody into one's home without any thought of recompense"

(Ben Jalloun 1999: 1). He argues that human beings should be valued in and of themselves, and that states should open their borders to migrants without calculation. Essentially, Ben Jalloun contends that institutional racism, in terms of both public reactions and legal instruments, should be held accountable to higher ethical standards.

The preceding discussion has shown that Italian immigration laws would not be considered hospitable under this definition. However, public reactions to migration differ greatly. Many scholars of Italian politics and society have argued that no single Italian culture exists; rather, Italy comprises numerous regional cultures. The subnational variance of Italian anti-immigrant reactions supports this assertion.

Continuing this discussion of stereotypes, one often hears that Southerners are "warmer" than the inhabitants of the North, who are characterized as aloof and arrogant. This generalization usually pervades immigration politics in the form of public reactions to illegal migration. In the North, anti-immigrant social movements have received regular support. Southerners view the absence of these movements in the South as proof that they are "less racist." Moreover, whereas Northerners have often reacted strongly against migration, Southerners are perceived as more sympathetic to illegal migrants due to the importance of emigration in the history of southern Italy and the region's relative poverty. In fact, the Italian government nominated the southern region of Puglia for the 1998 Nobel Peace Prize for its humanitarian work with illegal immigrants arriving from the Balkans, specifically from Albania.

Although stereotypes must always be taken with a grain of salt, public opinion data seem to support such views of Italian culture. According to a public opinion survey released in July 2000 by the research firm Centro Studi Investimenti Sociali (Censis), the greatest fear among Italian citizens is crime (37.1 percent). This response was dispersed evenly throughout Italy. In fifth place, after unemployment, urban traffic, and drugs, came immigration (21 percent). The distribution of the responses, however, seems to indicate the presence of such regional cultures in Italian immigration politics. In the Northeast, xenophobia reached 38.4 percent of the population. In the Center and Northwest it was measured at 23.8 and 21.5 percent, respectively, and it was only 9.5 percent in the South (Bellu 2000: 12).

Because anti-immigrant opinions were expressed three times as strongly in the North as in the South, this chapter will focus on local variations of xenophobia in the North, examining the electoral support shown across this region for the anti-immigrant Lega Nord. It investigates whether cultural variations regarding "hospitality" can be identified, and it then attempts to provide an explanation.

Italian Inhospitality and the Political Party System

At the conclusion of World War II, the radical right was effectively marginalized from European party systems. The Cold War froze European party politics, creating a system that pitted secular or Christian conservative parties against various parties of the left. The radical right remained a negligible force, achieving modest results in postwar elections despite the rise of immigration and the implementation of the guestworker system that were driven by the massive economic reconstruction of Western Europe.

During the past twenty years, two significant developments in European politics and society greatly improved the fortunes of the radical right and led to a renaissance of nationalism. The first was a rise in mass migration to Western Europe propelled by increased access to transportation, the unequal international distribution of wealth, and the rise of ethnic conflict in the Balkans. These developments occurred during a period of economic recession and increased unemployment, and foreigners were blamed for adding to the pressures on European labor markets. Second, the end of the Cold War led to a thaw in European party systems. According to many scholars of Western European party politics, these systems were characterized by dealignment, evidenced by lower rates in voter turnout, ideological shifts within the established party families of the left and center-right, and the appearance of new parties, such as the Greens and the radical right. In Italy, dealignment was caused by the Tangentopoli scandal and the dissolution of the left-wing bloc into various smaller parties.

The spaces left by these radical changes in the Italian party system opened opportunity structures to right-wing populism for the first time since the fall of Fascism. It is within this context of political transformation that mass migration began. Given the major changes occurring in the Italian political system, immigration was obviously considered a secondary issue. However, as migrants became more visible within Italian society, the question began to appear on the political agenda. Already in a 1990 opinion poll, 75.4 percent of respondents agreed that "there were too many foreigners in Italy" (Bonifazi 1992: 28). Nonetheless, no nationalist, anti-immigrant party ever formed in the new political system. This is likely the case because, first, anti-immigration reactions among political elites crossed party lines; and second, Italy's neo-fascist party, the Alleanza Nazionale, was trying to shed its reputation for extremism.

The Lega Nord quickly filled the vacuum created by the lack of a nationalist, radical right position on immigration. The Lega was born in 1989 as the collective force of autonomous local movements. Its appearance is one of the most significant results of the transformation of the party system. One could argue that Forza Italia has occupied the spaces previously filled by the Christian Democratic, Socialist, and various minor parties that dominated the center. Conversely, by introducing a regionalist political ideology, the Lega opened a new position in the party spectrum and prevented the formation of a new bipolar system. The Lega's platform originally focused on the center-periphery cleavage that resulted from Italy's late and incomplete unification. Specifically, it denounced the economic differences between the North and South, which the Lega views as an economic drain. However, this economic argument was often tinged with ethnic overtures, and the Lega successfully transformed this political issue. The party was not merely defending the interests of the northern regions, but also the identity and rights of citizens of those areas who had been "colonized and oppressed" by Rome.

With regard to immigration, the embrace of identity politics also led to the formation of strong nativist positions. The Lega contested all values that were not Padanian, whether southern Italian or foreign. Article 6 of the Padanian Citizens' Bill of Rights states: "The community of Padanian citizens is open to all other women and men, but they retain the right to establish regulations aimed at preventing the deterioration of their ethnic and cultural heritage." Specifically, the Lega focused its xenophobic, anti-immigrant platform on two issues: criminal activity among immigrants and the growing presence of Islam in Catholic Padania.

This rhetoric has been translated into significant political action and even public policy in those cities and towns where the Lega has won local elections. The party has organized protests and public masses against the construction of mosques in major cities such as Rome, Turin, and Brescia. During a recent protest in Lodi, march organizers promised to "take apart the mosque, brick by brick." At the local level, authorities affiliated with the Lega in the smaller towns of the Northeast have utilized health and housing ordinances to close lay structures utilized by Muslim immigrants as makeshift mosques and to prevent the establishment of Muslim places of worship. Not even local officials from Alleanza Nazionale have attempted to utilize such measures in the cities they govern in the South, which, incidentally, is where most of Italy's Muslim population is concentrated.

Table 7.1. Regional Distribution of Lega Nord Vote and Selected Variables

Region	Lega Nord Vote 1996 (%)	Immigrants as Percent of Total Population	Immigrants as Percent in Crime Figures	Presence of Islam[a]	Unemployment Rate (%)
Piemonte	18.4	1.2	11.8	1	7.2
Lombardia	24.6	2.5	11.7	0	4.8
Trentino Alto-Adige	13.2	2.9	10.3	0	3.5
Veneto	29.9	1.6	12.3	0	4.5
Friuli Venezia Giulia	23.2	2.6	10.6	0	5.6
Liguria	10.2	1.4	25.3	0	9.9
Emilia Romagna	7.2	1.8	10.8	1	4.6
Toscana	1.8	1.8	11.1	0	7.2

[a] A value of 1 was assigned to those regions where Muslims outnumbered Christian immigrants. A value of 0 represents those regions where Christian immigrants outnumber Muslims.

Explaining Anti-Immigrant Sentiment in Northern Italy

Numerous studies of the Lega Nord (Diamonte 1993; D'Alimonte and Bartolini 1997; Moioli 1990) have shown that patterns of support do not follow the trends that seem to characterize the distribution of the radical right vote in most European countries. Unlike the French Front National, the Lega does not seem to gain strength in frontier areas. Also, given its views on the North-South cleavage, it is a nonentity in Italy's poorer regions (unlike the case in Germany). Finally, this party does not seem to excel in areas with an international economy, which many authors have identified as a leading contributing factor to the success of the radical right. What, then, explains the Lega's success in Italian politics?

Most studies of the radical right in Europe focus on structural explanations for its recent success. Table 7.1 examines the distribution of the Lega vote at the regional level, along with many of the structural factors tied to immigration that are usually proposed as explanatory variables. The table demonstrates essentially two geographic areas of support for the Lega. In Italy's Central regions—Liguria, Toscana, and Emilia Romagna—levels of support for the Lega are considerably reduced. Conversely, one finds elevated support for the Lega in four northern regions: Lombardia, Veneto, Piemonte, and Friuli Venezia Giulia.

The first three explanatory variables presented in the table focus on regional characteristics pertaining to immigration: the percentage of immigrants in the total population, the percentage of immigrants among the total of those charged with committing crimes, and the importance of Islam within regional migrant populations. Neither the overall presence of immigrants nor the presence of Islam seems to influence the success rate of the Lega. Also, no patterns exist between overall unemployment levels and the Lega vote. However, this table and figure 7.1 both indicate that there does seem to be a relationship between variations in immigrant criminal activity and the strength of the Lega vote. Also, a negative relationship seems to exist between the Lega vote and the economic integration of immigrants. Table 7.2 presents the official regional requests for foreign labor submitted in 2000. One finds elevated support for the Lega Nord in three regions—Veneto, Piemonte, and Friuli Venezia Giulia—where the services of immigrant workers are highly desired. Even demographically, recent studies have shown that all of the regions in this area have among the lowest labor substitution rates in Italy (Koff 2001).

The contradiction between the economic need for migrant labor and the Lega Nord's electoral success is even more evident when analyzed at the provincial level. Tables 7.3 and 7.4 present the provincial distribution of the Lega vote in the two regions where this party is strongest, Lombardia and the Veneto. These data reinforce the pattern indicated at the regional level, which suggests that the Lega does well in areas where immigrants are most needed to support the local economy. Figures 7.2 and 7.3 graphically display the fit between the two sets of data, with the one exception of Milano in Lombardia, where the Lega has had reduced electoral success.

The Lega Nord and Political Culture

As an indicator of the distribution of anti-immigrant votes in Italy, the Lega's success cannot be explained by political economy analyses. This is even more evident when the socioeconomic backgrounds of Lega voters are taken into account; one finds numerous entrepreneurs and businessmen,[1] the very people who most benefit from migrant labor (see D'Alimonte and Bartolini 1997; Koff and Koff 2000). Thus attention must be turned to cultural factors and the so-called hospitality discussed above. These variables best explain the Lega's success in northern Italy.

The Lega's response to Islam is a significant indicator of its electoral base. In fact, studies of the Lega have found that religion is a relevant factor to its success, given that the party's electorate is characterized by a strong adherence to Catholicism. In general, the Lega's best results have occurred in the "white" areas of the Northeast. Specifically, the party has done extremely well in electoral districts that had previously been dominated by the Christian Democrats before this party's disintegration. According to Ilvo Diamanti, in the 1992 parliamentary elections, the Lega won approximately half of its seats in districts previously represented by the Christian Democrats (Diamanti 1993: 37).

This does not totally explain the Lega's success, however, nor its strong response to immigration. In fact, the Lega has broken with the Church on the immigration issue, which has provoked extensive criticism from Catholics. If the Lega vote were merely based on religion, the party should lose votes in these districts.

Analysis of election data also indicates that Lega supporters are concentrated in traditional societies. Figures 7.4 and 7.5 illustrate the provincial distribution of the Lega's electoral results in Lombardia and Veneto versus those for the provinces' capital cities. It is evident that the Lega has achieved more success in less populated areas than in urban settings. Moreover,

---

[1] The obvious explanation for this is that they support the Lega's fiscal policies.

Table 7.2. Immigrant Residents and Need for Foreign Labor by Region

Region	Immigrant Residents[a]	Number of Foreign Employees Requested[b]
Valle D'Aosta	1	17
Piemonte	79	5,230
Lombardia	255	869
Trentino Alto Adige	22	12,812
Liguria	29	730
Friuli	23	7,000
Veneto	97	5,100
Emilia Romagna	93	810
Toscana	82	692
Umbria	21	687
Marche	29	920
Lazio	195	1,370
Abruzzo	18	268
Molise	1	0
Campania	43	877
Basilicata	2	161
Puglia	28	995
Calabria	15	88
Sicilia	60	1,120
Sardegna	12	228
TOTAL	**1,105**	**39,974**

Source: Corriere della Sera, July 16, 2000.

[a] Statistics from Ministry of the Interior for December 31, 1999.

[b] Statistics from Ministry of Work relative to official requests from business.

Table 7.3. Provincial Distribution of Immigrant Labor and Votes for the Lega in Lombardia

Province	Number of Immigrant Employees	Lega Vote 1996 (%)	Lega Vote 2001 (%)
Bergamo	4,307	29.75	20.26
Brescia	7,186	34.50	16.46
Como	3,200	34.00	16.81
Cremona	701	22.47	9.70
Mantova	156	21.43	8.73
Milano	11,197	16.69	7.33
Pavia	662	20.30	7.68
Sondrio	232	41.35	20.20
Varese	2,014	33.39	16.66

Table 7.4. Provincial Distribution of Immigrant Labor and Lega Vote in Veneto

Province	Number of Immigrant Employees	Lega Vote 1996 (%)	Lega Vote 2001 (%)
Belluno	922	41.55	9.85
Padova	2,223	23.70	7.54
Rovigo	169	15.67	5.47
Treviso	4,526	42.22	16.92
Venezia	1,051	22.10	6.03
Verona	3,496	25.81	10.1
Vicenza	7,767	36.23	13.00

the gap between the Lega vote in the capital city and the province widens as the size of the capital's metropolitan area increases. In Treviso, Venezia, and Vicenza in Veneto, and in Milano, Brescia, and Bergamo in Lombardia, these differences are more pronounced. By contrast, the smaller provincial capitals closely reflect overall provincial percentages.

The data presented in this section indicate the presence of significant subnational variation in Italian reactions to migration. First, they suggest that varying levels of "hospitality" can be identified in Italy's North, Center, and South. Moreover, nativist reactions in the North are strongest in the region's rural and Catholic areas. Second, the data on Lega support in northern Italy seem to confirm the comparative work of Herbert Kitschelt (1995) and others who argue that the radical right can be best analyzed in terms of nativist fears of cultural internationalization, represented in this case by immigration. This fear of social and cultural globalization seems to explain why local cultures are significant variables.

DOES HOSPITALITY TRANSLATE INTO INTEGRATION? EVIDENCE FROM THE ITALIAN REGIONS

The Lega Nord, like its radical right counterparts throughout Europe, has often argued that immigrants are degrading national society and culture. As a result, Lega-run municipal governments have often implemented policies aimed at socially excluding migrants from local societies. Examples include the removal of benches in public places where migrants congregate and the closure of buildings that migrants use for social activities. There is no doubt that the distribution of xenophobia has some policy implications in Italy, especially at the local level. However, the question that this section addresses is: can one identify a general relationship between the distribution of xenophobic attitudes and integration policies? Obvi-

ously, one would expect less stringent implementation of integration policies in areas where nativist reactions have been strongest. In Italy, the prevailing logic would expect dedication to integration principles to be highest in the "more hospitable" South and less developed in the North, where
statistics and voting patterns suggest stronger nativist reactions.

Integration Strategies among the Italian Regions

Given the overall strength of regionalism in Italian politics and the importance of local and regional governments in implementing migrant integration policies, it is not surprising that these policies vary throughout Italy.
The foregoing discussion has shown that Italian immigration legislation
includes a stronger legal commitment to integration than that found in
Japan. Yet integration policies differ across Italy because the implementation of these legal objectives has varied by region. In part, this can be explained by the disparate commitment to "hospitality" demonstrated above.
However, as discussed below, integration policies are also significantly
affected by questions related to institutional governance.

Scholars of Italian immigration politics have generally identified three
approaches to the integration of non-EU migrants since the 1980s. These
strategies can be called custodial, assistential, and promotional (Zanfrini
1998). The first, custodial, follows a logic based on defending the host society from migrants who are increasingly perceived as criminals or deviants.
Assistential strategies view immigrants as members of a poor underclass
and promote policies aimed at addressing social emergencies and marginalization. Finally, promotional approaches view integration as a social
right and include notions of cultural exchange, political representation, and
migrant agency. These strategies are summarized in table 7.5.

The first studies of Italian integration strategies, conducted in the mid-
1990s, indicated that not only did these different approaches exist at the
subnational level, they also were aggregated regionally. For example, a
research project on integration conducted by the Consiglio Nazionale
dell'Economia e del Lavoro (CNEL) studied different projects implemented
at the local level in the fields of housing, health, and education, and how
they were carried out. The study correctly noted that commitment to integration can be viewed by studying the budgets for these programs. Table
7.6 indicates that the cities, provinces, and regions of the Northeast and
Center provided greater funding (local budgets) and utilized more of the
alternative available funding for integration projects than did those in the
country's Northwest and South.

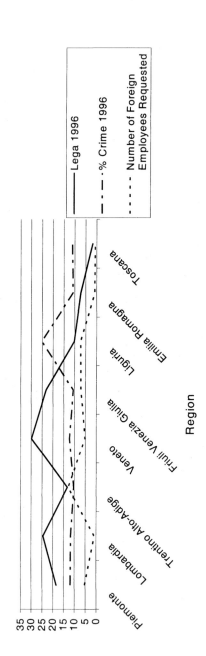

Figure 7.1. Regional Distribution of Lega Nord Vote, Immigrant Crime, and the Request for Foreign Labor

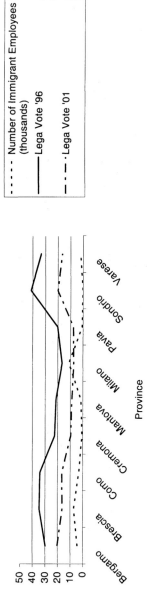

Figure 7.2. Provincial Distribution of Immigrant Labor and Lega Vote in Lombardia

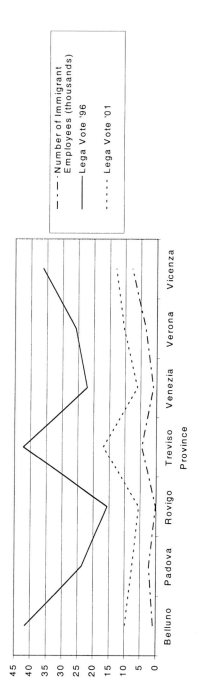

Figure 7.3. Provincial Distribution of Immigrant Labor and the Lega Vote in Veneto

Figure 7.4. Lega Vote, Province versus Provincial Capital in Lombardia

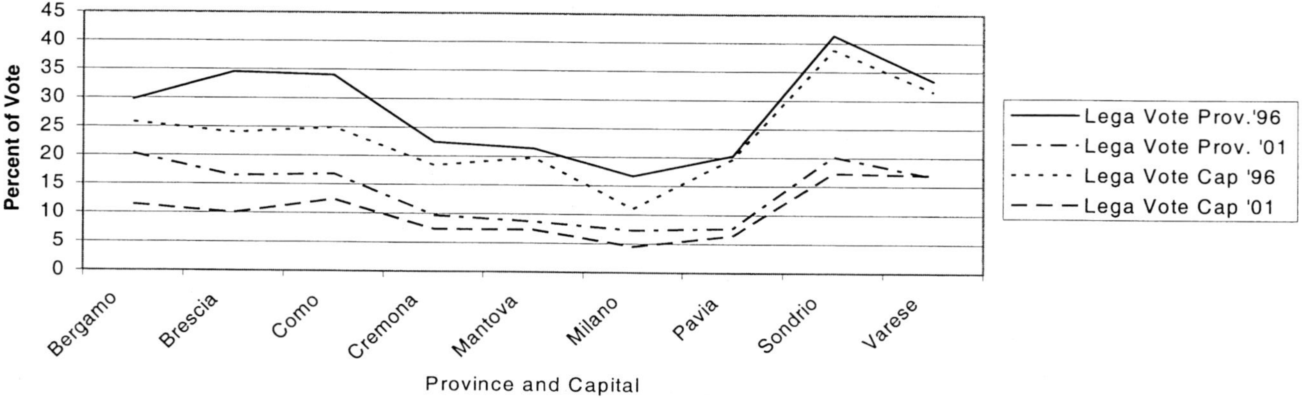

Figure 7.5. Lega Vote, Province versus Provincial Capital in Veneto

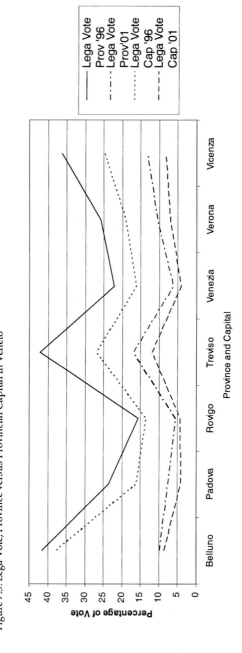

Table 7.5. Classification of Italian Integration Strategies

	Custodial Approach	Assistential Approach	Promotional Approach
View of immigrant	Potential criminal	Member of underclass	Socioeconomic actor
Objective	Defend host society	Address social emergencies	Integration as equals
Principal actors	Police and judiciary	Social services	Political parties and representative bodies
Logic of integration	Refusal of ghettoization	Temporary assistance	Social universalism

Source: Zanfrini 1998: 203.

Table 7.6. Economic Resources Used for Integration Strategies (percentage of funds used, by region)

	National Mean	Northwest	Northeast	Center	South and Islands
Local budgets	74.7%	63.6%	88.9%	80.0%	33.3%
Provincial contributions	12.6	4.5	13.9	25.0	—
Regional contributions	39.1	40.9	30.6	60.0	22.2
Private contributions	4.6	—	5.6	10.0	—

Source: CNEL 1995.

Table 7.7. Health, Housing, and Various Education Programs Established (average percentages, by region)

	National Mean	Northwest	Northeast	Center	South
Health programs	17.8%	15.2%	19.5%	16.6%	16.6%
Housing programs	31.5	30.7	34.7	33.8	16.5
Literacy programs	50.5	45.4	61.1	45.0	33.3
Elementary school programs	29.8	18.2	39.0	35.0	11.1
Professional training	24.1	13.6	27.8	30.0	22.2
Child care	47.1	36.3	44.4	65.0	44.4

Source: Data compiled by the author from CNEL 1995.

Furthermore, this report demonstrated that the cities and regions of the Northeast and Center implemented more social programs concerning housing, health, and education, which are traditional indicators of social integration. This is summarized in table 7.7, which illustrates the percentage of municipalities included in the study that have instituted projects in these fields. The table shows that the number of municipalities in the Northeast and Center having established social programs is greater than the national average, whereas the corresponding figures for the Northwest and South are generally less than this mean.

These trends, which divide Italy into four distinct regions, have persisted despite more attention at the national level to the integration of non–European Union immigrants. As noted above, following the passage of the 1998 law regulating immigration and the presence of foreigners in Italy, national legal responses to migration included significant attention to integration issues. In addition to a general amnesty, new rights for foreign residents included access to public housing lists, greater political representation at the local and regional levels, and an improved focus on education. The problem with Italian integration strategies has been that they have not been uniformly implemented. This is evident in the different ways in which regional authorities used funding from the national government directed specifically for integration programs. Table 7.8 examines the utilization of these funds by region. It shows that many of the southern regions and the Islands (Sicilia and Sardegna) did not even pass regional legislation enacting integration programs, despite the availability of funding. Those that did enact such programs tended to focus on human emergency issues, such as the construction of provisional shelters (assistential). In the Center-North, one finds a divergence between the regions of the Northwest, which established temporary, emergency measures (custodial model), and the regions of the Center and Northeast, which enacted strategies aimed at long-term integration (promotional model). By 2000, the second year after the law had been passed, the regional governments were better organized and had approved more programs, but the integration strategies employed followed similar geographic patterns in terms of objectives and content (table 7.9). These trends are still evident.

CONCLUSION: LESSONS FROM ITALY

This chapter is based on the premise that Italy is a country of paradoxes and contradictions. Rarely can stereotypes or generalizations accurately describe the complexity of Italian politics and society. In immigration politics, the differences that exist between regional responses are strikingly clear, and these differences demonstrate visible geographical distinctions within Italian migration politics. Public responses to immigration demonstrate the existence of three separate areas within the national borders. In the South, public opinion polls indicate relative tolerance of migration and less openly visible racism and xenophobia. In the country's Center, opinion polls illustrate higher levels of intolerance, but support for the radical-right Lega Nord remains low. Conversely, support for the Lega and openly voiced xenophobic opinions are most evident in the regions of the North, the part of Italy that observers have identified as the most "inhospitable." Moreover, this support is more affected by cultural concerns than by institutional or economic ones.

The largest seeming paradox of Italian immigration politics is the fact that the most progressive integration strategies can be found in the Center and the supposedly highly xenophobic Northeast. Due to their strong left-wing traditions, the regional governments of the Center would be expected to show interest in the social integration of migrants. However, the Northeast has never been a geographic area where social justice dominated the political agenda. What explains its commitment to migrant integration? Conversely, why have the "more hospitable" southern regions been slow to institutionalize public responsiveness to immigration?

These questions raise a theoretical point that has marked Italian immigration politics and has significance for Japan. "Hospitality" (as defined by Ben Jalloun) and "integration" are two distinct concepts. Public acceptance of immigration certainly provides government officials with wider opportunity structures in which to construct more innovative policy responses to immigration. However, integration objectives do not depend on public attitudes.

In Italy, one can identify four separate geographical areas delineated by the integration strategies followed within. In the South, regional governments have followed "assistential" strategies because migration flows have created emergency situations on the coasts of these regions. However, the administrative inefficiency and general systemic difficulties that characterize governance in these regions have created obstacles to the implementation of integration policies. Moreover, because these are Italy's poorer regions, many scholars, especially local ones like Cassano (1998), argue that many citizens are willing to support aid for those in emergency situations, but they do not agree with progressive strategies aimed at the socioeconomic integration of migrants, especially because many of these citizens are themselves unemployed or otherwise marginalized.

Table 7.8. Social Programs Enacted by Italian Regional Governments in 1998

Region	Contents of Programs
NORTHWEST	**CUSTODIAL**
Piemonte	Program not approved by regional government
Valle d'Aosta	General regional programming
Lombardia	Emergency housing, access to public housing
Liguria	Emergency housing and services, job training, crime prevention
NORTHEAST	**PROMOTIONAL**
Veneto	Emergency housing, access to public and private housing, research on regional immigration, institutional coordination of immigration-related activities, regional council of migrants
Friuli Venezia Giulia	Emergency housing, access to public and private housing, literacy programs, job training and professional education, education programs for migrant children, support for immigrant associations
Autonomous Province of Trento	General provincial programming
Autonomous Province of Bolzano	General provincial programming
Emilia Romagna	Emergency services for refugees from Kosovo, emergency housing, intercultural education programs (in general school curriculum), special education programs for migrant children, adult education for immigrants, social integration programs

CENTER	PROMOTIONAL
Toscana	Programs aimed at positive relations between peoples, equal opportunity, access to education, access to public and private housing markets, access to health and social services, youth programs aimed at crime prevention, special programs aimed at the abuse of women and children, services for migrants in prisons, the right to legal representation, assistance for foreigners coming from war zones in the Balkans requesting asylum
Umbria	Emergency housing, health and psychological services, information services, education programs, aid to asylum seekers from the Balkans
Marche	Social services, equal opportunity programs, information services, emergency housing and services, antidiscrimination programs, access to education (especially universities), access to public housing, special housing and services for women and victims of sex slavery
Lazio	Information services, emergency housing, literacy programs, social services, cultural programs aimed at promoting migrant cultures, religions, and languages, intercultural activities, antidiscrimination programs, aid for reentry to home countries
SOUTH AND ISLANDS	ASSISTENTIAL OR NONEXISTENT
Molise	Program not approved by regional government
Abruzzo	Emergency housing, access to public housing
Campania	Program not approved by regional government
Puglia	Emergency housing and services, intercultural activities
Basilicata	Program not approved by regional government
Calabria	Program not approved by regional government
Sardegna	Program not approved by regional government
Sicilia	Program not approved by regional government

Source: Compiled by the author from Zincone 2000.

Table 7.9. Social Programs Enacted by Italian Regional Governments in 1999–2000

Region	Content of Programs
NORTHWEST	CUSTODIAL
Piemonte	Reentry to country of origin, information system on migration, access to education, emergency housing and services, social integration initiatives
Valle d'Aosta	Immigrant assistance centers
Lombardia	Emergency housing, access to public housing, access to job markets, family assistance, special housing for victims of sex slavery, cultural mediators for social services, promotion of Italian language and culture, information services, support for immigrant associations, political representation
Liguria	Emergency housing and services, job training, crime prevention, education programs
NORTHEAST	PROMOTIONAL
Veneto	Emergency housing, access to public and private housing, research on regional immigration, institutional coordination of immigration-related activities, regional council of migrants, support for seasonal migrant labor
Friuli Venezia Giulia	Emergency housing, access to public and private housing, literacy programs, job training and professional education, education programs for migrant children, support for immigrant associations
Autonomous Province of Trento	Emergency housing and services, social services, social integration programs
Autonomous Province of Bolzano	General provincial programming
Emilia Romagna	Emergency services for refugees from Kosovo, emergency housing, intercultural education programs (in general school curriculum), special education programs for migrant children, adult education for immigrants, social integration programs, political representation

CENTER	PROMOTIONAL
Toscana	Programs aimed at positive relations between peoples, equal opportunity, access to education, access to public and private housing markets, access to health and social services, youth programs aimed at crime prevention, special programs aimed at the abuse of women and children, services for migrants in prisons, the right to legal representation, assistance for foreigners coming from war zones in the Balkans requesting asylum, social real estate agencies, political representation, emergency housing and services
Umbria	Emergency housing and services, health and psychological services, information services, education programs, aid to asylum seekers from the Balkans, programs aimed at facilitating social integration and cultural relations, social services
Marche	Social services, equal opportunity programs, information services, emergency housing and services, antidiscrimination programs, access to education (especially universities), access to public housing, special housing and services for women and victims of sex slavery, immigrants' rights initiatives
Lazio	Information services, emergency housing and services, literacy programs, social services, cultural programs aimed at promoting migrant cultures, religions, and languages, intercultural activities, antidiscrimination programs, aid for reentry to home countries

Table 7.9. (continued)

SOUTH AND ISLANDS	ASSISTENTIAL OR NONEXISTENT
Molise	Program not approved by regional government
Abruzzo	Emergency housing, access to public housing, information services, Italian language and culture courses, cultural mediation
Campania	Program not approved by regional government because overall regional budget not yet approved
Puglia	Emergency housing and services, intercultural activities, social integration programs
Basilicata	Information centers, education programs
Calabria	Information centers, emergency housing and services, education programs
Sardegna	Program not approved by regional government
Sicilia	Emergency housing and services, access to education, multicultural education programs, support for local nongovernmental organizations

Source: Compiled by the author from Zincone 2001.

Regions in Italy's Center and North provide different contexts for integration discussions. In the Center, one finds more responsive and better-organized political institutions, open economic markets, and the aforementioned left-wing traditions. The combination of these factors has naturally led to the creation of promotional integration strategies. Similarly, regional policy responses to immigration in the Northwest can be logically explained. In combination, the industrial recession currently being felt in these regions and a higher proportion of immigrant crime have created significant support for the Lega Nord and other anti-immigrant movements. Thus, high levels of intolerance have been translated into policy strategies, and the Lega is a partner, if not the controlling member, in many of the coalition governments in this area.

The geographic area that causes the most perplexity is the Northeast. Here one finds the highest rates of expressed intolerance to immigration and the strongest support for the Lega Nord. At the same time, these regional governments have implemented promotional integration strategies. Driven by economic needs, these regions have also been among the most vocal supporters of expanding Italy's immigration quotas. This would suggest that political lobbying by employers and industrial associations has outweighed public opinion in the decisions made by the region's leaders.

This situation demonstrates possibly the most important lesson that the Italian case presents. Integration need not come from cultural acceptance. In the case of the Italian Northeast, integration policies are the result of utilitarian logic. Unlike the Northwest, most of the regions in this area are currently enjoying periods of economic prosperity. Specifically, the sectors of heavy industry in the area need foreign workers to maintain current rates of growth. Many economists have noted that without migrant labor, the entire economy of this region would collapse. Thus local and regional governments promote progressive integration strategies because they are, in fact, self-beneficial.

Hospitality, defined as "the act of taking somebody into one's home without any thought of recompense," is clearly a superficial concept. Public attitudes toward migrants certainly influence government leaders by affecting their opportunity structures. However, integration is a question of access to political, economic, and social structures. In Italy, foreign residents are accepted in the South, but access to political representation, labor markets, and housing is limited by the generally closed and unresponsive nature of the area's political and economic systems. In the Northwest, intolerance has been fueled by relatively closed economic markets and the access immigrants have to criminal structures (unlike in the South, where Italian organized crime hierarchically controls organized criminal systems). The regions of the Center and Northeast have followed promotional strategies because regional governments have reacted to economic and social needs in the area. In exchange for migrant contributions to socioeconomic growth, they guarantee socioeconomic and political rights.

Much has been said about Japan's "inhospitability" toward migrants. However, because national immigration laws have not clearly defined integration strategies, one can already find subnational variance in responses to immigration. The Italian case shows that subnational actors should focus their efforts on questions related to opening access to political and socioeconomic systems. In specific areas, migrants to Japan may be tolerated or even accepted, but this does not ensure participation in the host society. Conversely, the Italian case shows that political and socioeconomic participation can be achieved in areas where nativism is significant. For this reason, Japanese integration strategies need to better reflect the needs of economic markets, especially at the local and regional levels.

References

Ambrosini, Maurizio. 2001. *La fatica di integrarsi.* Bologna: Il Mulino.

Balbo, Laura, and Luigi Manconi. 1990. *I Razzismi possibili.* Milan: Feltrinelli.

Bellu, Giovanni Maria. 2000. Tre italiani su quattro con l'incubo immigrati. *La Repubblica,* July 21.

Ben Jalloun, Tahar. 1999. *French hospitality.* New York: Columbia University Press.

Bonifazi, Corrado. 1992. Italian attitudes and opinions toward foreign migrants and migration policies. *Studi Emigrazione/Etudes Migrations* 24 (105).

———. 1999. *L'Immigrazione straniera in Italia.* Bologna: Il Mulino.

Calavita, Kitty. 1994. U.S. immigration and policy responses: The limits of legislation. In *Controlling immigration: A global perspective,* edited by Wayne A. Cornelius, Philip L. Martin, and James F. Hollifield. Stanford, CA: Stanford University Press.

Cassano, Franco. 1998. *Mal di Levante.* Bari, Italy: Cacucci.

CNEL (Consiglio Nazionale dell'Economia e del Lavoro). 1995. *Tempi e modi di esodo: Il rapporto sull'immigrazione nelle città italiane.* Rome: CNEL.

D'Alimonte, Roberto, and Stefano Bartolini, eds. 1997. *Maggioritario per case: Le elezioni politiche del 1996.* Bologna: Il Mulino.

Della Porta, Donatella. 2000. Immigration and protest: New challenges for Italian democracy. *South European Politics and Society* 5 (3):108–32.

Diamanti, Ilvo. 1993. *La Lega.* Rome: Donzelli Editori.

Kitschelt, Herbert. 1995. *The radical right in Western Europe*. Ann Arbor: University of Michigan Press.

Koff, Harlan. 2001. Immigration or integration? Examining political events of the year 2000. In *Italian politics*, edited by Mario Caciagli and Alan Zuckerman. Oxford: Berghahn.

Koff, Sondra Z., and Stephen P. Koff. 2000. *Italy: From the First to the Second Republic*. London: Routledge.

Moioli, Vittorio. 1990. *I nuovi razzismi: miserie e tortune della Lega Lombarda*. Rome: Edizioni Associate.

Papademetriou, Demetrios G., and Kimberly A. Hamilton. 1996. *Converging paths to restriction: French, Italian, and British responses to immigration*. Washington, DC: Carnegie Endowment for International Peace/Brookings Institution.

Pugliese, Enrico, ed. 2000. *Rapporto immigrazione: Lavoro, sindacato, società*. Rome: Ediesse.

Tsuda, Takeyuki, and Wayne A. Cornelius. 2004. Japan: government policy, immigrant reality. In *Controlling immigration: A global perspective*, edited by Wayne A. Cornelius et al. 2d ed. Stanford, CA: Stanford University Press.

Watts, Julie R. 2002. *Immigration policy and the challenge of globalization: Unions and employers in unlikely alliance*. Ithaca, NY: ILR Press.

Zanfrini, Laura. 1998. *Leggere le migrazioni*. Milan: Franco Angeli.

Zincone, Giovana, ed. 2000. *Primo rapporto sulli integrazione degli immigrati in Italia*. Bologna: Il Mulino.

———. 2001. *Secondo rapporto sulli integrazione degli immigrati in Italia*. Bologna: Il Mulino.

CHAPTER 8

Nongovernmental versus Governmental Actors? Multilevel Governance and Immigrant Integration Policy in Spain

BELÉN AGRELA AND GUNTHER DIETZ

In the last two decades, Spain has rapidly evolved from its former status as a classic country of emigration—toward the countries of Northern and Western Europe and Spain's former colonies in Latin America—to become a new "pole of attraction" for immigration into the European Union (EU). Slowly and reluctantly, Spain has become a "recent country of immigration." Despite its still relatively limited numbers of immigrants, Spain holds importance as a country of immigration on the broader European level. This importance stems from its geostrategic position as a double frontier: on one hand, Spain is the southern gate of entry to the European Union, and on the other it is the symbolic frontier where "Western" civilization meets the "Muslim" world, two civilizations that are assumed to be in conflict, especially in the aftermath of the terrorist events of September 11, 2001.

The first part of this chapter analyzes the demographic, social, and economic dimensions of Spain's evolution to a country of immigration, sketching out a particularly Southern European "model" (King 2000) of precarious, unstable, cyclical, and service-sector-driven labor market integration. The second section focuses on policymakers' reactions to the shift from emigration to immigration processes. These reactions are characterized by the early "problematization" of the migratory phenomenon in both security and cultural terms. This problematization justifies and legitimates policy shifts with regard to the distribution of responsibilities between the central government and emerging regional and local-level policy, leading to a complex and asymmetrical regime of "multilevel governance" in the domain of migration. The complexity of this regime is exacerbated by the trend toward "public-private partnerships" in minority integration policy. Since the very beginning of immigration into Spain, this diversification of responsibilities among different levels of government has been crosscut by powerful and omnipresent nongovernmental actors, as church-run, faith-based, and non-confessional immigrant support groups and NGOs have emerged as specialized counterparts actively promoting the diversification and multiculturalization of the services they provide to their migrant beneficiaries. This pattern of crosscutting processes results in an often conflictive and sometimes contradictory division of labor between the domains of migration control and immigrant integration, which are unequally distributed between governmental and nongovernmental actors. Finally, the consequences that this complex set of different levels and kinds of actors holds for the future of migration policy in Spain are highlighted in the context of post–September 11, 2001, public opinions toward immigration.

CHANGING MIGRATION PATTERNS

Due to the remarkable increase in Spain's immigrant population in recent years, it has been widely claimed that Spain is now a "country of immigration" (Colectivo IOE 1987; Izquierdo 1992, 1996; Cornelius 1994; Martínez Veiga 1997; Arango 2000). During the 1980s, Spain—like other countries in Southern Europe—experienced decreasing emigration while becoming a destination for new immigrants. Nevertheless, this was no mere "one-way process" of substitute migration; the migratory process is much denser than such a Manichean emigration-versus-immigration categorization would suggest. Rather, this "uneasy transition" (Cornelius 2004) reflects a highly heterogeneous migration pattern comprising at least four different, crosscutting processes:

- Although many Spanish emigrants have been settling down definitively in their Western and Northern European host countries (Ruiz Garzón 2001), the second and even the third generation of former Spanish emigrants are not completely abandoning their ties to their country of origin. They are traveling frequently to Spain and maintaining kin and/or communal ties to their villages of "origin." This new generation of rather well-integrated but hyphenated emigrants (Spanish-Germans, Spanish-French, Spanish-Swiss) cultivates an identity that is characterized by a diasporic longing for their ancestors' Mediterranean roots.

- Spanish "guestworkers" who migrated to Western and Northern Europe but did not fully integrate into their host society tend to re-migrate to their regions of origin when they retire. Sometimes they return alone, but they also often come together with their children, who settle down in a home country that the second generation knows only from short holiday trips.[1] Their integration into either the Spanish school system or the labor market is increasingly problematic.

- Retirement migration is not limited to Spanish "guestworkers"; it also dominates intra-Europe migration to Spain. Although marginally perceived as part of the overall immigration phenomenon, European "trans-migrants" (Pries 1999; Smith and Guarnizo 1999) — many of whom spend half the year in their country of origin and half on the Canary or Baleares Islands or on Spain's Mediterranean shores — make up nearly half of the migrant population residing in Spain (Jurdao Arrones and Sánchez 1990; Fernández Cordón et al. 1993).

- Finally, non-European immigrants[2] are increasingly choosing Spain as a point of transit or as a destination. On one hand, this kind of immigration reflects Spain's enduring postcolonial links with its former Latin American and North African territories. On the other hand, however, immigration to Spain is beginning to diversify. As a result of Spain's integration into the European Union and its participation in the Schengen Treaty, its southern shores have become a strategic "port of entry" not only to Spain but to the entire EU Schengen territory (Arango 2000; Zapata-Barrero 2001).

---

[1] There are currently no systematic data available on the amount and extent of this "remigration" integration phenomenon. For an exploratory case study from north-central Spain, see Hannken 1994.

[2] After the Treaty of Maastricht (1992), the bases were set for European citizenship; the main distinction was drawn between European and non-European citizens (the latter also defined as citizens of "third countries"). Thus emerged the concept of "non-Community immigration," a legal-political aspect that, on one hand, defines foreign people residing in Spain as those whose nationality is not any of the nationalities that compose the European Community. The notion is defined as much in terms of opposition ("non-Community nationality" versus "European or Community citizenship") as in terms of exclusion ("beneficiaries of all rights" versus "limited rights"). On the other hand and from a more anthropological perspective on immigration policy, this concept recounts a new categorization that emerges forcefully in the political and institutional discourse about foreigners and what it means to those who are "other immigrants," as differentiated from Europeans.

Despite the heterogeneity of Spain's migration patterns and despite problems of accuracy and reliability in the official data on migration, it is nevertheless clear that Spain is becoming a country of immigration. Available data show that there are more than a million foreigners with residence permits living in Spain (by contrast, more than two million Spaniards are living abroad; Gil Araujo 2002a). Yet the number of immigrants is not sufficiently large to justify the alarmist rhetoric of "massive invasion" that predominates in the political discourse on immigration. Immigrants account for only some 2 percent of Spain's total population, placing Spain among the European countries with the lowest percentages of immigrants.[3]

The total non-EU population living in Spain—including documented and undocumented, residents, and holders of work permits—is estimated at around 1.3 million. These immigrants come primarily from North Africa (especially Morocco and Algeria), Latin America (in particular, Peru, the Dominican Republic, and Colombia), Asia (basically China and the Philippines), and South Africa (mostly Senegal and Nigeria). Immigration from certain countries is increasing particularly rapidly; this is the case for Ecuador,[4] China, and some Eastern European countries, including Romania, Poland, and the Ukraine. Most immigrants, especially Maghrebi migrants, have shifted from viewing Spain as a point of transit on the way to France or Belgium to seeing it as a place for permanent settlement. The most outstanding feature of this immigration model is its newness. The fact that migrants have just begun settling in recent years has produced an "age effect" (Arango 2002), meaning that immigrant groups are composed predominantly by young people.

Two basic elements shape the demographic and social profile of immigration to Spain. First, although the immigrant population as a share of the total population remains low, its composition is highly heterogeneous, with notable differences between nationalities in terms of gender composition, skills, migratory projects, and degrees and types of labor market integration. Second, the migrants' distribution throughout the country is very uneven, and their labor market integration is limited to a reduced number

---

[3] The highest percentages of foreigners, approaching 4 percent, are found in the Canary and Baleares Islands, where EU citizens make up the overwhelming majority of foreign residents.

[4] The case of Ecuador is representative of this changing demographic trend of replacing "classical" countries of origin. Formerly of little or no significance as a region of origin, Ecuador has recently become the second-most-important country of origin of immigrants in Spain (Arango 2002).

of sectors that are showing a rapid tendency toward segmentation. Foreign workers are in demand in labor niches where there are insufficient numbers of local workers—that is, for jobs that domestic workers do not want because of economic and/or social reasons or labor conditions. Consequently, immigrants end up working in less desirable niches such as agriculture, construction, manufacturing, domestic service, or the broader service sector, creating immigrant enclaves in the secondary labor market (Piore 1975; Piore and Berger 1980) that are characterized by unstable and short-term employment, high worker rotation, low salaries, and a nearly total lack of upward mobility (Herranz 2000). In addition, most of these jobs are in the shadow economy, where exploitation and abuses frequently occur but there are few or no labor inspections. Consequently, the foreign workers' integration into these occupations contributes even more to their stigmatization as a marginal group, working at the fringes of the labor market in some specific geographic areas. The legal category of "foreigner" is thus complemented by connotations of marginality and inferiority.

THE PROBLEMATIZATION OF IMMIGRATION AND THE EMERGENCE OF MIGRATION POLICY

Spain's admission into the European Union overlapped the increase in the number of Third World immigrants. Hence we need to understand Spain's migration policy within the ideological framework of the EU, a context that helps explain much of the contradictory discourse and policy that emerged in Spain. Spain's political agenda with regard to immigration has been largely conditioned by this country's relationship to the European Union (Colectivo IOE 1999). Accordingly, "migration" became an institutional policy issue in the 1980s. The political redefinition of immigration and the related governmental practices are directly linked to Spain's "strategic position" as the southern entryway to "Fortress Europe." Spain has become the EU's southern gate in a pragmatic sense because of its geographic position, but also in an ideological sense in that the EU's position is being used politically to justify Spain's policy of "closing its doors" (Agrela Romero 2002a). Control of Spain's borders thus takes on European dimensions as definitions and policies are adapted to European Community accords.[5] In this process of accommodation, discourses on immigration are

---

[5] These include the Treaty of Rome (1957), TREVI Group (1976), Schengen Treaty (1985), Dublin Convention (1990), Maastricht Treaty (1992), Treaty of

embedded in a policy of closing the EU's external borders, a policy that is closely tied to ensuring security within the EU. This means that immigration is implicitly being linked to crime, terrorism, and drug and human trafficking (Gil Araujo 2002a).

Bommes and Geddes (2000) analyze how national responses to immigration differ enormously in terms of social inclusion and exclusion depending on a country's organizational and decision-making infrastructures. In countries with weak welfare traditions, such as Spain, the main policy reactions to immigration have placed a stronger emphasis on restriction than on social integration. In addition, the "social integration" of noncitizens can become highly controversial in these "fragile states," leading the public apparatus to shy away from direct intervention in this process.

Spain issued its first immigration law, the Ley de Extranjería, immediately following the signing of the Schengen Treaty in 1985. The rigidity of the Spanish law, one of the strictest immigration laws in Europe, is due more to Spain's need to satisfy European requirements than to real migratory pressure. Indeed, Spain's "tough" immigration policy seems excessive when we consider that immigration was still at very low levels when the law was issued. Because Spain was a "latecomer" to an EU policy context dominated by mostly northern European "early starters,"[6] Spain began by adopting norms, restrictions, and strategies that are the classical features of traditional countries of immigration. Therefore, Spain's national policy responses to changing migration patterns do not correspond at all well to Spain's particular situation and real needs. This is reflected in important social and political outcomes, including the creation of obstacles to the successful implementation of both immigration control and the social integration of immigrants. In order to justify the introduction of this "policy import" into the national political arena, Spanish policymakers quickly redefined immigration as a "problem" and made it an appropriate object of government intervention on the public's behalf. The "problem" is defined along different dimensions—social, economic, political, identity-related, ethnic, and so on. However, two dimensions are central in public discourse on non-European immigration to Spain: immigration as a security problem and immigration as a cultural problem.

Amsterdam (1997), European Council in Tampere (1999), Council in Laeken European Council (2001), and the Seville European Council (2002).

[6] These terms were used in a similar context about forty years ago by Alexander Gerschenkron (1962; cited in Arango 2002).

Immigration as a Security Problem

Much of the current debate about immigration revolves around the idea of security, with widespread claims of a connection between the increasing influx of immigrants and rising insecurity (higher rates of robbery, murder, rape, and so on). In line with successive European Community agreements, measures related to immigration and the presence of "third country" citizens have increasingly become a "safety" matter, prompting an immigration policy based on mistrust of settled immigrants and rejection of would-be immigrants wanting to enter (Calavita 1998).

Facing the symbolic threat of an "invasion," Spain supposedly needs to reinforce its borders to counteract the country's "call effect" among people of the Third World. To hold off this "ghost" incursion, Spanish immigration policy is moving from the pull of a "call effect" to the push of a "kick effect." Officially, the link between immigration and citizen insecurity is justified by the need to "guarantee coexistence inside Spanish society" (GRECO 2000: 6). This "law and order" discourse became explicit in early 2002 when the then-minister of the interior, Mariano Rajoy, publicly linked rising crime rates with rising immigration.[7] In the opinion polls conducted shortly thereafter by the Centro de Investigaciones Sociológicas (CIS 2001, 2002),[8] the lack of citizen security ranked as the "third-most-important problem faced by citizens."

Beginning with the signing of the Treaty of Amsterdam in 1997, everything related to borders in EU countries became "community-wide" through the European police and judicial cooperation in criminal matters, emphasizing the control and criminalization of immigration. This approach requires stronger enforcement of the EU's external borders. This strategy is acknowledged in the 2000 National Program for the Integration of Immigrants (Programa Nacional de Integración de Inmigrantes), which notes: "It is essential to address immigration from a global perspective ... in the framework of our membership in the European Union and the obli-

---

[7] Just recently, the central government offered "citizen insecurity" as the justification for a comprehensive anticrime program. This program, which substantially increases the number of police and modifies the Penal Code, again links immigration with insecurity. Migrants who are convicted of crimes and sentenced to less than six years in prison must now be deported to their country of origin (El Mundo, January 1, 2003).

[8] CIS is a dependency of the Spanish Ministry of the Presidency. It employs polls to study Spanish society and issues a monthly "barometer" on various current social, economic, and political topics.

gations acquired by our country in this context" (GRECO 2000: 6), as well as in its more pragmatic aspects such as the economically important investment in the establishment and launching of the complex Integrated System of External Vigilance (Sistema Integrado de Vigilancia Exterior).[9]

The prevailing "police approach" to immigration reflects pressures at both the national and the European level. At the EU level, there is the strengthening pressure to fortify external borders.[10] And at the national level, Spain's conservative government (which came to power after fourteen years of Socialist government) has introduced an even more restrictive immigration law and enacted a new national integration program, the Programa GRECO. In the framework of this political turn toward "closing doors," the GRECO Program is less directed to immigrant integration in the strict sense and more to regulating the influx of migrants and controlling borders.[11] "Security-inspired" immigration control is thus the central government's core concern. The "lighter" domains of social and labor-

---

[9] Cf. Agrela Romero 2002b. A key axis of current immigration policy, as expressed in the GRECO Program, is the "regulation of migratory inflows in order to guarantee coexistence within Spanish society." In order to achieve this coexistence, a measure was introduced to strengthen border control through the Integrated System of External Vigilance (SIVE). The SIVE "involves the step-by-step establishment of sensors, radars, optronics, control and command centers, communications tools, and the strengthening of interception units at different points on Spain's borders. Through this system, all external Spanish borders will be comprehensively monitored" (GRECO 2000: 37). For a graphic representation of the system's functioning, see the multimedia gallery linked to the special issue of El País on immigration in Spain; http://www.elpais.es/multimedia/espana/sive.html.

[10] An example of this desperate strategy to contain immigration was the British and Spanish prime ministers' proposal for the last EU council in Seville (2002), which recommended using warships and military airplanes to control and protect borders. The immigration issue has become one of the most important topics on the EU agenda.

[11] The former plan, the 1995 "Plan for the Social Integration of Immigrants," had been conceived as an integration and development tool, and subdivided into six main targets and their respective domains and measures of integration. By contrast, the GRECO Program of 2000 is structured as a "global program," in which "integration" is only one of four basic concerns and in which the regulation of migratory inflows and borders is highlighted. This declining importance of integration measures and migrants' rights is also reflected in the fact that migrants are mentioned in only four domains: health, education, family reunification, and religious freedom.

related integration policy are only considered insofar as they may become "risk factors" for national security.

As will be discussed below, NGOs and lower-level government agencies end up stepping in to develop more comprehensive integration measures. The central government's new policy focus on border control has had an important impact on the symbolic construction of migrants, creating three new categories in public discourse: these individuals are considered potentially "dangerous" (linked to crime and trafficking); are labeled as "immigrants" (non-EU citizens) in contrast to EU "foreigners"; and are viewed as inherently "different" because of their cultural otherness (Agrela Romero 2002b). It is on the basis of these three identifiers—dangerous, foreign, and different—that the practices of governance are redefined and constructed and the practices of intervention are distributed between governmental and nongovernmental actors.

Immigration as a Cultural Problem

Because immigrants and their cultures are defined and perceived as "other" —unlike "us," the bearers of Spanish culture—constructing immigration as a problem relies particularly on construing immigrants' "culture" as an obstacle to integration and a threat to national security. Any problems that can be linked to immigrants are seen as a consequence of their cultural distance and difference. Thus, in and of itself, the discourse on "non-EU" immigration generates a distinctive social category in the interaction between public administration and foreign immigration, in which "cultural differentialism" (Gallini 1993) or "ethnicism" (Van Dijk 1991) gradually becomes predominant.

Accordingly, "immigration" takes on a gloss of "foreignness" and "strangeness." With passage of Spain's first immigration law, foreigners began to be called non-EU immigrants, a label that carries a strong sense of judicial and sociocultural externality and that is reserved for persons from the Third World who come to Spain because they are "poor." In addition, immigrants came to be perceived as dangerous because they are "invaders" and because they arrive in Spain looking for work—presumably aiming to take a Spaniard's job.

Moreover, the culture ascribed to the immigrants is deemed inferior and backward. According to this discourse, "culture" is something you are born into, and consequently something that is resistant to change. Following this argument, "modern Spanish culture" is being threatened by the primitive behaviors and practices of the immigrants' less developed cultures. Moreover, immigrants' cultural patterns are understood as deficient and deviant with regard to the norms of the host society (Santamaría 2002).

In general, policy reactions to the increasing diversification and "multi-culturalization" of migrant flows tend to establish an ethnicized hierarchy of migrants and the "problems" related to immigration (Agrela Romero 2002a). At the top of this hierarchy, the large numbers of intra-EU migrants are made "invisible" statistically and politically by excluding them from official immigration data, from the discourse on migration, and from government integration measures.

Their immigration is challenged in situ by those who were traditionally and symbolically defined as "cultural others" and "Third World primitives," currently encroaching on the "First World" of the civilized. The resulting discourses and intervention and integration measures reflect the difficulties of recognizing the existence of an increasingly diverse and plural society (Gregorio and Franzé 1999). How immigration is perceived and dealt with is officially and artificially focused on south-north migration (Gil Araujo 2002b). In this regard, the formal and legal classifications of migrants—as refugees or asylum seekers, as permanent or temporary immigrant workers, as "undocumented" immigrants, and so on—are combined with ethnocultural and symbolic differentiations that reflect a shared and implicit ethnoreligious hierarchy of "others." In this hierarchy, the lowest position is ascribed to Spain's numerous and historically important *gitano* or Roma community. Next up the ladder we find people of Arabic origin and/or Muslims, a group that is ranked worse than immigrants in general.

In sum, the political reaction to immigration in Spain is generating a culturalist view of migrants: "exclusion has been culturalized" (Gil Araujo 2002b: 180). Migrations are represented as phenomena that are completely disconnected from any other international trends. Accordingly, migration becomes an issue of controlling and regulating borders and, simultaneously, a "humanitarian issue" requiring assistential interventions. This discourse—concerned with addressing the threats to public safety that supposedly result from immigrants' "otherness" and the need for culturally sensitive compassion and paternalism—again reflects the divide between migration control policies of the central government and the focus on integration measures that prevails among nongovernmental and regional and local public agencies.

The resulting public discourse of immigration as a "problem" revolves around three rhetorical elements: the invasion threat, destabilization of the labor market, and difficulties arising from migrants' integration and socio-cultural adaptation. Policymakers take advantage of these perceptions to legitimate measures based on the principles of (1) stability and security (vis-à-vis an absence of public order and control sparked by "invasion"); (2) efficiency (vis-à-vis the need to rationalize labor market resources); and (3) cohesion (vis-à-vis situations of exclusion and racism).

POLICY REACTIONS TO THE CHANGING MIGRATION PATTERN

Within the framework of the changing perspectives on immigration, policy-makers' reactions are characterized by two main features: (1) the central state's determination to rely solely on migration control and border enforcement mechanisms, using its legislative and executive powers to this end; and (2) the hesitant and reluctant redesigning of former public emigration assistance institutions, which are becoming the starting point for the government's still weakly developed immigrant integration facilities. Far from reflecting the current reality of non-EU immigration to Spain, these public institutions are still shaped by the "Fordist" nature of the post–World War II emigration of Spaniards to Northern Europe and by the traditional "alliance" of Spain's Labor Ministry, entrepreneurs, and trade unions during the Franco regime.

Under the new pattern of in-migration, the diversification of jurisdictions and policies among the various levels of government—national, regional, and local—has been crosscut by powerful and omnipresent nongovernmental actors. Ad hoc immigrant support groups, neighborhood associations, community organizations, trade union sections, and church-run, faith-based, and non-confessional groups have all emerged as knowledgeable and competent counterparts (Dietz 2000, 2004) whose specialized social service and legal assistance skills and experiences are much more developed than those of the government. In this network of governmental and nongovernmental actors, an implicit division of labor has emerged among the various kinds of actors: the task of controlling migratory flows and preventing the illegal entry of immigrants falls solely to the public administration, whereas the tasks of socially integrating migrants and dealing with the "humanitarian problem" that immigration poses has been handed over to NGOs as more suitable cultural "translators" and "mediators." Within the context of the subcontracting and privatizing of public administration, these NGOs are becoming strategic, sometimes even "monopolistic," pillars of the immigration policies of Spain's central state, regions, and municipalities.

The following presents an analysis of Spanish political and institutional reactions to the country's increasingly heterogeneous migration patterns, ascribing these reactions to three different but closely interrelated axes of policymaking, which combine and redistribute traditional responsibilities in both migration control and immigrant integration policies: (a) the centralism-federalization axis, (b) the statism-privatization axis, and (c) the universalism-multiculturalization axis.

Public Policymakers: Institutional Actors and Structural Changes, Centralism vs. Federalism

Spain became a newcomer to immigration and migrant integration at approximately the same time that it became a newcomer to democracy and multilevel governance inside the European Union. Spain's legacy of nationalist centralism and the concomitant pressures for homogenization have been deeply questioned in the post-Franco process of "transition" and democratization. Since Franco's death in 1975, and especially with the writing and passage of a democratic constitution in 1978, Spain's traditional centralism has been gradually but entirely transformed (Solé Tura 1985; Pérez-Díaz 1993). The 1978 Constitution redefines Spain, the oldest nation-state in Europe, as a "state of autonomous communities" whose responsibilities are distributed through a slow process of administrative decentralization, which de facto ends up federalizing the state as a whole (Resina 2002).[12]

Nevertheless, from the very beginning, this federalization has not been conducted evenly, nor are there any mechanisms for interregional compensation or exchange. Instead, the Constitution distinguishes between two types of regions: those shaped by "historical nationalisms" and their distinctive cultural and linguistic features, on one hand, and those that lack any cultural idiosyncrasies and/or ethno-nationalist identities, on the other (Constitución Española 1991). As a result, the process of devolution from Madrid to the regions that began in the late 1970s and early 1980s was asymmetrical and ethnically biased. The official distinction between "fast-track" and "slow-track" regions immediately "ethnicized" subnational conflicts and the negotiations on devolution and delimitation of jurisdiction between the different levels of government (Conversi 1997). Accord-

---

[12] "Federalization" is used here not only in the sense of administrative decentralization, but also as encompassing a profound redefinition of the relationship between the central, regional, and local levels of government.

ingly, in several "autonomous communities," the emerging regional elites adopted a strategy of "pragmatic radicalism" in order to justify their claims-making.

In this context of "competitive ethnicizing" of subnational claims-making, immigration quickly becomes a major concern, both for anti-immigrant ethnic regional nationalisms and for anti-centralist multiculturalist regionalisms. Thus, beginning in the late 1990s, regions like Catalonia, the Basque Country, and Andalusia started developing their own "migration policies," which are de jure limited to migrant integration services but which de facto try to influence the central state's immigration policy as well. The "contingent" distribution negotiations, the struggle concerning "regularization campaigns" for undocumented immigrant workers, and the recent establishment of quota systems for temporary agricultural laborers all became battlegrounds between the central and regional governments (Dietz 2004). It is not surprising that regions that have been more successful in claiming, negotiating, and obtaining devolved authority from the central government are also the pioneer regions in the development of their own (formal or informal) migration policies. For instance, due to the importance in Catalonia of protecting Catalan from the dominant "state language" (Spanish), the Catalan regional government and several Catalan municipalities have taken early initiatives to implement linguistic, cultural, and social integration programs targeted at newly arriving immigrants. The migrants' "obligation" to learn Catalan is justified in this region—in contrast to the situation in the Basque Country—by a "civic," French-inspired notion of citizenship and participation. These integration "duties" are to be "rewarded" by the granting of full citizenship rights, which, however, can only by given by the central government. Therefore, the most proactive regions in the sphere of integration policies are also those that more convincingly claim the transfer of comprehensive migration policy responsibilities.

Nevertheless, under Article 149 of the 1978 Constitution, the state holds exclusive jurisdiction in the areas of nationality, immigration, emigration, and asylum law; that is, it is the only entity empowered to control the country's entry and exit points and to authorize work and residence permits for foreigners. However, it is local administrations that de facto are dealing with immigrants. In the course of the decentralization and deconcentration processes that have completely reshaped public administration in Spain, it has been the municipalities that have taken over executive responsibilities and developed the global politics of intervention and service delivery. These local governments have taken responsibility for implementing compensatory measures targeted at social groups and communities that display specific needs, and these groups commonly include immigrant populations.

Paradoxically, the central state's devolution of responsibility for migration issues to the subnational level is hindered by the supranational pressures of EU harmonization. Because European efforts to coordinate and harmonize immigration policies are still controlled by the member states' central executive branches and not by the EU Commission or the European Parliament, "EU pressure" or the "European framework" is often tendered as a justification for more restrictive migration control and border enforcement policies, on one hand, and for retaining or regaining central state authority in migration policy issues, on the other.[13]

This is evident in the two latest major shifts in Spanish migration policy: the shift from the traditional laissez-faire approach to undocumented migrants who were identified as such but not deported (and who immediately entered the shadow economy) to harsher enforcement measures, and the shift from using temporarily legalized, mostly Moroccan immigrant workers already in Spain to temporarily "importing" mostly Eastern Europeans on seasonal contracts to work in agriculture. In both cases, which are fiercely debated in the political arena, the central government claimed that the European Union pressures forced Spain to tighten its immigration control measures (Gil Araujo 2002b).

Thus, ironically, multilateral and supranational measures such as the Schengen Accords end up restricting the federalization of migration policy in Spain. And there are sharp differences between the dimensions of the central state's immigration policies and the interests of Spain's subnational governments, as expressed by the Autonomous Communities. Yet despite official and legal restrictions, regions such as Catalonia, Andalusia, and Madrid are starting to develop their own de facto migration policies, focusing on immigrant integration, especially migrants' integration into the regionally and sectorally differentiated and segmented labor markets. At the same time, regional and local governments are forced to shoulder the core financial and infrastructural burdens that result from the central

---

[13] This European framework and its relationship to Spanish migration legislation and policy are detailed in Colectivo IOE 2001. Monereo Pérez and Molina Navarrete (2001) and Bontempi (2001) offer juridical analyses of this supposed "communitarization" of Spanish migration laws.

state's migration control measures, even though these governments have no policy-making authority over these measures.

Consequently, local governments are managing and financing settlement camps, housing, schooling, and health care for both legal migrants and detained undocumented migrants. However, in order to establish these integration and/or compensation measures (and to develop social policies on the municipal level more generally), local governments depend heavily on subsidies from higher levels — from regional or national administrations or even from the European Union. The fact that both the inception and maintenance of these integration measures rely on the (generally yearly) renewal of subsidies indicates that the social intervention projects targeted to migrant populations are not viewed as essential and unchallengeable policy elements, but instead are mere signs of political goodwill subject to higher-level discretion. In this context, social service agencies must fight to defend these programs year after year.

Over the course of recent years, local and regional actors have developed substantial expertise in all of these integration policy domains — more so, in fact, than the national agencies that remain formally in charge of many of these integration measures (Morén-Alegret 2002). It was not until the present decade that immigration was finally officially perceived and analyzed from a structural dimension, as a "matter of state" (Zapata-Barrero et al. 2002). The previous institutional setting surrounding integration policies had allowed for political arbitrariness and a lack of coordination, which together prevented the emergence of a common policy and frame of reference.

Even though the central government created the "Inter-Ministry Commission on Foreigners" in 1992, the "Permanent Observatory on Immigration" in 1994, and the "Plan for the Social Integration of Immigrants"[14] in 1995, the institutional structure of immigration governance on different governmental levels is more recent. As noted above, it is the regional governments of Andalusia, Catalonia, and Madrid that are leading in the creation of their own institutional structures and developing their own programs, agencies, and delegations to design, manage, and implement policies to respond to the challenges posed by immigration.[15]

---

[14] This was conceived as a comprehensive regulatory instrument for the development of administrative and integration measures for foreign immigrant populations on the national, regional, and local levels.

[15] Although the three Autonomous Communities differ in terms of their responsibilities, power vis-à-vis the central government, economic develop-

After two decades of changing migration patterns and highly impro-
vised and atomized policy reactions, it is only now that the structural
changes in Spanish society are beginning to be accompanied by structural
changes in the country's institutional setting on the various macro, meso,
and micro levels: "There is a link between social conflicts [social change]
and structural reactions. The majority of these social and institutional reactions occur simultaneously" (Zapata-Barrero et al. 2002: 108).

Private Policymakers: The Nongovernmentalization of Migration Policy, Statism vs. Privatization

Spain's multilevel regime of migration-related public governance is crosscut by powerful and omnipresent nongovernmental actors. The latter have
taken on responsibilities in this arena primarily because of the government's lag in redesigning former emigration assistance institutions to serve
as immigrant integration facilities.

Despite the above-mentioned government attempts at institutionally
recovering comprehensive control over integration policy, the public administration responses in the various domains of integration and social
services are still slow to develop (Aragón Bombín 1997). Increases in the
number of the government's social service delivery projects and programs
do not erase the fact that the vast majority of specific measures to attend to
and integrate immigrant populations are initiatives by nonprofit, nongovernmental, private entities (Agrela Romero and Villanueva García 1999).

Thus, paradoxically, the central government's deeply rooted "statist"
and "industrialist" bias has prevented it from implementing suitable integration programs and measures, providing nongovernmental actors with
"room to maneuver" and to develop expertise in the provision of specialized social services, health care, and legal assistance (Domingo, Kaplan,
and Gómez Gil 2000). In some cases, regional governments have copied the
initiatives developed by these pioneering NGOs. Such was the case with
the *tarjeta sanitaria*, an unofficial "social security card" that enabled undocumented migrants to access primary health care. This card system,
developed by an Andalusian network of NGOs, was then incorporated
into the regional government's immigrant integration program and, in

---

ment, and demographic profile, they lead in the development of institutional
integration policy frameworks because all are affected by immigration in
similar ways; that is, the majority of non-EU immigrants tends to settle in
these three regions.

2002, was adopted as part of the national GRECO Program.[16] Such "adoptions" necessarily create policy contradictions: the central government seeks to privatize certain immigration-related services, turning them over to NGOs, but in the process of devolution and federalization these same NGO services are "re-statized" by regional or municipal governments. Thus federalization and privatization do not always occur simultaneously, and we can often see "back-and-forth" movement between public and private actors at the lower levels of immigration policy and immigrant integration measures.

Officially, attending to immigrants' needs is supposed to be the purview of the public administration in its role as provider of social security and protection. In fact, however, public social service agencies form a network of "primary" or "basic" social service provision only. This network of basic services operates as a "point of entry" to nongovernmental agencies, which have been given responsibility for delivering "specialized" services. Immigrants should by right have access, first and foremost, to the primary social services. However, because of their popular portrayal as "others" (as noted above), they are in fact channeled toward the special needs programs developed by local governments (FEMP 1995) but generally implemented by private agencies and NGOs. Not only does this trend imply a separation between native and immigrant beneficiaries of social services, but it also means the privatization of measures to attend to the needs of immigrants.

Despite comprehensive framework programs issued on the national and/or regional level, the policy trend is not for government agencies to "reconquer" the de facto areas of NGO responsibility. On the contrary, the "nongovernmentalization" of Spanish migration policy has been decisively supported by the administration's rush toward subcontracting and privatization. Thus migration policy has become, *avant la lettre*, a test case for "lean government." In the course of this shift toward out-sourcing and subcontracting immigrant integration measures, government agencies dealing with migrant populations on the national, regional, or local level sharply distinguish between "friends" and "foes," between "private and NGO assistance and service delivery" and "claims-making immigrant support movements," the last of which are not eligible for state funding (Dietz 2000).

---

[16] Cf. Cornelius 2004. Blanco Fernández de Valderrama (2001) provides a critical analysis of the GRECO integration measures.

However, official attempts to "privatize" and "depoliticize" NGOs are doomed to failure; nongovernmental actors only succeed in their specific intermediation functions with their (often undocumented) immigrant constituencies if they offer alternative channels for claims-making and participation. Consequently, NGOs cannot be reduced to "private," market-driven forces. Rather, they are becoming strategic and sometimes even "monopolistic" pillars of the immigration policies of the central state, the regions, and the municipalities. They deliver services in such diverse domains as housing (as landlords, informal mediators, and legal guarantors), health care (through their own network of volunteer physicians and nurses, as well as the aforementioned health card), legal assistance (through specialized volunteer lawyers), and education (through literacy and language courses and pioneering intercultural education projects in certain "magnet" schools). Sometimes, however, NGOs perform tasks in which immigrant integration and migration control functions overlap. For example, in order to alleviate overcrowding in camps of undocumented migrants on the border between Morocco and the Spanish enclaves of Ceuta and Melilla, several Spanish NGOs participated in a contingent distribution measure that involved the temporary relocation of undocumented migrants to various cities of the Spanish mainland. The participating NGOs, each of which "adopted" a certain number of undocumented migrants, received government funding to house the migrants and help them adjust to their new local host contexts, but the funding was only forthcoming if the NGOs also took over surveillance and policing tasks with regard to their group of immigrants. Such officially approved overlapping of migration control and immigrant integration often divides migrant-support organizations and weakens their advocacy capabilities.

Policies of Equality and Difference with Regard to the Cultural "Other": Universalism vs. Multiculturalization

As noted earlier, one way of identifying immigration as a "problem" is to treat it in cultural terms—that is, in terms of the supposed distance and differences between immigrant and national culture. In the course of this "culturalization" of immigrants, the institutional delimitation of immigrants as a group and the corresponding assignation of behavioral determinants to this group are used as a legitimate instrument for regulating the interaction between the native and immigrant populations. From this perspective, there is the risk that immigrants' vulnerability and exclusion will be viewed and analyzed solely in terms of their presumed cultural difference (de Lucas 2002). The resulting public policies and social practice are based on a number of contradictory discourses related to: (1) averting the transmission of the "problematic" immigrants' "contaminated culture"; (2) paternalist solidarity toward those considered inferior, less developed, or defenseless; (3) the obligation to "forcibly assimilate" those evaluated as dysfunctional or maladjusted; and (4) intolerance of cultural relativism toward those considered unchangeable and bounded in their difference.

Once cultural difference had been interpreted in terms of conflictiveness, two mutually exclusive approaches were developed to address the challenge of immigrant integration: a politics of equality versus a politics of difference. This polarization reflects the dilemma of universalism versus multiculturalism — that is, the broader issue of the need to define programs and measures for immigrant populations in generalist or in particularistic terms. Thus, in recent years, the combination of the centralism/federalization and statism/privatization axes has promoted a third trend in Spanish migration policy: a gradual move away from universalistic and generalist approaches and toward particularized and "multicultural" integration measures.

The process of very gradual and unequal devolution of authority and responsibility to the Autonomous Communities and the long periods of overlapping jurisdiction between central and regional agencies have often resulted in parallel integration measures, as in vocational training and labor market promotion. The official position of most affected public administrations seems to be in favor of gradually extending generalized services while limiting specialized programs and measures to a minimum. This position, which is also favored by civil servants working in the generalist agencies, contrasts sharply with the actual practice of immigrant integration. The practice of developing highly specialized and individualized measures for different target immigrant communities, a practice pioneered by NGOs, is still being justified by the supposedly inherent differences among immigrant groups and between them and the host population.

This pattern has been reinforced by NGOs' developing expertise in certain service delivery domains (Dietz 2000) as they strive to individualize and "multiculturalize" their activities in order to adapt general social service, education, training, and even legal assistance functions to specific clienteles. The underlying argument is as follows: developing culturally sensitive integration services depends on input from the target immigrant population. Only the immigrant population is in a position to identify its own basic needs and determine how these can be met. Therefore, the delivery of specific services should be realized by professionals who are compatriots of the program's beneficiaries; only they will be sensitive to their fellow nationals' "culture of origin" and the need to preserve it, and hence only they can create appropriate spaces for immigrant associations. The same line of argument is used to justify the training of immigrants as "intercultural mediators" who participate in intercultural negotiations both within particularistic NGO service deliverers and within generalist public social service agencies. It is via this new kind of "professional immigrant" that the culturalist view of integration policies has gained a foothold among governmental actors, despite their traditionally universalist attitudes. One key result is that the emerging "multiculturalist" niche sectors of social service provision are not integrated into the comprehensive mainstream welfare system. Instead, because they are officially associated with "cultural others," they tend to be watered-down versions of their parallels in the mainstream system, especially when government services are outsourced to more "efficient" (read cheaper) NGO service providers. Again, this trend toward asymmetrical multiculturalism ends up paternalistically ascribing certain features, "problems," and "needs" to particular groups and communities.

Over the last decade, nationality, ethnicity, religious affiliation, legal status, and gender have all emerged as defining features of ever more subdivided measures. While some NGOs work with particular national or ethnic groups, others focus on specific domains, such as the secondary labor market, professional training, regularization assistance, linguistic and/or religious instruction, health issues, and so on. NGOs and many of their constituent organizations—such as Moroccan sections in trade unions and associations of Senegalese tradesmen or Muslim women—justify this particularistic approach in terms of empowerment, as a strategy aimed at integration through the recognition of difference. Governmental institutions are actively promoting this trend though out-sourcing and subcontracting policy domains, but for these actors it is efficiency, not "empowerment," that is driving the increasing "multiculturalization" of integration measures.

PUBLIC OPINION AND IMMIGRATION POLICY IN THE SHADOW OF SEPTEMBER 11

Ever since the *reconquista* (Christian reconquest) of the Iberian Peninsula was accomplished with the final fall of Granada, the Spanish nation-state project has been founded on a mixture of ethnically based "Arabophobia" and religiously motivated "Islamophobia" (Stallaert 1998).[17] The construction and imposition of a common Spanish-Castilian hegemonic identity has always relied on measures of religious persecution such as the Inquisition and "ethnic cleansing," implemented since 1492 through "laws of blood purity" which blur biological, ethnic, and religious terminology.

Strangely, the confusion of ethnic, religious, and phenotypic differentiation persists into the present (Dietz and El-Shohoumi 2002; Dietz 2004). A major quantitative study, conducted prior to September 11, 2001, under the auspices of the Spanish Ministry of Labor and Social Affairs (ASEP 1998), tried for the first time to break down the diverse elements that make up anti-immigration attitudes in Spain. On the basis of these statistical data— collected through scalings of "positive," "negative," and "indifferent" opinions about certain minorities (including different nationalities, ethnic minorities such as gypsies, racialized terms such as *negros*, and religious classifications such as Jews and Muslims)—it is possible to detect elements of this deeply rooted and historically transmitted stigmatization of "the other."

Despite the variations observed in the study that can be linked to the educational level of the Spanish interviewees, the degree of contact they maintain with minority populations, and other indicators, these stigmatization processes reflect a shared, implicit ethno-religious hierarchy of common "others." In this hierarchy, the lowest position is still ascribed to the Spanish Roma community, followed by a generalized negative attitude toward people of Arabic origin and/or Muslims,[18] a label that is ranked worse than "immigrants" in general. The comparison of attitudes toward "others" prevailing in "high-immigration" versus "low-immigration" regions of Spain shows that this persistent Arabophobia/Islamophobia does not merely reflect recent immigration trends (ASEP 1998): the native population of regions with nearly no immigration shows an "index of xenophobia" that is similar to that of regions affected by immigration (2.47 versus 2.32 index points, respectively), whereas the main attitudinal differences are perceivable between urban and industrial "high-immigration" regions such as Madrid, on one hand (1.98 index points), and rural and agricultural

---

[17] The term "Islamophobia" was coined in the British debate (cf. Runnymede Trust 1997, Halliday 1999).

[18] Unfortunately, the study fails to adequately differentiate ethnic and religious classifications, as, by example, asking interviewees to rank Arabs and Muslims as one minority group (ASEP 1998: 23).

"high-immigration" regions such as Andalusia, on the other (2.33 index points).

Since the attacks of 9/11, Islamophobia-cum-Arabophobia has reappeared openly in the media, with supposed Al-Qaeda sleepers or network units suspected to exist in nearly every Muslim immigrant community in Spain. It has also resurfaced in opinion polls; post–September 11 opinion polls (published in monthly demoscopic barometers by the governmental Centro de Investigaciones Sociológicas) show a dramatic increase in anti-immigrant attitudes.[19] The historically rooted fear of the reconquered, then expelled, and afterwards colonized "other" is discursively channeled through the combination and overlapping of the rather different issues of external security, internal security and criminality, and migration control. In this context, a U-turn occurs in the public debate on Islam, migration, and integration policies. Suddenly the economic and demographic benefits Spain is gaining from immigration disappear from the debate and are replaced by arguments about security menaces and challenges posed by the *musulmaneidad* of many immigrants. Samuel Huntington's (self-fulfilling?) prophecy of a "clash of civilizations" (Huntington 1996) and Giovanni Sartori's (2001) thesis on the degree of "cultural distance" and the "integrate-ability" of certain kinds of immigrant groups that are viewed as "enemies of the West" have become attractive and oft-cited frameworks for the discussion. Culturalist rhetorics of exclusion proliferate; Mikel Azurmendi, former Spanish government–appointed chair of the "Forum on Immigrant Integration," called multiculturalism "a gangrene in society" (*Estrella Digital*, March 13, 2002). This scenario of Islamophobia, Arabophobia, and anti-immigrant attitudes, long present in Spain, resurged there in the aftermath of September 11, stressing the "limits" of the country's ability to absorb a "flood of immigrants" — this in a country where immigrants account for only about 2 percent of the population and where the birthrate is one of the lowest in the world!

This climate favors a discourse that interprets Muslim immigrant groups' adherence to certain cultural and religious norms as evidence of their failure to integrate into European societies, "a discourse that ends up filtering into the principles that form the basis for local integration policy"

---

[19] National opinion polls issued by the Centro de Investigaciones Sociológicas (CIS 2001, 2002) and the Spanish portions of the monthly EU "Eurobarometer" reflect this increasing concern with "immigration as a threat," and not matter of factly, as it had previously been viewed by the majority of the Spanish population, well accustomed to their own migratory experiences.

(Moreras 2001: 2). Cultural difference is increasingly advanced as a potential source of conflict and a key obstacle to immigrant populations' integration, where cultural characteristics are defined as conditioning behavior. Religious identity constitutes a powerful device identifying alterity, with "Muslim" becoming the identifier for diverse immigrant groups in Europe. Islam has replaced communism as the main threat to Western civilization, in a sort of return to the Crusades (Agrela Romero and Gil Araujo 2004). As Nash (2001) notes, today's spaces of conflict lie on the frontier of cultural difference.

One of the most visible impacts of this new Islamophobia is the way in which politicians explain away measures that arbitrarily limit citizenship. The differing requirements for access to citizenship, as well as the supports provided to immigrants from Spain's former colonies in Latin America and elsewhere, suggest a link between cultural attributes and access to Spanish citizenship. The central state facilitates entry to the political community for individuals who are presumed to share a common cultural heritage, which includes the Castilian-Spanish language and Catholicism. Statements by various government representatives confirm this bias, as do recent regularization programs. Jordi Pujol, former president of the Catalan legislative assembly, has also suggested that the Muslim identity of most immigrants' regions of origin poses a difficulty for these individuals' integration.[20] Similarly, immigrants from the Maghreb are being portrayed as representatives of the most radical kind of "otherness."

Spain's still weakly developed immigrant integration model (which adheres more closely to a political, rather than an ethno-cultural, notion of citizenship) is subtly radicalizing its discourse in cultural terms – in the process, strengthening and accelerating the shifts in migration and immigrant integration policies discussed above. The widening divide between the migration control and policing functions of the central state, on one hand, and the immigrant integration measures handled by NGOs and lower levels of government, on the other, is driving the concomitant shift from generalist to multiculturalist service provision; and this is happening in the midst of a discourse about the dangerous and disruptive consequences of multiculturalism! These shifts, and their perpetuation after

---

[20] Regarding integration, the president affirmed that "South American immigrants and sub-Saharan Maghrebi immigrants in Madrid, and Pakistani immigrants who live in Catalonia" were very different due to cultural factors: "An Ecuadorian transplanted to Madrid feels right at home ... he is not noticeable" (*La Vanguardia* and *El País*, May 21, 2002).

September 11, risk replicating and deepening the hierarchy of rights referred to above (Zapata-Barrero 2001). Currently, migrants' access to political participation and citizenship rights is markedly segmented in Spain,
not only in terms of legal restrictions imposed "from above" through national and EU legislation but also increasingly through national, ethnic,
religious, and gender-based distinctions that are acknowledged "from
below."

The consequences of this confluence of distinctions and hierarchies
become evident in the images of "migrant others" presented in the Spanish
media and opinion polls. A relatively well-articulated discourse is emerging within the host society, in which only certain migrant groups are identified with insecurity, criminality, and a terrorist threat (Gil Araujo 2002a).
The media's constant blending of images of "illegal entry," undocumented
seasonal work, shadow economic activities, petty criminality, and large-
scale drug trafficking results in a xenophobic short-circuit that creates a
chain linking immigration to informality to illegality to insecurity. As these
"short-circuits" redefine existing asymmetries of migration versus integration policies and public versus private jurisdictions and responsibilities,
the newly emerging, complex "Spanish model" of a multilevel and gov-
ernmental/nongovernmental migration policy regime risks being caught
up in the EU-wide tendency to promote a "fortress" approach to the challenge of immigration.

As a result, the balance between immigration control and immigrant
service provision has changed. The linking of immigration, Muslim identity, and terrorism that is contained in the dominant political discourse has
created public insecurity and fear, and this is being exploited to reinforce
restrictive border controls and immigration measures. Paradoxically, immigration was one of only two topics (the other was Basque "terrorism")
on the government's agenda on which the main two political parties (the
governing Popular Party, or PP, and the opposition Socialist Labor Party,
PSOE) were in accord, agreeing to undertake another reform of the Immigration Law.[21] Furthermore, in 2003 the Ministry of the Interior issued a
Plan to Counter Delinquency that links immigration to public insecurity
and crime, and a reform of the Penal Law has been introduced that would
accelerate the sanctioning and deportation of foreigners convicted of
crimes.

---

[21] Reform of the Ley Orgánica 14/2003 (November, 20, 2003).

The events of September 11, 2001, have returned the security-freedom debate to the policy agenda, often in highly simplified form, and some governments seem to be accepting the dangerously xenophobic "terrorism, crime, immigration" equation (Aguelo Navarro 2002). Under the pretext of fighting an external threat, governments are enacting emergency laws and border controls that ultimately contravene any democracy's legal guarantees. In Spain and elsewhere, physical, legal, and symbolic frontiers are being strengthened in the name of fighting both "terrorism" and the "cultural invasion."

In sum, the problems of post–September 11 immigrant integration in the Spanish and European contexts are usually explained as the product of preexisting differences—differences that the migrants carry with them—while differences that are imposed or constructed by institutional policy are ignored (Agrela Romero and Gil Araujo 2004). Therefore, the debate is formulated within a framework of cultural incompatibilities (Moreras 2001). It is this construction of incompatibilities that allows immigration to be formulated in terms of limiting tolerance, on one hand, and, on the other, of maintaining an unequal distribution of the "burden" of control and integration policies between governmental and nongovernmental entities and between central, regional, and local actors.

References

Agrela Romero, Belén. 2002a. La política de inmigración en España: reflexiones sobre la emergencia del discurso cultural. *Migraciones Internacionales* 1 (2):93–121.

———. 2002b. Spain as a recent country of immigration: How immigration became a symbolic, political, and cultural problem in the "new" Spain. CCIS Working Paper No. 57. La Jolla, CA: Center for Comparative Immigration Studies, University of California, San Diego. http://www.ccis-ucsd.org/PUBLICATIONS/wrkg57.PDF.

Agrela Romero, Belén, and Sandra Gil Araujo. 2004. Constructing otherness: The management of migration and diversity in the Spanish context. *Migration: European Journal of International Migration and Ethnic Relations* 43–44.

Agrela Romero, Belén, and Ma. Angustias Villanueva García. 1999. Las políticas sociales de intervención con la población inmigrante extranjera: una aproximación desde el trabajo social. *Cuadernos Andaluces de Bienestar Social* 1:31–58.

Aguelo Navarro, Pascual. 2002. Los derechos de los inmigrantes tras el 11 de septiembre. *Reicaz* 10. http://www.reicaz.es.

Aragón Bombín, Raimundo. 1997. Bases y objetivos de la política de inmigración en España. Paper presented at the I Congreso sobre Inmigración en España, Madrid.

Arango, Joaquín. 2000. Becoming a country of immigration at the end of the twentieth century: The case of Spain. In *Eldorado or fortress? Migration in Southern Europe,* edited by R. King, G. Lazaridis, and C. Tsardanidis. Hampshire and New York: Macmillan/St. Martin's.

———. 2002. La inmigración en España a comienzos del siglo XXI: un intento de caracterización. In *La inmigración en España: contextos y alternativas,* edited by F. J. García Castaño and C. Muriel López: Granada: Laboratorio de Estudios Interculturales.

ASEP (Análisis Sociológicos, Económicos y Políticos, S.A.). 1998. Actitudes hacia los inmigrantes. Madrid: Ministerio de Trabajo y Asuntos Sociales-Observatorio Permanente de la Inmigración.

Blanco Fernández de Valderrama, Cristina. 2001. La integración de los inmigrantes: fundamentos para abordar una política global de intervención. *Migraciones* 10:207–48.

Bommes, Michael, and Andrew Geddes. 2000. *Immigration and welfare: Challenging the borders of the welfare state.* London: Routledge.

Bontempi, Rinaldo. 2001. Hacia una política europea de inmigración y un régimen común en materia de asilo. *Revista Cidob d'Afers Internacionals* 53. http://www.cidob.es.

Calavita, Kitty. 1998. Immigration, law, and marginalization in a global economy: Notes from Spain. *Law and Society Review* 32:529–66.

CIS (Centro de Investigaciones Sociológicas). 2001. Resultados de los barómetros: año 2001. Madrid: CIS. http://www.cis.es.

———. 2002. Resultados de los barómetros: año 2002. Madrid: CIS. http://www.cis.es.

Colectivo IOE. 1987. Los inmigrantes en España. Documentación Social, 66. Madrid: Cáritas Española.

———. 1999. *Inmigrantes, trabajadores, ciudadanos: Una visión de las migraciones desde España.* Valencia: Universidad de Valencia.

———. 2001. Política migratoria española en el marco europeo. *Studi Emigrazione* 38 (144):855–68.

Constitución Española. 1991. In Declaración universal de los derechos humanos — constitución española — Estatuto Autonómico de Andalucía, edited by Editorial Arguval. Málaga: Arguval.

Conversi, Daniele. 1997. *The Basques, the Catalans, and Spain: Alternative routes to nationalist mobilisation.* London: Hurst.

Cornelius, Wayne A. 1994. Spain: The uneasy transition from labor exporter to labor importer. In *Controlling immigration: A global perspective,* edited by Wayne A. Cornelius, Philip L. Martin, and James F. Hollifield. Stanford, CA: Stanford University Press.

———. 2004. Spain: The uneasy transition from labor exporter to labor importer. In *Controlling immigration: A global perspective*, edited by Wayne A. Cornelius et al. 2d ed. Stanford, CA: Stanford University Press.

de Lucas, Javier. 2002. Cultura, inmigración y Estado. In *Políticas sociales y estado de bienestar en España: Las migraciones*, edited by C. Clavijo and M. Aguirre. Madrid: Fundación Hogar del Empleado.

Dietz, Gunther. 2000. *El desafío de la interculturalidad: el voluntariado y las organizaciones no-gubernamentales ante el reto de la inmigración.* Granada and Barcelona: Laboratorio de Estudios Interculturales/Fundació "la Caixa."

———. 2004. Frontier hybridization or culture clash? Trans-national migrant communities and sub-national identity politics in Andalusia. *Journal of Ethnic and Migration Studies* 30 (5).

Dietz, Gunther, and Nadia El-Shohoumi. 2002. Door to door with our Muslim sisters: Intercultural and inter-religious conflicts in Granada, Spain. *Studi Emigrazione* 39 (145):77–106.

Domingo, Andreu, Adriana Kaplan, and Carlos Gómez Gil. 2000. *Chivos expiatorios fáciles: inmigrantes sin papeles en Europa. Informe sobre España.* Barcelona and Alicante: Centre d'Estudis Demogràfics/Alicante Acoge.

FEMP (Federación Española de Municipios y Provincias). 1995. *Los municipios y la integración social de los inmigrantes: análisis y propuestas de actuación.* Madrid: FEMP.

Fernández Cordón, J. A., et al. 1993. *Informe sobre extranjeros de tercera edad en España.* Madrid: Instituto de Demografía.

Gallini, Clara. 1993. Del racismo científico al diferencialismo cultural. Paper presented at the ICE Seminar, Universidad de Lleida, April.

Gil Araujo, Sandra. 2002a. Extranjeros bajo sospecha: lucha contra el terrorismo y política migratoria en EEUU y la Unión Europea. In *De Nueva York a Kabul: Anuario CIP 2002*, edited by M. Aguirre and M. González. Madrid and Barcelona: Centro de Investigación para la Paz/Icaria.

———. 2002b. Políticas públicas como tecnologías de gobierno: Las políticas de inmigrantes y las figuras de la inmigración. In *Políticas sociales y estado de bienestar en España: Las migraciones*, edited by C. Clavijo and M. Aguirre. Madrid: Fundación Hogar del Empleado.

GRECO. 2000. *Programa global de regulación y coordinación de la extranjería y la inmigración (Greco).* Madrid: Ministerio del Interior/Delegación del Gobierno para la Extranjería y la Inmigración.

Gregorio, Carmen, and Adela Franzé. 1999. La intervención social con población inmigrante: esos "otros" culturales. *Intervención Psicosocial* 8 (2):163–75.

Halliday, F. 1999. "Islamophobia" reconsidered. *Ethnic and Racial Studies* 22 (5): 892–902.

Hannken, H. 1994. *Migrationsbewegungen in einem altkastilischen Dorf.* Münster: LIT-Verlag.

Herranz, Yolanda. 2000. Inmigración e incorporación laboral. *Migraciones* 8: 127–64.

Huntington, Samuel P. 1996. *The clash of civilizations and the remaking of the world order*. New York: Simon and Schuster.

Izquierdo, Antonio. 1992. *La inmigración en España 1980–1990*. Madrid: Trotta.

————. 1996. *La inmigración inesperada: La población extranjera en España (1991–1995)*. Madrid: Trotta.

Jurdao Arrones, F., and M. Sánchez. 1990. *España, asilo de Europa*. Barcelona: Planeta.

King, Russell. 2000. Southern Europe in the changing global map of migration. In *Eldorado or fortress? Migration in Southern Europe*, edited by R. King, G. Lazaridis, and C. Tsardanidis. Hampshire and New York: Macmillan/St. Martin's.

Martínez Veiga, Ubaldo. 1997. *La integración social de los inmigrantes extranjeros en España*. Madrid: Trotta.

Monereo Pérez, José Luis, and Cristóbal Molina Navarrete. 2001. *Comentario a la Ley y al Reglamento de Extranjería e Integración Social (LO 4/2000, LO 8/2000 y RD 864/2001)*. Granada: Comares.

Morén-Alegret, Ricard. 2002. *Integration and resistance: The relation of social organisations, global capital, governments and international immigration in Spain and Portugal*. Aldershot, UK: Ashgate.

Moreras, Jordi. 2001. El factor religioso musulmán en la definición de las políticas locales de integración. Presented at the workshop Prioridades de una política europea de inmigración, Instituto Internacional de Sociología Jurídica, Oñati, May 10–11.

Nash, Mary. 2001. Diversidad, multiculturalismos e identidades. In *Multiculturalismos y género*, edited by M. Nash and D. Marre. Barcelona: Bellaterra.

Pérez-Díaz, Víctor M. 1993. *The return of civil society: The emergence of democratic Spain*. Cambridge, MA: Harvard University Press.

Piore, Michael. 1975. Notes for a theory of labor market stratification. In *Labor market segmentation*, edited by R. C. Edwards, M. Reich, and D. M. Gordon. Lexington, MA: Lexington Books.

Piore, Michael, and S. Berger. 1980. *Dualism and discontinuity in industrial societies*. Cambridge: Cambridge University Press.

Pries, Ludger. 1999. New migration in transnational spaces. In *Migration and transnational social spaces*, edited by Ludger Pries. Aldershot, UK: Ashgate.

Resina, Joan Ramón. 2002. Post-national Spain? Post-Spanish Spain? *Nations and Nationalism* 8 (3):377–96.

Ruiz Garzón, F. 2001. *De la primera a la segunda generación: Identidad, cultura y modo de vida de los emigrantes españoles en Hamburgo, Alemania*. Granada: Asociación Granadina de Emigrantes Retornados.

Runnymede Trust. 1997. *Islamophobia: A challenge for us all*. London: Runnymede Trust.

Santamaría, Enrique. 2002. *La incógnita del extraño: Una aproximación a la significación sociológica de la "inmigración no comunitaria."* Barcelona: Anthropos.

Sartori, Giovanni. 2001. *La sociedad multiétnica.* Madrid: Taurus.

Smith, Michael Peter, and Luis Eduardo Guarnizo. 1999. *Transnationalism from below.* New Brunswick, NJ: Transaction.

Solé Tura, Jordi. 1985. *Nacionalidades y nacionalismos en España: Autonomías, federalismo, autodeterminación.* Madrid: Alianza.

Stallaert, Christiane. 1998. *Etnogénesis y etnicidad en España: Una aproximación histórico-antropológica al casticismo.* Barcelona: Proyecto A.

Van Dijk, Teun. 1991. Discours de l'élite et racisme. *Cahiers de Praxématique* 17:49–71.

Zapata-Barrero, Ricard. 2001. *Ciudadanía, democracia y pluralismo cultural: Hacia un nuevo contrato social.* Barcelona: Anthropos.

Zapata-Barrero, Ricard, et al. 2002. Estructuras institucionales y redes de actores en las políticas de acomodación de los inmigrantes en España: Cultura de acomodación y cambio estructural. In *La inmigración en España: Contextos y alternativas*, edited by F. J. García Castaño and C. Muriel López. Granada: Laboratorio de Estudios Interculturales.

CHAPTER 9

NGOs, Transnational Migrants, and the Promotion of Rights in South Korea

TIMOTHY C. LIM

As late as 1987 there were only a few thousand foreign migrants working in South Korea, and most of these were professors, language teachers, researchers, and other skilled professionals. Only a decade later, however, there were more than 245,000 foreign or transnational migrant workers in the country, the large majority of them there "illegally," working in low-skilled factory jobs in the so-called 3D (dirty, difficult, and dangerous) industries. The financial crisis of late 1997 led to a rapid and dramatic exodus of foreign workers from South Korea, but by early 2002 the number had climbed back to a record high of some 384,000, including at least 189,000 illegal or undocumented workers. The actual number of transnational migrant workers may be even larger. According to at least one knowledgeable source, Korea may be host to as many as 500,000 transnational migrant workers today.[1] Although this figure is not terribly impressive by U.S. or European standards (or even by the standards of other Asian countries, including Malaysia and Singapore),[2] the presence of so

[1] This figure was cited by Father Jack Trisolini, director of the Labor Pastoral Center for the Archdiocese of Seoul (author interview, June 2002, Seoul). Lee Kyu Yong, a senior researcher at the Korea Labor Institute and one of the leading authorities on foreign worker migration in Korea, agreed that the figure of 500,000 is not an unreasonable estimate. He could not, however, confirm its accuracy (author interview, June 2002, Seoul).

[2] At one point in 1999, the number of migrant workers in Malaysia was about 1.7 million: 700,000 documented workers and 1 million undocumented migrants. As a result of a government "amnesty" program, which promised not to fine, imprison, and/or "cane" those who did not leave voluntarily, however, about 300,000 illegal workers left between March 22, 2002, and July 31, 2002, with another 50,000 more expressing a readiness to leave. Almost im-

many "outsiders" is extraordinary for an ostensibly homogenous and traditionally insulated society like Korea's.

The reason for the large inflow of transnational migrants is not difficult to discern: South Korea is undergoing a transition, largely due to unavoidable changes in the structure of the national economy and demographic profile. Specialists refer to this phenomenon as the "migration transition." For South Korea, the migration transition began in the late 1980s and is symbolized by Seoul's hosting of the 1988 Olympic Games. Significantly, the impact of this transition is no short-term phenomenon; indeed, combined with parallel changes in its demographic profile, it is almost certain that South Korea will need to continue to "import" more and more foreign labor for many decades to come. The key question that faces South Korea, then, is not *whether* it will become a "land of immigration"[3] but *what kind* of immigration country it will be. Of course, this concern is not unique to Korea. Throughout the world, but especially in Western Europe, the United States, and Canada, countries have long had to grapple with questions of immigrant/migrant rights. In Western Europe and the United States, as Joppke (2001) cogently argues, the expansion of immigrant/migrant rights has been tied to domestically based legal sources, and particularly to the courts (which have often acted against the wishes of "restriction-minded state executives").[4] As my analysis will show, this

---

mediately, though, the government reversed itself (largely as a result of pressure from domestic businesses), and between August 14 and 23, 2002, it approved applications to bring in an additional 500,000 foreign workers (*Bernama* [Malaysian National News Agency], September 17, 2002; retrieved from the Lexis-Nexis Academic database, https://web.lexis-nexis.com/universe).

About 750,000 of the 4.1 million Singapore residents are foreigners (*Migration News*, December 2001; http://migration.ucdavis.edu:80/mn/archive_mn/dec _200116mn.html).

[3] I use the word "immigration" loosely. In general, immigration refers to the entry and *permanent* settlement of non-native peoples in another country or region, whereas migration refers to a temporary movement of people across distinct geographic spaces. In Korea it is still not certain that large-scale permanent settlement by "non-native" peoples will take place; it is certain, however, that relatively large-scale migration will continue for several decades to come.

[4] Joppke distinguishes between legal and political or social sources of rights. To Joppke, political and social sources of rights expansion are "grounded in conflict and the mobilization of interest groups, parties, or protest movements." Conflict and mobilization, in other words, precede and directly lead to legal change and rights expansion. In contrast, when courts act independently of

phenomenon is not unique to the West; in South Korea the courts have played an important role in the expansion of immigrant/migrant rights. At the same time, I argue that courts have not necessarily been the primary — and clearly not the *original* — source of rights expansion in South Korea. An equally if not more important source is political. More specifically, in South Korea, I contend that *political activism* — carried out by transnational migrant workers themselves, *in conjunction* with a network of domestically based but internationally oriented civil and religious organizations (or NGOs) in Korea — has been a crucial source of rights expansion.

With this in mind, this chapter begins with an overview of transnational worker migration to South Korea, which includes a brief discussion of (1) the scope and nature of this phenomenon, (2) the general factors that have opened South Korea up to transnational worker migration, and (3) Korea's initial policy toward transnational migrant workers and its response as a "host country." In the next section, I examine the changing status of transnational migrant workers in Korea. As we will see, the changes have been significant. Beginning from a situation in which transnational migrant workers had few — essentially no — protected rights, these workers are now *legally entitled* to most of the same labor rights as local Korean workers. The more important question, of course, is just how this (still developing) transformation took place. This is the subject of the last two substantive sections of the chapter, in which I first delineate the context of political and social change in Korea and then examine the central role that political activism — carried out by the transnational migrant workers themselves and a network of socially conscious, rights-oriented nongovernmental organizations (NGOs) in Korea — has played in expanding immigrant/migrant rights in Korea.

TRANSNATIONAL LABOR MIGRATION TO SOUTH KOREA: AN OVERVIEW

The reason behind the increase in transnational worker migration to South Korea, as noted above, is hardly novel. As with many other industrializing countries, it is part and parcel of a larger economic and demographic process. The most salient part of this process is South Korea's rapid industriali-

---

popular, political, or bureaucratic will, the source of change is legal. Moreover, when the source of change is grounded in national legal norms and precepts, one can say it is domestic rather than transnational or international (as in the concept of international or universal human rights).

zation, which began in the 1960s and accelerated in the 1970s and 1980s. This rapid industrialization led to an increasingly tight labor market: between 1980 and 1995, the unemployment rate for the economy as a whole declined from 5.2 percent to a mere 2.0 percent (see table 9.1); the latter figure was actually below the "natural" rate of unemployment. Significantly, for "low-skilled" and "unskilled" workers, the labor market was even tighter. In 1991—the peak year—the labor shortage rates for low-skilled and unskilled workers in the manufacturing sector were 10.4 percent and 20.1 percent, respectively (table 9.2). The shortage of labor in the manufacturing sector (especially for small and medium-sized enterprises) persisted despite intense efforts by the government to expand the domestic labor pool. At one point, for example, the government offered to exempt military draftees from regular army service providing they signed up for five years of work in factories, on construction jobs, or as merchant seaman (Jameson 1991). Despite a huge pay differential—a private first class in the Korean army earned only $10.83 a month (in 1991), while factory wages averaged $820 a month—few draftees accepted the offer. Indeed, the labor shortage for low- and unskilled positions was hardly affected by this new government policy (as well as other policies designed to bring more women and young people into the "economically active" workforce).

The inability of the government to resolve the country's labor shortage through an expansion of the domestic workforce reflects the demographic changes that had been taking place in Korea. As Yoo and Uh (2001) point out, the most relevant of these changes were a decline in the labor market participation rate of men and women between the ages of 19 and 24 and a rapid improvement in educational levels. In addition, South Korea also experienced a rise in the proportion of older workers in the labor force (between 1980 and 2000, the ratio of workers over age 55 to total employment increased from 10 to 17 percent) (Yoo and Uh 2001). The first two changes, of course, are strongly related. That is, a general increase in educational levels—especially in postsecondary and higher education—invariably means that fewer young people will be available to join the workforce. In South Korea, the improvement in the educational level was both dramatic and fairly rapid: between 1985 and 1995 the percentage of college graduates among total workers increased from 10.3 to 18.8 percent, whereas the percentage of middle school graduates among total workers declined from just under 59 percent to 37.7 percent (Yoo and Uh 2001). The significance of the improvement in South Korea's educational level is even more apparent in comparison to other countries: in 1999, among all OECD

Table 9.1. Changes in Employment and Unemployment, 1975–2000 (1000s and percentages)

	Labor Force		Participation Rate (%)	Unemployment Rate (%)
	Employed (1000s)	Unemployed (1000s)		
1975	11,692	501	58.3	4.1
1980	13,683	748	59.0	5.2
1985	14,970	622	56.6	4.0
1990	18,085	454	60.0	2.4
1991	18,677	438	60.6	2.3
1992	19,033	466	60.9	2.4
1993	19,328	551	61.1	2.8
1994	19,905	490	61.7	2.4
1995	20,432	420	61.9	2.0
1996	20,817	426	60.7	2.0
1997	21,106	556	62.2	2.6
1999	20,281	1,353	60.5	6.3
2000	21,061	889	60.7	4.1

Source: National Statistical Office (South Korea), cited in Yoo and Uh 2001: 12.

Table 9.2. Labor Shortage Rates in Manufacturing, by Skill Level (percentages)

	Craftsman	Skilled	Low-Skilled	Unskilled
1985	1.23%	1.99%	2.19%	4.90%
1986	1.26	2.27	3.31	8.34
1987	1.42	3.56	5.30	11.12
1988	2.49	3.94	5.27	12.29
1989	4.05	3.60	5.25	11.82
1990	4.45	5.31	7.92	16.23
1991	5.94	7.32	10.39	20.13
1992	1.74	6.97	6.58	10.86
1993	1.75	5.07	6.35	14.74
1994	4.16	4.45	7.21	12.90
1995	2.87	4.97	7.80	11.41

Sources: Korea Labor Institute, Labor Statistics, 1993: 31 and 1996: 32.

countries, South Korea had the second-highest proportion of 18- to 21-year-olds enrolled in postsecondary institutions—51.4 percent. (Greece was first at 54.1 percent.) Korea was also ranked high in the proportion of 22- to 25-year-olds in postsecondary education: 26.2 percent, which was fourth behind only Finland (35.1 percent), Norway (28.0 percent), and Denmark (26.6 percent) (National Center for Education Statistics 2001).[5]

Given these trends, the turn toward nondomestic sources of labor was practically inevitable. At the same time, Koreans—both within and outside government—were hardly enthusiastic about the prospect of "hosting" tens of thousands (still less, hundreds of thousands) of ethnic and cultural "strangers," especially those with little money. Like many of their Asian neighbors (including, most notably, Japan), Koreans feared that having too many "strangers" in their society would threaten to rend the country's tightly knit social fabric. The apparent solution to this dilemma was to encourage the influx of ethnic Koreans from China, known in Korea as *chosun jok*. (Not coincidentally, this same strategy was used by the Japanese, who actively encouraged South Americans of Japanese ancestry to work in Japan.) For Koreans, this strategy was only partly successful. It was successful in that it tapped into a steady, geographically close, and essentially unlimited source of workers willing to fill positions in labor-short areas of the Korean economy. In 1991, for example, more than 18,400 Korean Chinese found work in South Korea (although almost all did so illegally). By 1996 the cumulative number of Korean Chinese workers had risen to more than 40,000 and, except for 1998, has continued to increase (see table 9.3). By mid-2002 the figure stood at slightly less than 80,000. Significantly, however, the percentage of Korean Chinese among the total population of transnational migrant workers in Korea has fallen from a high of 40.6 percent in 1991 to only 25 percent in 2000.

The proportional decline of Korean Chinese workers is due to a variety of factors. But almost certainly one of the more important is that the chosun jok did not fit seamlessly into the fabric of Korean society (as many Koreans assumed they would). Far from it. Indeed, the relationship between the chosun jok and their Korean "hosts" soured almost from the very beginning, despite the fact that the chosun jok were initially considered and actively portrayed (in Korea's mass media) as long-lost "brethren." It is in this regard that Korea's strategy of encouraging the influx of

---

[5] The original source of the statistics is the Organisation for Economic Co-operation and Development (OECD), *Education at a Glance*, various years.

ethnic Koreans from China was a failure. For the Korean Chinese were expected to do the jobs that most South Koreans utterly disdained. Moreover, they were expected to do these jobs at a lower rate of pay, without basic labor rights, and without even minimal legal protection against abusive employers (who frequently slapped, kicked, punched, sexually assaulted, or verbally insulted migrant workers, whether "brethren" or not).[6] This was true both for those Korean Chinese who worked in Korea as so-called industrial trainees and for those who worked in Korea "illegally" — that is, without a proper visa but *with the tacit consent* of the government. In short, despite "blood ties" and an initial sense of cultural affinity, the harsh realities of migrant work in Korea simply did not mix with the ideals of brotherhood and assimilation. Thus, while the chosun jok continue to come to Korea to work, today there is little sense left that they are appreciably different than workers from Nepal, Bangladesh, Indonesia, Vietnam, the Philippines, and elsewhere (other than the fact that the chosun jok, as a group, tend to have more familiarity with the Korean language). Indeed, according to a recent survey of small factory owners in South Korea, the chosun jok are not even the most "favored" foreign workers; this "honor" belongs instead to workers from Indonesia (workers from China, who are not necessarily ethnic Koreans, and Vietnam were second and third, respectively).[7]

It is significant that the large majority of transnational migrant workers, including the Korean Chinese, continue to work in Korea "illegally." At one point in 1991, in fact, more than 90 percent of all transnational migrant workers in Korea were undocumented (more recently, the figure has

---

[6] It is difficult to gauge with any certainty the extent of physical and verbal abuse by Korean employers. In one survey conducted in 1995, for example, two Korean professors found that 42 percent of a random sample of 185 foreign workers had been beaten on the job (in Cheesman 1995). In another, more extensive survey conducted by S. W. Park, C. K. Lee, and D. H. Seol (1995) the same year, however, the figures were much lower. These researchers found, for example, that only 2 percent of Korean Chinese respondents had suffered physical abuse. At the same time, the issue of workplace beating was sufficiently important that the Korean Federation of Small Businesses (KFSB) felt it necessary to publish a pamphlet that advised employers, among other things, not to beat their workers (in Lim 1996).

[7] The survey was conducted by the KFSB, which queried 1,286 small and medium-sized enterprises: 30.6 percent favored workers from Indonesia, 17.2 percent favored workers from China, and 13.7 percent favored workers from Vietnam (*Korea Times* 2002a).

Table 9.3. Number and Share of Korean Chinese Workers in Korea, 1991–2001

	Number of Korean Chinese Workers					Share of Korean Chinese Workers in Total Foreign Workers				
	Total	Professionals	Post-Training Workers	Industrial Trainees	Undocumented	Total	Professionals	Post-Training Workers	Industrial Trainees	Undocumented
1991	18,436	7	0	12	18,417	40.6%	0.2%	-	2.0%	44.0%
1992	27,240	7	0	287	26,946	36.9	0.2	-	5.8	41.1
1993	23,286	14	0	1,885	21,387	35.1	0.4	-	23.4	39.2
1994	21,441	31	0	4,317	17,093	27.6	0.6	-	18.0	35.4
1995	32,365	47	0	6,612	25,706	22.7	0.6	-	12.6	31.4
1996	40,286	101	0	8,112	32,073	19.1	0.8	-	11.9	24.9
1997	40,323	131	0	10,334	29,858	16.4	0.8	-	12.7	20.2
1998	35,310	166	0	8,956	26,188	22.4	1.5	-	19.1	26.3
1999	57,507	178	0	15,160	42,169	26.5	1.4	-	19.2	31.2
2000	77,779	268	196	19,967	57,348	25.0	1.7	9.5%	19.0	30.3
2001	93,736	338	1,670	19,396	72,332	24.4	1.8	19.3	28.3	24.4

Sources: Ministry of Justice, *Statistical Yearbook of Departures and Arrivals Control*, various years. From Seol and Skrentny 2004.
Note: The number of migrants calculated as of December 31 of each year listed, except for 1992, when the tally was made on July 31.

ranged from 60 to 70 percent; see table 9.4).[8] This does not mean, as I suggested above, that they are working in Korea against the wishes of the government, for the presence of undocumented workers in the country has been essentially condoned and even encouraged by the Korean authorities since the very beginning of large-scale foreign worker migration. (In this regard, it would be fair — and probably far more accurate — to say that undocumented or illegal foreign workers are, in fact, "tacitly approved" foreign workers.) The reason for this is clear, if not banal: "illegal" workers are easier to exploit and, in principle, easier to control than authorized workers. One official in the Ministry of Justice was quite blunt on this point; as he put it, "As far as we know, the United States also relaxes control on illegal Mexican workers during its orange-harvesting season. Afterwards, it repatriates them on the reports of employers. *That could be cited as a model case for maximizing the nation's interest*" (*Korea Herald* 1998, emphasis added). From this perspective, it is reasonable to conclude that the presence of so many "illegal" workers is a fully *intended* outcome of government policy.[9] Still, it is important to recognize that other significant aspects of government policy — and small business policy — toward foreign migrant workers have clearly *not* achieved their intended results; the reason for this goes back to the main argument of this chapter, namely, political activism on the part of transnational migrant workers and a network of Korean NGOs.

The tacit approval of "illegal" or undocumented worker migration to South Korea was, and is, not the only policy designed to deal with the labor shortage in the country's small and medium-sized enterprise (SME) sector. The other major policy scheme — also clearly borrowed from Japan — is the industrial "training program," which allowed the government

---

[8] In March 2002, the Ministry of Justice/Bureau of Immigration implemented a "Voluntary Reporting Program" for undocumented foreign workers. Those who voluntarily reported — about 256,000 at the end of registration period — were given permission to stay and *work* in Korea for up to one year. Practically speaking, then, those workers who registered are no longer unauthorized or "illegal" (although, as the Ministry of Justice was careful to note, "In principle, the foreigner is [still] not allowed to work. But if he/she works in the workplace of the owner who issues a report on his/her establishment of the unauthorized foreigner, he/she can only work in the designated workplace prior to voluntary departure").

[9] The relevant visa classifications are: University Teacher (E-1), Language Teacher (E-2), Researcher (E-3), Technology Instructor (E-4), Professional (E-5), Entertainer (E-6), and other specific positions, including Airline Pilot (E-7).

Table 9.4. Numbers of Migrant Workers in Korea, 1987–2001[a]

	Total[b]	Industrial Trainees	Undocumented	Percent Undocumented
1987	6,409	0	4,217	65.7%
1988	7,410	0	5,007	67.5
1989	14,610	0	12,136	83.0
1990	21,235	0	18,402	86.6
1991	45,449	599	41,877	92.1
1992	73,868	4,945	65,528	88.0
1993	66,323	8,048	54,508	82.1
1994	77,546	24,050	48,231	62.2
1995	142,405	52,311	81,866	57.4
1996	210,494	68,020	129,054	61.4
1997	245,399	81,451	148,048	60.3
1998	157,689	47,009	99,537	63.1
1999	226,875	78,945	135,338	59.7
2000	311,544	104,847	188,995	63.6
2001	383,695	100,344	255,206	66.5

Source: Seol and Skrentny 2004, calculated from the Statistical Yearbook of Departures and Arrivals Control, released by the Ministry of Justice.

[a] Number of migrant workers calculated as of December 31 of each year listed, except for 1992, when the tally was made on July 31.

[b] Total includes "registered migrant workers" (that is, professionals and post-training workers).

Note: In 2002, the Ministry of Justice and Bureau of Immigration implemented a "voluntary registration program" for undocumented workers. By the end of the registration period, more than 256,000 individuals had registered. Technically speaking, the percentage of undocumented workers for 2002 would be under 5 or 10 percent (and perhaps lower).

and SMEs (led by the Korean Federation of Small Business, or KFSB) to circumvent the prohibition in Korea's immigration and emigration law against the employment of unskilled or low-skilled foreign workers. (The law only permits "professional and technical workers," such as professors, researchers, or entertainers to work legally in Korea.)[10] The Industrial

---

[10] The 1991 system was initially restricted to foreign nationals who were already employed in Korean-owned companies located overseas. Since almost all of these were large companies, however, the 1991 law creating the trainee system did not provide small and medium-sized companies with the labor

Technical Trainee Program (ITTP), which was introduced in 1991,[11] allows the government and SMEs to circumvent existing immigration law by creating a convenient and cynical fiction: under this program, those who enter Korea to take up positions in labor-short areas are not defined as "workers" but as "trainees." The implications of this semantic difference are significant. For while government-sanctioned *workers* would be (albeit not necessarily) entitled to basic labor protections, market-based wage rates, and freedom to change jobs, "trainees" are not. Instead, under the ITTP, trainees were (originally) restricted to an assigned "training facility" and provided a government-mandated "stipend," which was far below the prevailing wage rate (compared to both native Korean workers and even undocumented workers doing the same job). Trainees, moreover, were not entitled to basic labor protections, and they were required to leave Korea immediately after completing their "training."

The aim of the ITTP, as with the tacit approval of "illegal" worker migration, was obvious, namely, to institutionalize and legitimize an unequal, "flexible," and highly exploitative employment system for foreign nationals, one that would remain separate from and clearly subordinate to the employment system for Korean citizens. This goal, however, was challenged—to a significant extent, by transnational migrant worker themselves—from the very beginning. Moreover, while the ITTP was still in place as of late 2002, these challenges have been effective, even *very* effective (a point I take up in a subsequent section). Indeed, over the past decade or so, the ITTP has undergone significant changes, a number of which have unequivocally undermined the original intent of the program. Still more, the very existence of the program is in doubt, which, I argue, is the product of unremitting pressure (political activism) applied by Korean NGOs and transnational migrant groups on the Korean government. Certain parts of the government—in particular, the Ministry of Labor and, to a lesser extent, the executive branch—have been receptive to this pressure, while other parts of government (most notably, the Ministry of Justice) remain resistant. But the primary obstacle has been the KFSB (a private

---

they required. For this reason, the law was amended in 1994 to allow SMEs to use "trainees." The KFSB was put in charge of this newly revised system and given authority to recruit foreign nationals from a number of approved countries (Park 1995: 373–74).

[11] In some cases, albeit based on a high level of overtime work, undocumented workers are able to earn upwards of 1.2 million won a month (author interviews with foreign workers in South Korea, June 2001 and June 2002).

industry organization), which has engaged in its own, equally determined, and hitherto more effective brand of political activism.

The nature and extent of the political activism exercised by both proponents and opponents of change are, of course, central to the argument I advance here. Before I discuss the activism surrounding migrant/immigrant rights in South Korea, however, it would be useful to look first at the changes that have actually taken place thus far.

THE CHANGING STATUS OF TRANSNATIONAL MIGRANT WORKERS

In the early 1990s, transnational migrant workers had few protected rights in Korea. This was equally true for both legally sanctioned trainees and undocumented workers. The unprotected status of transnational migrants left them highly vulnerable not only to economic exploitation—including substandard pay, nonpayment of wages, no overtime pay, excessive work hours (usually mandatory), inadequate or nonexistent compensation for industrial accidents or occupational illness, and extremely unsafe working conditions—but also to racial and ethnic discrimination and to physical, sexual, and verbal assault (typically by their own employers and/or other Korean employees working in the same company). Transnational migrants, moreover, had (and continue to have) extremely limited access to health care and social services. As noted above, most of this was a largely intended outcome, particularly from the standpoint of those companies that hire foreign trainees. On this point, it is useful to consider a recent survey in the *Korea Times* (2002a), which indicates that almost 86 percent of SME owners find the ITTP the "most suitable [employment system] for Korean society." Their reasoning is telling: any change to the system might oblige them to provide the same treatment to foreign industrial trainees as to Korean employees, which, in turn, could lead to unionization and greater financial burdens.

The fact that ITTP, along with the criminalization of foreign labor, defined Korea's migration/immigration policy for more than two decades does not mean that nothing has changed. As I have already suggested, a great deal has changed, both in transnational migrant workers' day-to-day conditions and in their legal status. On an everyday level, one of the most significant changes—from the standpoint of transnational migrants—has been a gradual but meaningful increase in their rate of pay. In 2002, undocumented foreign workers received an average monthly wage of more than 858,000 won (based on a 60-hour workweek).[12] Although still below the average monthly earnings of all wage and salary workers in Korea—which stood at 1.28 million won in March 2002 (KLI 2002)—858,000 won per month is comparable to the wage received by native Korean workers doing the same type of work for the same number of hours.[13]

Industrial trainees continue to receive less than their counterparts working "illegally," but their basic wage or "allowance" has also increased significantly over the past several years. According to one recent survey, industrial trainees receive an average of 823,000 won per month (based on a 69-hour workweek) (*Korea Herald* 2002a). In the early years of the trainee program, the basic allowance was less than 50 percent of the wage level for domestic workers, but, according to Yoo and Uh (2001), trainee wages had grown to about 80 percent of this level by 2000. It is also worth noting that, although industrial trainees are still not formally recognized as workers, since 1999 they have been covered by South Korea's basic Minimum Wage Act (KFSB 2002). The increase in the price of labor, it is important to understand, is not strictly or even mostly a function of market forces, especially for industrial trainees. On this point, recall the primary rationale for the ITTP, which was (and still is) to institutionalize a nonmarket-based employment system—that is, one in which wages are intentionally depressed and the entry and mobility of workers tightly regulated. The increase in trainee wages, therefore, suggests that nonmarket (political) forces are at play.

Legally, the changes for transnational migrant workers have been just as important. The first significant legal development occurred in 1993, with a decision by the Seoul Superior Court (Case No. 93 Ku 16774) establishing the right for undocumented foreign workers to receive compensation for industrial injury. A few years later, in 1995, a special court was created to deal exclusively with the problems of foreign workers, such as wage issues and severance pay (*Korea Economic Daily*, January 20, 1995). Another important case was decided by the Seoul Supreme Court in 1997 (Case No. 97

---

[12] Estimates for the average monthly earnings of undocumented workers need to be viewed with caution. The figure cited in the text is *Korea Herald* 2002a. Sr. Josephina Cheong, who counsels transnational migrant workers on a daily basis for the Foreign Workers Labor Counseling, cited a similar figure (author interview, June 2002).

[13] Sr. Cheong pointed out that, while the basic monthly wage is similar, foreign workers generally do not receive yearly bonuses, which can amount to more than a full month's wage.

Ta 18875). This decision affirmed the right of illegal aliens employed in Korea to receive severance pay.[14] Meanwhile, a series of similar cases by lower courts eventually compelled the government to adopt a more general policy position.[15] As result of all this, on October 14, 1998, the Ministry of Labor announced that all undocumented immigrant workers in Korea would be protected under the Labor Standards Act.[16] According to a Ministry spokesperson, the Act was amended because, "The relevant Supreme Court's judicial precedents regard illegal foreign workers as workers to whom the Labor Standards Act applies…. Accordingly, when employers … violate the Labor Standards Act against illegal foreign workers, the employers are subject to the same level of punishment as that against domestic workers" (Ministry of Labor Press Release, October 14, 1998). This decision, while undoubtedly significant, was still only a qualified victory since the Act applied to companies with five or more employees, but a large proportion of undocumented workers in Korea work in companies with fewer than five employees. In July 2000, however, this limitation was partly overcome when the occupational accident law was extended to cover workers in all companies, regardless of size.[17]

Of course, recalcitrant employers (and their supporters in the government) can sidestep court decisions. This has certainly been the case: employers continue to withhold pay, to deny responsibility for industrial accidents and injuries, to physically abuse their employees, and so on.

---

[14] In this case, South Korea's Supreme Court upheld a lower court decision that ruled that all foreign workers, *including those working illegally,* deserve severance benefits. More specifically, the court ruled that, even though a foreign worker (Mohamed Abdul Kalek from Bangladesh) clearly violated immigration control laws, his employment contract was valid and he was, therefore, entitled to 3.67 million won in severance benefits from his former employer (*Korea Herald* 1997a).

[15] In 1996, to cite one example, a Korean Chinese woman, who had already returned to China, sued the Labor Welfare Corporation, arguing that it had no right to deny her compensation for an injury she suffered in 1994. According to a government directive, only foreign workers injured after March 1995 (when the law was changed) were eligible for compensation. A three-judge panel, however, ruled that the Ministry guideline had no legal force, and therefore the plaintiff was fully entitled to compensation for her injuries (*Korea Times* 1997).

[16] The full text of the Labor Standards Act is available at http://www.globalmarch .org/virtuallibrary/ilo-natlex/korea-standards.htm.

[17] Author interview with Sr. Josephina Cheong, June 2002, Seoul.

Unlike the early 1990s, however, the bureaucratic system is now generally, albeit not entirely, obliged to protect the rights of foreign workers, which frequently means working against the interests of small and midsize businesses. This represents a marked contrast to the early 1990s, when the relevant agencies perceived their mission primarily in terms of protecting Korean society *from* foreign workers, or in terms of maximizing the exploitation of foreign workers to the benefit of Korean business. The shift in bureaucratic perceptions (and actions) is, of course, a matter of degree and not a complete reversal. It is also uneven. The Ministry of Labor, as I have suggested, has proven to be a relatively strong and consistent advocate of rights for transnational migrant workers. But even the Ministry of Justice, the Bureau of Immigration (which is under the jurisdiction of the Justice Ministry), and the Small and Medium Business Administration (SMBA) are clearly moving away from their clear-cut suspicion of (if not outright hostility toward) transnational migrant workers. In early 2002, for example, the Ministries of Justice and Labor and the SMBA announced a proactive joint effort to begin "surveillance" of businesses that treat foreign workers poorly.[18] Around the same time, the Ministry of Commerce, Industry, and Energy announced its plans to create "working rules" (in collaboration with the private sector) that would guarantee the protection of "non-native laborers' human rights" (*Korea Herald* 2002c). To reinforce all this activity, the Ministry of Labor also announced its intention to establish, by the end of 2002, counseling booths exclusively for foreign workers in all of its regional offices (*Korea Herald* 2002d). Previously, the "counseling" of transnational migrant workers had been the exclusive domain of Korea's secular and religious NGO community.

The change in bureaucratic attitude toward transnational migrant workers is also reflected in a general unwillingness to crack down on legally prohibited but politically sensitive activities. In 2001, for example, a small group of undocumented foreign workers established a union for migrant workers; according to Korean law, neither industrial trainees nor undocumented workers are permitted to join labor unions. This union,

---

[18] According to the plan announced by the SMBA, businesses violating the rights of foreign workers (for example, by delaying payments or physically assaulting, confining, or sexually harassing them) would be barred from receiving various forms of financial support, such as the operation stabilization funds from the government. The agency also said it would limit the distribution of industrial trainees and specialized industrial workers to companies that violate the rights of foreign workers (*Korea Herald* 2002b).

which was established as a branch of the Seoul-Kyonggi-Inchon Region Equality Trade Union (SKIRETU, a regional union affiliated with the progressive Korean Confederation of Trade Unions), has only a very small membership, estimated at fewer than 150. Still, neither the Labor Ministry nor the Justice Ministry has been willing to act against the union. In fact, the Ministry of Labor practically endorsed the union by stating that foreign workers are "entitled to organize themselves." The Justice Ministry was more circumspect but still indicated that it would not interfere with the operation of the union unless the activities of the foreign workers made them "visible."[19]

The most recent change is the creation of the "Work Permit System for Foreigners," which debuted in 2004. This system allows transnational migrants to work legally in South Korea for three years, during which time they are fully protected by Korean labor law (the Labor Standards Act). The system also forbids discriminatory wage treatment, except where it is possible to "differentiate the wage level ... due to gaps in productivity" (Human Resources Development Service n.d.). This system, however, represents a clear compromise. On one hand, it does not go nearly far enough from the perspective of the transnational migrant workers and their supporters in Korea. The three-year limitation, for example, is explicitly designed to prevent "permanent settlement" in South Korea, which especially hurts those workers who have already been there for an extended period (some as long as twelve years). Moreover, only workers from countries that have signed a Memorandum of Understanding (MOU) with Korea can take advantage of the provisions of the system. (As of July 2004, only the Philippines, Mongolia, Thailand, Vietnam, and Sri Lanka had signed an MOU; Indonesia and China were expected to complete an agreement before the end of the year [*Hanguk Ilbo* 2004].) On the other hand, it is clear that advocates of the industrial trainee program preferred the old system, which limited wages and worker rights. In sum, the work permit system is an ambiguous development with regard to the changing status of transnational migrant workers. At best, it will leave many underlying issues unresolved for years to come.

Whatever the case, the creation of the work permit system and all other changes in the status of transnational migrant workers reflects a deeply politicized process, one in which the key agents of change were not necessarily the bureaucratic agencies that shape and enforce policy nor the

---

[19] For details, see *Korea Herald* 2001a, 2001b, 2001c.

courts (although they have clearly played a central role in many aspects of the process thus far). Rather, the main sources of change, as I have repeatedly suggested, are the transnational migrants themselves and a network of secular and religious nongovernmental organizations in Korean society. It is, of course, not obvious that this is the case. Thus, in the remaining sections, I endeavor to show how political activism—sometimes subtle and sometimes quite conspicuous—has served as the crucial source of rights expansion for transnational migrant/immigrant workers in Korea.

THE CONTEXT OF POLITICAL AND SOCIAL CHANGE IN SOUTH KOREA

The role of political activism in South Korea cannot be properly understood without an appreciation of the context of political and social change in this country. A crucial aspect of this context is Korea's authoritarian past, which lasted from 1961 to 1987. Although it is beyond the scope of this chapter to cover this period in any depth or detail, it is important to note that during the years of dictatorship, the suppression of political participation and "popular will" created a particular dynamic leading to the development of a fragmented but strongly determined and effective "civil society." South Korea's civil society, as Kim Sukhyun (1996) explains it, is presently composed of three main actors: newcomers, "old radicals," and converts. As a product of Korea's authoritarian past, these main actors— while not always in agreement on basic principles and strategies—did share a common opposition to dictatorship and a common desire for democracy. The shared struggled *against* dictatorship and *for* democracy, not surprisingly, was broadly based. In other words, it was not just one segment of Korean society that was involved in this struggle, but multiple segments: radical students, churches and other religious groups, workers, and, perhaps most importantly, a politically liberal but fairly broad segment of the middle class—white-collar workers, academics, lawyers, technicians, independent businesspeople, and low-ranking public servants (Kim Sukhyun 1996).

The sheer breadth of the pro-democracy struggle meant that, once the goal of a democratic society was realized, Korea's activist "civil society" would not immediately fade away. In fact, the collapse of the authoritarian system led to a proliferation of civil groups, particularly groups associated with the more moderate citizen's (*simin*) movement, as opposed to the more radical people's (*minjung*) movement: in the late 1980s, only a handful of civic organizations or NGOs existed, but by 2000 there were an estimated 70,000 civic groups in Korea (Narkarmi 2000). While the vast majority of these groups have scant political weight, the largest and best-established organizations have proven to be quite effective in pushing for social, economic, and political reform. One reason for this, argues the Reverend Kyung-Suk Soh (1994), general secretary of the Citizens' Coalition for Economic Justice (CCEJ)—one of the largest civic organizations in Korea—stems from the ability of some Korean NGOs to transcend the class-based divisions that used to characterize South Korean society.[20] Forging links between the middle class and working class, in other words, has enabled certain NGOs to develop broad-based consensus and legitimacy, which has translated into political power. It is useful to remember that this, too, is a legacy of Korea's authoritarian past.

Korea's authoritarian past also has been instrumental in shaping another significant aspect of the country's political and social context, namely, its receptiveness to international or transnational norms, specifically norms regarding human rights and worker rights. As Gurowitz correctly points out, we can neither assume that international or transnational norms have the same effect across countries nor that they even have a positive impact on the treatment of both citizens and noncitizens. Instead, "[w]e need to look at concrete domestic contexts to understand how norms are mobilized or not, and are useful or not, in different countries and across different issue areas" (2000: 877). In looking at the Korean context, it is clear that the pro-democracy/anti-authoritarianism movement has had a profound impact; the movement itself often, and even necessarily, relied on international norms as a key source of political legitimacy. This was true, in large part, because the struggle against authoritarianism invariably elicited state repression in the name of anti-communism and "national security." The main actors in the struggle, therefore, had to establish an alternative ideological (or discursive) position, one that clearly insulated them from charges that they supported communism. This alternative position was one that concentrated on human rights, the situation of workers, and political democratization (Kim Sukhyun 1996). On this point, too, it is important to highlight the nexus between human rights and worker rights; both are inextricably connected in the Korean context since labor played a decisive role in paving the road to democracy (Moon 2000).

---

[20] The CCEJ is also extremely influential. According to an annual survey conducted by the well-regarded *Sisa Journal* (October 21, 1993), the CCEJ was ranked as *the* most influential organization in South Korea. Significantly, the survey put the CCEJ above the Federation of Korean Industries (FKI), which is composed of Korea's largest and most powerful business groups.

Finally, it is worth noting that the legacy of Korea's authoritarian past is clearly reflected in the composition of the government. Kim Dae Jung, South Korea's president from 1998 to 2003, is a former leader of the pro-democracy struggle and a leading advocate of human rights. The minister of labor during Kim's presidency, Bang Yong Seok, was a union leader who played a key role in Korea's labor movement during the 1970s and 1980s. Moreover, throughout the government, there is a keen sensitivity to the issue of human and labor rights—and to Korea's international image as a country that pays heed to these international/transnational norms. (South Korea's current president, Roh Moo-hyun, was also a noted human rights and pro-democracy activist during the country's authoritarian period.)

POLITICAL ACTIVISM AND THE EXPANSION OF MIGRANT RIGHTS

The (legal) expansion of rights for transnational migrant workers in Korea, which began in 1993 (as noted above), was *preceded* by political activism and unequivocally ran counter to the interests of small businesses (in particular, the KFSB) and their allies in the government. The first manifestation of this activism, however, was not in the form of a public protest, sit-in, or other type of demonstration. Instead, it was based on the activities of the Archdiocese of Seoul and the Labor Pastoral Center (LPC). The LPC, which was established in 1979 to assist local Korean workers, has long relied on a particular political strategy, one focused on using existing legislation to protect and expand worker rights. For local Korean workers, this normally entailed an appeal to domestic law; but in the case of transnational migrant workers, the LPC appealed to international labor standards and norms, and specifically to the standards articulated by the International Labour Organization (Korea became a member of the ILO in 1991). In appealing to international norms, the LPC made the case that even if foreign workers were in Korea illegally, the fact that they were employed made their work contracts legal.[21] In other words, the LPC argued that

---

[21] This particular strategy should be credited to Professor Sohn Ch'ang-hee, a member of the Seoul Archdiocesan Labor Pastoral Commission and formerly professor of labor law at Hanyang University. According to Fr. J. Trisolini, director of the LPC, Professor Sohn "always insisted in public talks that, although migrant workers were undocumented, their labor contract was valid under international norms" (personal e-mail communication, October 14, 2002).

international labor standards dictate that work contracts (whether implied or explicit) must be honored and protected by domestic authorities regardless of the worker's legal status.[22] Although is it not possible to link this strategy with a particular change in government policy, it most likely "played an important role in the first court decision [November 1993] establishing the legal right for foreign workers to receive compensation for industrial injuries."[23]

The LPC's legal strategy has been effective, in part, because Korean officials are (for reasons discussed above) extremely sensitive to situations in which domestic laws or practices contradict international standards, especially standards by which the government has agreed to abide. Interestingly, but for slightly different reasons, the same strategy has worked in Japan. In Japan, the Zentoitsu Labor Union (ZWU) has used Article 3 of Japan's Basic Labor Law to promote and expand the rights of transnational migrant workers. Article 3 states that an employer shall not engage in *discriminatory treatment* with regard to wages and working conditions by reason of nationality or social status. The use of this clause effectively gave foreign workers in Japan the same legal standing with regard to labor rights as native workers.[24] In both Japan and Korea, however, the appeal to existing laws or international standards is limited to the extent that employers and even bureaucratic agencies are able to subvert or ignore legal strictures. This problem is exacerbated in Korea because "there is no American style system of judicial precedent and a decision of the Supreme Court does not have the binding force of precedent in subsequent cases of a similar nature. It merely has a persuasive effect."[25] This means that, by themselves, court rulings do not guarantee the protection, much less expansion, of migrant/immigrant rights in Korea.

Thus, despite important legal decisions — such as the 1993 case establishing the right for foreign workers to receive compensation for industrial injury — many (if not the majority of) small factory owners simply ignored changes in the law. It is partly for this reason that the estimated 150 civil and religious organizations that assist transnational migrant workers in Korea devote the bulk of their efforts to "labor counseling" — that is, to

---

[22] Author interview with Fr. Trisolini, June 2001.

[23] Personal e-mail communication with Fr. J. Trisolini, October 14, 2002.

[24] Author interview with Torii Ippei, secretary general of the ZWU, June 2002.

[25] "Korean Legal System — the Judiciary," *Korean Legal Resources on the Internet.* At http://www.siu.edu/offices/lawlib/koreanlaw/.

helping foreign workers collect unpaid wages or severance pay; obtain medical assistance and financial compensation for work-related accidents; deal with housing and medical problems or with violence in the workplace; and so on. *The very existence of these organizations, in other words, reflects the practical limitations of court decisions designed to protect transnational workers.* For much of the 1990s, moreover, the government's attitude and behavior encouraged small business owners to maintain a hard-line stance, even if, in so doing, they violated the law. The Ministry of Justice and Bureau of Immigration, for example, regularly deported foreign workers who attempted to assert their legal rights.

This ongoing resistance on the part of small business owners and segments of the Korean government inspired a second — and more common — form of political activism, namely, public demonstrations and protests. The first significant protest occurred in 1994, when a small group of workers from Nepal, Bangladesh, the Philippines, and Ethiopia staged a sit-in at the headquarters of the Citizens' Coalition for Economic Justice. These workers had all suffered serious industrial injuries (one woman from Nepal had lost all her fingers on one hand); yet despite the 1993 court decision, none had been able to receive compensation from their employers. To make matters worse, their companies refused to return their passports, meaning that the workers could not even leave Korea.[26] Given their situation, the workers, in collaboration with members of the CCEJ, decided that their only recourse was to stage a (decidedly nonviolent) sit-in. The CCEJ and the workers, moreover, quite consciously decided to draw on the issue of human rights; one of the signs used by the workers stated simply, "We are human."[27] The sit-in, which the CCEJ also helped to publicize through its network of contacts in the Korean media, lasted for twenty-nine days and ended when the Ministry of Labor agreed to "improve the human rights problem of foreign laborers."[28] The success of the protest, however, was extremely limited; the only enduring change was the admission by government officials that a serious problem existed. Most of the concrete promises the government made, by contrast, were simply not kept. Despite this limited success, the sit-in encouraged more public activism.

---

[26] Author interview with We Jung-Hee, director of the Buddhist Coalition for Economic Justice, June 2001, Seoul.

[27] In my June 2001 interview at the CCEJ, We Jung-Hee stated clearly that the appeal to the global discourse of human rights was a strategic decision; she knew it would be one of the most effective strategies for the workers to use.

[28] For additional details, see *Civil Society* 1994.

Indeed, less than a year later, in January 1995, a second, more public protest was staged, this time by a group of thirteen Nepalese "trainees" demonstrating at the Myongdong Cathedral. During this very quiet protest—in which the CCEJ also played an important role—the workers made only a few public statements. In one joint statement, they said, "We may be from a poor country, and that's why we are working here in Seoul like slaves. But we have our basic human rights as well" (*Reuters World Service* 1995). For the most part, though, their point was made with a series of posters that contained statements (with photographs) such as: "I lost three fingers on my right hand working in a factory. What will I do for the future?" "Please don't beat me," and "We are not slaves."[29] This sit-in, too, ended when the government—along with the KFSB—agreed to implement stronger measures to protect industrial trainees from beatings and sexual assault and to provide compensation for work-related injuries (the 1993 court decision did not apply to industrial trainees). The government also agreed to allow trainees to retain possession of their passports and to be paid directly. Again, though, the government's promises proved to be largely empty. (Moreover, the thirteen trainees were all deported after the end of the sit-in.)

Still, while this second protest also had limited results—it did not lead to any dramatic changes in government policy and practice—it did spark an upsurge of interest within the Korean NGO community. Hitherto, only the Archdiocese of Seoul and a few other organizations—most notably, the Association for Foreign Workers' Human Rights (part of the Labor Human Rights Center)[30]—were actively and significantly involved in assisting transnational migrant workers. Shortly after the 1995 sit-in, however, the number increased rapidly. As noted above, most of these organizations were established to provide "labor counseling" and/or other forms of social assistance. Most, too, were and are church-based: the Christian Institute for the Study of Justice, for instance, lists a total of 101 church-based organizations (86 Protestant, 12 Catholic, 2 Buddhist, and 1 Islamic) set up to assist foreign workers (http://www.jpic.org/eindex.html). A smaller

---

[29] Based on the author's personal observation; translations by the author.

[30] The director of the Association for Foreign Workers' Human Rights, Pak Seok Woon, claims that his was the first organization devoted to the protection of foreign workers in South Korea. The organization was established in 1992, which is about the same time the LPC began to work closely with foreign workers (author interview, June 2001, Seoul).

number of organizations, however, are also sharply focused on the broader goal of rights expansion. The CCEJ (along with its Buddhist counterpart, the Buddhist Coalition for Economic Justice, or BCEJ) and the Archdiocese of Seoul/Labor Pastoral Center are two of the main actors in this regard. But they are not alone. Another extremely important organization is the Joint Committee for Migrant Workers in Korea (JCMK), a coalition of like-minded NGOs committed to the "improvement of working conditions and [to the] elevation of [the] political, economic, social status of migrant workers."[31]

The JCMK was founded in 1995 in direct response to the 1994 and 1995 sit-ins. According to Ahn Seoung-Guen, a former coordinator of the JCMK, the limited and short-lived success of the two sit-ins demonstrated the need for more coordinated efforts; accordingly, the JCMK was explicitly created to act as an umbrella organization (author interview, June 2001). The first major activity of the JCMK was to push for a new law specifically protecting foreign migrant workers. Actually, this effort was initiated almost two years earlier by a key member of the JCMK, the Labor Human Rights Center (LHRC), which originally proposed a new law for foreign workers in 1995. According to the director of LHRC, Seok Won Park, this new law was to include the following provisions: (1) abolition of the trainee system, which unjustly and disingenuously classifies full-fledged workers as "trainees"; (2) implementation of a work permit system, which would also extend domestic labor rights to all foreign migrant workers; (3) provision of social welfare benefits to foreign workers; and (4) a grant of full amnesty to all foreign migrant workers in Korea "illegally" (author interview, June 2001). The establishment of the JCMK (with ten original members; the current membership stands at thirty-four [table 9.5]) gave added strength and vigor to this effort. Yet it was not enough to win passage—or even serious consideration—of a new law. One reason for this was the still strong and active resistance by the Ministry of Justice and the KFSB against any changes in the treatment of transnational migrant workers; another reason, perhaps, was simply the indifference of other segments of the government, including the executive branch, to the problems faced by foreign workers in Korea.

---

[31] Author interview with Kim Mi Sun, director of the Public and International Department, JCMK, June 2002.

Table 9.5. Members of the Joint Committee for Migrant Workers in Korea
(as of June 2002)

Organization	City
Ansan Migrant Shelter	Ansan
Ansan Migrant Workers' Center	Ansan
Asan Migrant Workers' Center	Asan
Association for Foreign Workers	Gwang-ju
Association for Foreign Workers' Human Rights	Seoul
Buceon Migrant Workers' House	Bucheon
Daegu Migrant Workers' Counseling (Shelter) Center	Daegu
Emmaus	Suwon
Galilea	Ansan
Gwanggu Migrant Workers' Center	Gwang-ju
Ilsan International Workers' Counseling Office	Koyang
Inchon Migrant Workers' Center	Inchon
Jinchon Migrant Brothers' House	Jincheon
Korea Migrant Workers' Human Rights Center	Inchon
Korean Church Women United	Seoul
Kwang Myong Foreign Workers' Center	Kwangmyeong
Kyungsan Migrant Workers' Church	Kyung-san
Legal Aid Center for Foreign Migrant Workers	Ujieongbu
Medical Mutual-Aid Union for Migrant Workers in Korea	Seoul
Migrant Workers' Counsel Office	Chang-won
Migrant Workers' House/Korea-Chinese House	Sungnam
Migrant Workers' House/Korean Chinese House	Seoul
Migrant Workers' Human Rights and Culture Center	Kimpo
Pyongtaek Migrant Worker Center	Pyongtaek
Seoul Migrant Workers' Center	Seoul
Shalom House	Seoul
Suwon Migrant Workers' Center	Suwon
The Diocese of Busan's Labor Apostolate and the Apostolate of Salaried Workers	Busan
The House of Shalom	Namyangju
Welfare Mission Center for Korean Chinese	Seoul
Women's Center for Migrant Workers	Namyangju
Won Buddhism Seoul Foreigners' Center	Seoul
World Neighbors Seongdong Migrant Workers' Center	Seoul
Yangsan Foreign Workers' House	Yangsan

Pressure and activism by the JCMK, however, was constant: from 1996 to 1999, the JCMK organized a series of demonstrations (including a hunger strike and a "driving demonstration"), signature campaigns, and public hearings pushing for a new law. In addition, other organizations not affiliated with JCMK independently pressed for the same or similar changes in government policy.[32] Then in March 2000 the JCMK published a white paper entitled *The Report on Oppressed Human Rights of the Migrant Trainee Workers (Weiguk-in sanop kisul yonsusaeng ingwon paekso)*. The JCMK sent this report directly to President Kim Dae Jung, whose initial response was extremely positive. Indeed, shortly after receiving the report, Kim ordered both his own party (the Millennium Democratic Party, or MDP) and the Ministry of Labor to study the foreign worker issue and develop recommendations.[33] Somewhat later, the head of the MDP and the minister of labor announced that the government would enact a new law to abolish the trainee system and legalize transnational migrant work in Korea; the government's proposal was quite close, though not identical, to the proposal put forth by the JCMK. The new law was set to take effect in July 2000 but was later postponed until January 2001.[34]

The postponement proved fatal; the MDP announced in January 2001 that the new law would be shelved indefinitely (*Korea Times* 2001). It is not certain why the MDP suddenly shifted its position, but constant pressure by the KFSB no doubt played a role. Indeed, political activism by the KFSB has been an integral part of the entire process of migrant/immigrant rights expansion in Korea. I will take up this issue shortly; first, however, it is important to understand that the failure—thus far—of the JCMK and other NGOs to abolish the trainee system and to create a legal work permit system for transnational migrant workers in South Korea does not mean their activism has been irrelevant. Far from it. The unremitting pressure for sweeping change has clearly had an impact on governmental and social views of the foreign worker issue. At a minimum, this pressure has suc-

[32] The Archdiocese of Seoul Labor Pastoral Commission, in particular, issued several formal statements—and one petition to the National Assembly—on the need for a law to protect foreign migrant workers (Foreign Workers' Labor Counseling Office 2002). It is likely, too, that Cardinal Kim and the other auxiliary bishops of Seoul have spoken officially or off the record with government officials on the situation and rights of migrant workers (personal e-mail communication with Fr. Trisolini, October 14, 2002).

[33] Author interview with Ahn Seoung-Guen, June 2001.

[34] For additional details, see *Korea Economic Daily* 2000.

cessfully and unequivocally framed the problems faced by transnational migrant workers as a "human rights issue." For this reason alone, the foreign worker issue is difficult to ignore within Korea. According to Lee Yong Kyu, a senior researcher at the Korea Labor Institute (and someone intimately familiar with governmental discussions on the foreign labor issue), "virtually everyone" in the government realizes that "something must and will be done" to reform the trainee system—even among those who generally support the interests of the KFSB. More significantly, perhaps, Dr. Lee readily acknowledges that the motivation for change within the Korean government is the belief that Korea must be a "modern country," which means treating foreign workers as "human beings" rather than as merely "cheap labor" (author interview, June 2002).

In the meantime, the trainee system—still in place and still highly exploitative—has been revised on several occasions. I have already discussed the gradual but nonetheless striking increase in the basic "allowance" for trainees. This increase is almost certainly due to the "activism" of the transnational migrant workers themselves (à la Scott's [1985] "everyday forms of peasant resistance"), namely, their propensity to simply walk away from low-paying trainee positions. Indeed, according to a report in the Korea Herald (October 2, 1997), upwards of 60 percent of foreign trainees—and probably many more—abandoned their positions in the early years of the program. It was only after the "allowance" was significantly increased that the desertion rate came down to acceptable levels (but never disappeared). Also, as I have suggested, trainees have obtained some protections under the Labor Standards Act, the Minimum Wage Act, and the Industrial Accident Compensation Insurance Act; and those who complete their "training" are now eligible to become "post-training" workers, which would provide them the same rights as native workers. (Ironically, undocumented workers already have these rights; post-training workers, however, would not be subject to deportation.)[35] None of these reforms satisfy the transnational migrant workers or the NGOs,[36] but all represent

---

[35] This position was created by the Working After Training Program for Foreigners bill, which was introduced in April 1998. Under its provisions, trainees who pass a skills test after a two-year training period can continue to work for one year as regular "workers." In 2000 (the first year of eligibility), there were 2,068 post-training workers (Seoul and Skrentny 2004).

[36] In the most recent signature campaign organized by the JCMK (the "Campaign on Opposing Discrimination against Migrant Workers," which began in May 2002 and was scheduled to coincide with the Korea/Japan World

an effort by the government (particularly the Ministry of Justice) and the KFSB to mollify and address the activism of their antagonists. From this perspective, one can argue that the piecemeal, ad hoc, and essentially defensive approach adopted by the Labor Ministry and KFSB is a clear demonstration of the effects of unremitting political activism on the part of the NGO network and the transnational migrant workers themselves.

The foregoing discussion, I should emphasize, also helps us see that the constant pressure for sweeping change has not occluded the day-to-day struggle for *incremental* change. Consider, for example, the legal decisions that have expanded the rights of foreign migrant workers to date. All of these decisions are based on the step-by-step and persistent efforts of Korean NGOs. I have already discussed the role of the LPC in this regard, but a range of other NGOs have also aided in the legal struggle. One of the most important of these is Minbyun (Lawyers for a Democratic Society). Minbyun was established in 1986 by thirty lawyers, most of whom had already been active in defending the rights of "prisoners of conscience" during the democratization movement. After the collapse of the authoritarian system, the organization began to focus primarily on defending and promoting human rights in Korea and in assisting other NGOs working for social progress. While the organization's efforts with transnational migrant workers are limited, its staff of volunteer lawyers has handled at least 421 cases and assisted 972 individual workers since 1988. (In addition, Minbyun is currently collaborating with the JCMK and the Korean Confederation of Trade Unions to introduce another proposal for a labor permit system in Korea.)[37] The legal assistance provided by Minbyun should not be underestimated. Indeed, in a country that has only 4,200 lawyers,[38] pro

---

Cup tournament), the trainee system was portrayed by the organizers as "nothing more than the modern-day slavery system" ("Signature Collecting Campaign on Opposing Discrimination against Migrant Workers," May 7, 2002, public statement, photocopy).

[37] The attorney preparing the draft proposal for Minbyun is Kim Jin. According to Ms. Kim, the Minbyun proposal differs from the current government proposal in several respects. Specifically, it would permit foreign workers to work in any company, with certain restrictions. In addition, it would allow a longer stay: two years initially, followed by three one-year extensions, for a total of five years. After five years, foreign workers would receive a special labor permit, which would enable them to work in any type of industry (no restrictions) (author interview, June 2002).

[38] Of this number, about 350, or 8.8 percent of all lawyers in Korea, are members of Minbyun. Even more impressive is the fact that not only are members

bono legal assistance and representation is an extraordinarily valuable commodity. Nor is Minbyun the only attorneys' organization that provides pro bono legal assistance to foreign workers; the Seoul Bar Association has been running a Legal Center for Migrant Workers since December 1994 (*Korea Herald* 1997b). In addition to the legal assistance provided by these organizations, many practicing attorneys and law professors volunteer their services on an individual basis to the NGOs working with transnational migrant workers (various interviews by the author).

As I suggested earlier, this ongoing legal assistance—combined with the advocacy and on-the-ground activism of the service-based NGOs—has helped ensure that rights extended by the courts (or via public policy) have been translated into concrete action. This remains important, for even to-day companies continue to flaunt laws protecting transnational migrant workers. But unlike the not-so-distant past, it is becoming more and more difficult for these companies to evade their legal obligations, particularly when confronted by knowledgeable NGOs.[39] Indeed, for the most recent two years, the LPC's Foreign Workers' Labor Counseling Office—the largest and busiest labor counseling center for foreign workers in Korea—claims a 100 percent success rate in resolving complaints regarding industrial accident compensation.[40] Ten years earlier, by contrast, few industrial accident claims were granted. Just as important, undocumented workers who bring claims are no longer subject to automatic deportation, since their complaints are no longer forwarded to immigration authorities.

---

of Minbyun asked to provide pro bono legal assistance, they are also required to pay monthly membership dues of 100,000 won (about US$80).

[39] Many transnational migrant workers, however, are still not aware of their legal rights or of the many NGOs set up to assist them. Surprisingly, the same is true for the representatives of several countries whose citizens are working in Korea. During my interview with Albert Yankey, the minister-counselor for the Embassy of the Republic of Ghana, for example, the minister described his frustration in helping two Ghanaian citizens receive compensation for industrial injuries they had suffered; one had been severely scalded by molten plastic and had been left completely disabled. All of his efforts as a representative of the Ghanaian government to gain compensation failed. Mr. Yankey was not aware, however, that the workers were legally entitled to compensation, nor was he aware of the NGOs available to assist him or the workers directly (author interview, June 2002, Seoul).

[40] This figure, for the years 1999 and 2000, was provided by Benedict Choe, general secretary of the LPC (author interview, June 2001). Among NGOs providing labor counseling, however, none claimed a similar success rate. Still, all felt that the situation had significantly improved over the years.

OBSTACLES TO CHANGE

The main obstacle to the expansion of migrant/immigrant worker rights in Korea should already be apparent: the KFSB. The reason for the KFSB's opposition, however, is not obvious at first glance, but comes down to a common, even trite, set of interrelated issues: money and client politics. To see this, it is important to understand that the current system, which is focused on the Industrial Technical Trainee Program, is far more than a way to bring needed workers into the Korean economy. It is also a cash cow — a very big cash cow — for the KFSB. Indeed, it would not be too much to state that the entire ITTP is set up as a highly profitable money-making enterprise. The contours of the system are straightforward. To begin, the KFSB, which, we should recall, is a *private* industry association, has responsibility for administering the ITTP (under the nominal supervision of the Small and Medium Business Administration, or SMBA). In this role, according to Seol Dong-Hoon, the KFSB deals directly with recruiters in sending countries. It is also given authority over placing "trainees" in positions with Korean companies and collecting a monthly fee from the trainees (via twenty specially designated "consulting" agencies). This system has resulted in a net profit of 56.5 billion won between 1996 and 2001 (author interview, June 2002; also see Seol 1999). Of this amount, according to an SBA report, approximately 32.67 billion won was in commissions from agencies training unskilled migrant trainees; 10.63 billion won were deposits that companies seeking foreign workers paid to cover the risk of trainee flight from workplaces; and 13.23 billion won were interest earnings from the funds (*Korea Times* 2002b). Thus the KFSB makes a profit even when a foreign trainee abandons his or her assigned position, since the company hiring that trainee forfeits its deposit (about US$300 per person) to the federation if this happens.

Given the KFSB's financial interest in maintaining the current system, it is easy to understand why it is vehemently opposed to any changes. But others benefit as well, including government officials and politicians. The benefits to individuals in government, however, are typically in the form of bribes or kickbacks, a few cases of which have been publicly exposed. The Ministry of Justice, for its part, has not been implicated in any corruption scandals, but several retired officials of the Ministry of Justice's Immigration Bureau have served as chairmen of the Korean International Training Cooperation Corps (KITCO), which was created by the KFSB to oversee the process of trainee recruitment and selection. And several top KITCO officials have been arrested on bribery charges.

However powerful, the flow and exchange of money is not the only factor keeping the system in place. Another important obstacle to change is the more general fear of the damage that the large-scale inflow of "oustsiders" would do to the cohesion and harmony of Korean society. This "fear of foreigners" was first manifested, as noted above, in the effort to limit worker immigration to Chinese of Korean ancestry, the so-called chosun jok. Ironically, it was this initial effort that helped strengthen the public and popular perception that immigrants — if not strictly controlled — would bring harm to Korean society; this perception was reinforced when the harsh realities of life in Korea, combined with a sense of betrayal among many Chinese Koreans, led to frequent outbreaks of violence. In one particularly notorious case, the captain of a South Korean fishing boat, the *Pescamar 15*, was murdered, along with ten other crewmen (seven Koreans and three Indonesians), after the Chinese Korean crewmen complained about harsh working conditions. Unfortunately, this was not an isolated incident: in 1995 there were at least 125 violent incidents on Korean ships, resulting in the deaths of twelve Korean nationals (this number, I should emphasize, includes only incidents in which Korean nationals were attacked by foreign nationals, not the other way around). The situation became so bad, in fact, that the South Korean government was compelled to ban all crews in which foreign workers outnumbered native Koreans. Much, if not all, of the blame for this situation was placed squarely on the shoulders of the immigrant workers. This was certainly the view of one influential Korean newspaper editor, who, writing in the *Chosun Ilbo* on September 9, 1996, labeled ethnic Koreans in China as "two-faced" backstabbers. As he put it, "They realize economic benefits from South Korea, yet they denounce South Koreans. From the South Korean viewpoint, we are getting slapped in the face even though we are helping them."

By itself, this image of immigrant labor would represent a huge obstacle to change. But combined with (1) the KFSB's constant and politically savvy pressure on the government, which has included numerous public demonstrations in front of government offices such as the Blue House and the Tripartite Commission building;[41] (2) the contrived but nonetheless "illegal" status of most immigrant workers; and (3) the historical insulation of Korean society, it would be easy to assume any hope for far-reaching change to be naïve. Yet, as I have shown, significant change has already

---

[41] Author interview with Sun Han-Seung, chief expert adviser, Tripartite Commission of Korea, June 2002.

occurred, and even more significant change is not only likely but almost certain. The reason, to repeat, is clear: political activism exercised by both transnational migrant workers and the network of Korean NGOs devoted to the protection and promotion of migrant worker rights. Indeed, without the ongoing, focused, and indefatigable activism of these groups, it is quite likely that little or nothing would have changed. Certainly the KFSB and its allies in government, from the beginning until now, have been intent on maximizing and permanently institutionalizing the exploitation and subordination of foreign workers. The court system, for its part, has relied upon the network of NGOs and volunteer lawyers not only to bring cases but also to ensure that the decisions handed down are actually and meaningfully implemented.

Finally, it is important to recognize the role NGOs have played in minimizing public mobilization against transnational migrant workers. The conscious and strategic use of the global discourse on human rights and on appeals to international norms has effectively "humanized" the migrant worker community. Indeed, it would be fair to say that this strategy has turned the equation completely around, for the NGOs have turned transnational migrant workers from "threats against" to "victims of" Korean society.

CONCLUSION

Despite the strong conclusion I draw about the role of political activism in the expansion of migrant/immigrant rights in Korea, it is important to remember the particular social and political context in which this occurred. In other words, the argument I make here is not necessarily applicable—and clearly not generalizable—to other cases. At the same time, the Korean case provides a stronger delimitation to those arguments that focus on the legal (and domestic) sources of migrant/immigrant rights expansion. To be sure, such arguments also do not claim universal applicability (see, for example, Joppke 2001). Nonetheless, it is important to underscore this point, if only because migration/immigration is an increasingly complex global phenomenon, one that is likely to continue growing in intensity and scope in the years to come.

It is also important to emphasize that the expansion of rights is by no means a smooth, linear process. Indeed, recent events in South Korea have proven this to be the case. Beginning in the fall of 2003, for example, the government (in anticipation of the newly developed work permit system) announced a new crackdown on transnational migrant workers. The crackdown followed the implementation of an "amnesty" program (originally announced in late 2002) that encouraged non-documented foreign workers to register with the government. Those who registered (and who had been in Korea more than four years) were permitted to work in Korea legally until October 31, 2003, but once the deadline passed, the Ministry of Justice announced that those workers who did not leave voluntarily would be deported *and* fined up to 20 million won (or jailed for up to three years). In response, at least two migrant workers committed suicide (*Korea Times* 2003a), and countless others went into hiding, a situation that would likely lead to a diminution of their hard-won rights. Only a small proportion of transnational workers left voluntarily. Indeed, the announcement encouraged Korean firms hiring transnational workers to withhold pay and compensation for work-related accidents.

Significantly, though, the new crackdown on transnational migrant workers was met not only with passive resistance (that is, attempts to elude authorities; see *Korea Times* 2003b) but also with active resistance on the part of the workers and Korean NGOs. A few days after the government's announcement, for example, thousands of Korean Chinese migrant workers staged a rally in front of Korea's Constitutional Court in Seoul; other migrant workers engaged in sit-ins (the largest lasting from November 2003 to February 2004) and a hunger strike, which led to a surprise visit by President Roh (*Korea Times* 2003c). Hundreds of religious leaders and human rights supporters also staged protests calling on the government to bring an immediate end to the deportation policy (*Korea Times* 2003d). While the protests did not result in a fundamental change in the government's policy, they did at least compel the government to extend the period of voluntary departure to March 1, 2004, and allow those who left voluntarily to return after six months under the auspices of the new work permit system.

Recent events highlight the continuing importance of political activism, for in South Korea the expansion of immigrant/migrant rights is an incremental, hard-fought process with unremitting "backward" pressure. Every gain, in other words, is subject to an equal if not greater loss. The work permit system is a case in point. Though certainly an improvement over the industrial trainee program, at base the new system is designed to limit the rights and power of transnational migrant workers. Thus, if the workers and their allies in South Korea's civil society simply accept the work permit system as is, it is likely that the new system will devolve into a variant of the old trainee program. However, if the workers and their allies continue to exert pressure for change, the work permit system may prove to be a base for even greater progress.

References

Cheesman, Bruce. 1995. Plight of foreign workers: An issue ready to explode—Korea. *Reuters Textline (Australian Financial Review)*. March 21.

Civil Society. 1994. The abuse of foreign laborers' human rights. Vol. 1 (1).

Foreign Workers' Labor Counseling Office. 2002. History and mission statement. Unpublished report.

Gurowitz, Amy. 2000. Migrant rights and activism in Malaysia: Opportunities and constraints. *Journal of Asian Studies* 59 (4):863–88.

Hanguk Ilbo. 2004. Work permit system for foreigners to debut next month. July 7.

Human Resource Development Service of Korea. n.d. The employment permit system for foreigners. http://www.hrdkorea.or.kr:8080/www/english/english_sub_employment02.htm.

Jameson, Sam. 1991. Soldiers to help ease labor pinch in South Korea. *Los Angeles Times*, July 8.

Joppke, Christian. 2001. The legal-domestic sources of immigrant rights: The United States, Germany, and the European Union. *Comparative Political Studies* 34 (4):339–65.

KFSB (Korean Federation of Small and Medium Business). 2002. Information for selected persons—Procedures of industrial training in Korea.

Kim Sukhyun. 1996. Civil society in South Korea: From grand democracy movements to petty interest groups? *Journal of Northeast Asian Studies* 15 (2): 1–97.

KLI (Korea Labor Institute). 2002. Labor trends. http://www.kli.re.kr/english/labornews/09/subtrends.html.

Korea Economic Daily. 2000. New employment scheme for foreign workers to be introduced. September 4.

Korea Herald. 1997a. Illegal foreign workers awarded severance pay. August 8.

———. 1997b. Seoul bar association offers free legal assistance to foreign workers. April 22.

———. 1998. Justice Ministry postpones plan to expel illegal foreign workers. January 8.

———. 2001a. Move to form labor union for illegal foreign workers alerts employers. May 11.

———. 2001b. Migrant workers' labor union launched. May 28.

———. 2001c. Government officials accept foreigners' union "fait accompli." May 29.

———. 2002a. Migrant workers in Korea earn 7 times what they gain at home. May 10.

————. 2002b. Government reinforces surveillance on ill treatment of foreign workers. April 10.

————. 2002c. Government reinforces surveillance on ill treatment of foreign workers. March 25.

————. 2002d. Labor Ministry reinforces protection of migrant workers. May 21.

Korea Times. 1997. Court rules invalid gov't denial of foreign worker's right to industrial accident compensation. January 30.

————. 2001. MDP shelves introduction of work permit system. January 11.

————. 2002a. Indonesians most favored foreign workers. May 1.

————. 2002b. KFSB finds foreign workers attractive revenue source. September 17.

————. 2003a. "Korean Dream" turns into a nightmare. November 14.

————. 2003b. Illegal workers dodge crackdown. November 18.

————. 2003c. Roh makes surprise visit to protesting workers. December 1.

————. 2003d. Unions protest migrant worker policy. November 24.

Kyung-Suk, Soh. 1994. The meaning of "civil society" in the Korean context. *Civil Society* 1(1): 10–13.

Lim, James. 1996. Do not beat the foreign workers. *Asia Times*, October 31.

Ministry of Justice/Bureau of Immigration. 2002. *A guide book for voluntary reporting program*. Seoul: Ministry of Justice.

Moon, Katharine H. S. 2000. Strangers in the midst of globalization: Migrant workers and Korean nationalism. In *Korea's globalization*, edited by Samuel S. Kim. Cambridge: Cambridge University Press.

Narkarmi, Laxmi. 2000. The power of the NGOs: Civic groups are the new political force. *AsiaWeek.Com Magazine*, February 11. http://www.asiaweek.com/asiaweek/magazine/2000/0211/nat.korea.lobby.html.

National Center for Education Statistics. 2001. International comparisons of education. *Digest of Education Statistics 2001*. http://nces.ed.gov/ pubs2002/digest2001/ch6.asp.

Park, Seok-Woon. 1995. The situation of foreign workers in Korea and measures to ensure their protection. In *Policies and protective measures concerning foreign migrant workers*, edited by Korea Research Institute for Workers' Human Rights and Justice. Seoul: Friedrich-Ebert-Stiftung Korea Cooperation Office.

Park, Seok-Woon, Chong-Koo Lee, and Dong-Hoon Seol. 1995. A survey of foreign workers in Korea 1995. In *Policies and protective measures concerning foreign migrant workers*, edited by Korea Research Institute for Workers' Human Rights and Justice. Seoul: Friedrich-Ebert-Stiftung Korea Cooperation Office.

Reuters World Service. 1995. Cardinal Kim apologizes to foreign workers in Seoul. January 10.

Scott, James C. 1985. *Weapons of the weak: Everyday forms of peasant resistance*. New Haven, CT: Yale University Press.

Seol, Dong-Hoon. 1999. *Weiguk-in nodongcha wa hanguk sahwoe*. Seoul: Seoul University Press.

———. 2001. The labor policy for foreign workers and their rights to work in Germany, Singapore, Taiwan, Hong Kong, Japan, and Korea. In *International NGO forum for the rights of migrant workers* (Proceedings).

Seol, Dong-Hoon, and John D. Skrentny. 2004. South Korea: Importing undocumented workers. In *Controlling immigration: A global perspective*, edited by Wayne A. Cornelius, Takeyuki Tsuda, Philip L. Martin, and James F. Hollifield. 2d ed. Stanford, CA: Stanford University Press.

Yoo, Kilsang, and Soobong Uh. 2001. Immigration and labor market issues in Korea. Korea Labor Institute Issue Paper. http://www.kli.re.kr/issue1.html.

Part V

CONCLUSION

CHAPTER 10

The Limits of Local Citizenship and Activism in Japan and Other Recent Countries of Immigration

TAKEYUKI TSUDA

As the preceding chapters demonstrate, immigrants have considerable opportunities for local citizenship. Despite the dominant focus on nation-states as the source of citizenship, localities in recent countries of immigration have proven to be a much more inclusive, effective, and reliable source of rights and services for migrant workers. In contrast to national governments, which continue to view immigrants strictly as temporary labor power and as culturally alien outsiders, local governments and nongovernmental organizations (NGOs) have welcomed foreign residents into their communities as local citizens even though the nation-state has refused to do so. When the guarantees of local citizenship have been insufficient, NGOs and local activists have stepped in to defend and expand the rights of immigrants. As a result, migrant workers have been able to enjoy substantive citizenship rights even in the absence of nation-state recognition. Thus localities have come to the forefront of internationalization through their direct involvement in the governance of the ethnic diversity that global migration generates. Ironically, supposedly "provincial" localities in recent countries of immigration have been much more responsive to globalization than have nation-states.

As an alternative to the formal citizenship granted by the nation-state, local citizenship is more substantial and viable than the nominal and ultimately unenforceable rights of transnational and postnational citizenship. Nonetheless, our enthusiasm for local citizenship should not blind us to its serious limits. When citizenship is left to localities, each with its own local conditions and contingencies, it becomes subject to regional variation, ultimately sacrificing uniformity and quality. Even proactive local governments and NGOs have limited geographical jurisdiction and resources. In addition, foreign workers themselves do not always claim and exercise their local rights, partly because of their sense of social and cultural marginalization in the host country. Activism on behalf of migrant workers also faces constraints that limit its effectiveness.

THE LIMITS OF LOCAL CITIZENSHIP

Lack of Uniformity: Local Variation in Immigrant Rights

One of the hallmarks of formal citizenship is its geographical uniformity. National citizens receive the same rights and privileges regardless of where in the country they reside. Of course, those citizens who are ethnic minorities or members of the underclass do not always enjoy equal rights, but the unevenness of national citizenship derives from social group membership, not geographical location. Although a nation-state's nominal jurisdiction does not extend beyond its borders, national governments also protect their citizens residing abroad and guarantee them the same rights.[1] Likewise, the formal citizenship rights that nation-states grant to denizens and legal immigrants are also constant across geographical localities, as long as they remain within the country's borders. In the case of postnational/global citizenship, the same set of universal rights is, in principle, conferred to all human beings in all parts of the world.

In contrast, local citizenship rights lack geographical uniformity, even within the borders of a single nation-state, and they can vary considerably from city to city. Because a municipal government's jurisdiction is limited to a specific locality, it can only grant rights and services to immigrants who reside in the local community. Although NGO service providers are not strictly limited to the local community (especially when they advise immigrants over the telephone or through Web sites), most local NGOs have offices in only one location (at most, they have offices in a few cities), limiting the geographical range of their in-person services.

For instance, the local grassroots organizations that Keiko Yamanaka examines in her chapter in this volume offer services only to immigrants living in Hamamatsu City. There are very few nationwide NGOs that have

---

[1] Of course, citizens cannot always exercise these rights from abroad. As a result, various national governments have recently extended rights to their citizens living abroad that formerly could be exercised only by those residing in the nation-state. This includes expatriate voting through absentee ballots and the right to purchase land while abroad.

branch offices in all major cities and localities. Therefore, if immigrants move from a specific community, technically they lose the rights and services they were granted by that community's municipal government and local NGOs. Although they join a new community as local citizens, the rights that the new local authorities and organizations offer are likely to vary considerably in substance and quality. Therefore, in contrast to formal citizenship rights which remain constant across localities, local citizenship is geographically uneven and subject to regional contingencies and variation.

The chapters presented here document the substantial variation in citizenship rights that localities have offered foreign workers in recent countries of immigration, including countries in which the national government has developed (and subsidizes) a unified immigrant integration policy that supposedly applies across regions. However, the implementation of this national immigrant integration policy has been delegated to the localities, giving rise to considerable regional differences. In Italy, some regions have active and well-funded programs, while others have yet to pass legislation for such a program. The disparities in local citizenship policies are even greater in Japan, which has no national immigrant integration policy and no federal funding earmarked for developing such programs. Certain cities, such as Kawasaki in Kanagawa Prefecture, have promoted foreign residents' incorporation and civic participation through active welfare, language, counseling, educational, outreach, and intercultural programs, as well as through municipal antidiscrimination ordinances and even limited local political representation via advisory councils. Other cities with significant immigrant populations, such as Kawaguchi in Saitama Prefecture, have minimal incorporation programs that are limited to information brochures, language classes, and special events (see Tegtmeyer Pak 2000, 2001). In addition, a large number of migrant workers in Japan reside in cities with few foreign residents, and these cities offer virtually no rights and services specifically for this population.[2]

There are multiple reasons for the unevenness of immigrant citizenship and integration policies across localities in recent countries of immigration. Regionalism remains quite strong in all of the countries examined in this book. Both Italy and Spain were among the last Western European coun-

---

[2] The sixteen Japanese cities that meet regularly to cooperate on immigrant integration issues—and presumably have the most active programs—contain only 6.5 percent of the total foreign worker population in Japan (see Tegtmeyer Pak, this volume).

tries to be formally unified as nation-states, and they still have considerable regional disparities in economic development, ethnic composition and culture, and local histories, which influence their reception of immigrants. As Harlan Koff notes in his chapter, there are significant differences in regional hospitality toward immigrants in Italy.[3] Spain continues to have semiautonomous ethno-national regions that have been granted more local authority than other regions to develop their own immigrant policies. Regional disparities in economic development remain strong as well. As a result, more prosperous localities with greater need for foreign labor and larger immigrant populations have implemented more proactive integration programs than have less developed regions (see Koff, this volume). In addition, certain regions have received more central government funding for such programs, depending on the size of their immigrant populations, their proposed projects, and their political leverage.

Japan also has had a strong history of regionalism. For most of its modern history, it was divided into local kingdoms, and the country continues to display prominent regional differences in identities, dialects, cuisine, and local culture. In general, localities with more extensive historical experience with foreigners and immigrant minority groups, as well as more active local internationalization programs in the past, have been more receptive toward the recent wave of immigrants. Further, Japanese cities that have larger immigrant populations and that depend on and benefit economically from foreign workers generally have more developed immigrant citizenship policies and programs[4] and a greater number of active NGO service providers. Undoubtedly, more prosperous localities with correspondingly greater tax revenues are willing to commit more funds for immigrant programs and for NGOs. Finally, local governments in cities where migrant workers have a more positive image and are more locally visible (that is, more Japanese-descent nikkeijin, fewer illegals and sex work-

---

[3] However, Koff argues that local hospitality does not impact immigrant integration programs.

[4] Machimura (2000: 184–85) suggests that the political clout of local employers of foreign workers influences whether a city will have active immigrant integration programs. However, as noted in the introductory chapter, Tegtmeyer Pak (2000: 268–69) found that local officials did not directly link their incorporation programs to the local economic contribution of foreign workers. Instead, they implicitly assumed that such programs would promote the local economy and industries.

ers) also have more active immigrant incorporation programs (Tegtmeyer Pak 2000: 264–66).

In contrast, it could be argued that NGOs are more active in cities with *more* undocumented immigrants and foreign sex workers. Because these immigrants are the most victimized but also generally neglected by local governments, they have the greatest need for NGO services and protection. However, it is important to note that NGO services vary in scope and quality not only by locality but also from one organization to another in the same locality, depending on institutional and financial resources, staff competence and experience, and local government support.

Thus variations in immigrant rights and services across localities are very much a product of contingent local histories, economies, and foreign populations. As long as such regional differences exist, local citizenship for immigrants will continue to be geographically uneven. However, as Katherine Tegtmeyer Pak notes in her chapter, there has been considerable horizontal sharing of immigrant incorporation programs among local governments in Japan. According to Richard Samuels (1983), Japanese local governments have often relied on horizontal linkages and cooperation with other localities for policy-relevant information, and this "translocal policy interdependence" has been just as important, if not more important, than policy guidance from the national government.[5] The horizontal dissemination and adoption of policy ideas is most prevalent between neighboring local governments (which create regional councils for information and policy exchange) and between those with similar characteristics. It has also been driven by competitive rivalries among municipal governments (Muramatsu 1988: 51).

As Tegtmeyer Pak discusses in her chapter, there are numerous ways in which such horizontal policy sharing occurs with regard to immigrant citizenship and integration programs, including a committee for policy cooperation and coordination that links sixteen cities that have large concentrations of foreign workers. There is also a good deal of study, informal exchange, and emulation of policy innovations across city governments, with the largest cities exerting the most influence because of intergovernmental power hierarchies. The standard-bearer at the forefront of policy innovation is Kawasaki City, which frequently serves as a model for local governments developing their own immigrant incorporation programs.

---

[5] According to a study conducted by Muramatsu, a majority of local government officials claimed that the standards for their policy decisions came from other relevant city governments (1988: 51).

Such policy dissemination and sharing has made local immigrant citizenship more uniform across localities and less subject to regional contingencies and variables. The result has been an improvement in the quality and coverage of local immigrant citizenship nationwide.

A similar process is under way among NGOs that assist immigrants in Japan. They are beginning to collaborate across cities in order to share expertise and experiences, offer similar services, and assist one another in fund-raising (see Milly, this volume; Shipper 2002). Various NGOs have created support groups to accumulate and share new knowledge about assisting foreign workers and to strengthen their collective bargaining power on behalf of immigrants (Shipper 2002: 60–63). Annual meetings and conferences for NGOs have also been organized, bringing organizations together from across the country. Finally, NGOs are creating translocal (and even national) networks to improve collaboration, information sharing, and service delivery (see Shipper 2002; Milly, this volume). These networks have emerged not only among similar NGOs, but also among different types of NGOs. These collaborative efforts have likely created more evenness in the quality of local citizenship services that NGOs offer to foreign workers in various localities in Japan. Similar processes of policy emulation and information sharing may also exist among local NGOs in Italy, Spain, and South Korea, resulting in more uniformity in local citizenship programs in these countries.

Lack of Substantive Citizenship: Low Civic Participation among Foreign Residents

Another factor that hampers the effectiveness of local citizenship in recent countries of immigration is foreign workers' under-participation in integration programs and services. Citizenship is not simply a bundle of rights that governments or institutions bestow on individuals as members of a community. Citizenship is not *substantive* unless these rights are implemented and enforced (the problem with postnational/global citizenship). However, even if rights are put into force, citizenship is still not substantive unless these rights are actively claimed and exercised through individuals' recognition of their civic belonging and commitment. In other words, substantive citizenship also involves active civic participation by community members.

However, in many recent countries of immigration, foreign workers do not feel the strong sense of civic attachment and belonging to their residential communities that is necessary for effective local citizenship. Because migrant workers have not lived in these countries for an extended period, many view themselves as temporary sojourners[6] whose primary objective is to save as much money as possible in a short period of time. Their work-centered lives make them uninterested in utilizing the immigrant services and programs that municipal governments and NGOs offer, except for basic necessities such as health insurance or emergency medical care. Their general status as migratory transients also means that they are not yet involved in the local citizenship issues of concern to long-term or permanent immigrants, such as rights to equal employment, education, housing, institutional access, and local political representation.

In addition, foreign workers in recent countries of immigration often work on temporary contracts and/or switch jobs frequently in search of better wages or working conditions, leading them to move from one city to another.[7] They do not remain anywhere long enough to feel a sense of participatory belonging as local citizens. In contrast to national citizenship, which has become deterritorialized to a certain extent,[8] high mobility is antithetical to local citizenship, which is highly territorialized. Its rights can only be claimed and exercised by residents who remain grounded and committed to specific localities, not by shifting groups of migratory transients.

Moreover, foreign workers in recent countries of immigration tend to be culturally unassimilated and face significant cultural and linguistic barriers in the host society. As a result, they are socioculturally marginalized by the native residents in local communities and self-segregate in immigrant enclaves, further dampening their sense of civic community and engagement as local citizens. In fact, a certain amount of cultural citizenship may be a prerequisite for active substantive citizenship.

In sum, instrumental economic motives, sojourner mentality, and ethnic segregation have made foreign workers in recent countries of immigration

---

[6] Even immigrants who have settled in the host society with their families continue to regard themselves as sojourners who will soon return home (see, for example, Tsuda 1999).

[7] According to a survey of foreign workers in Hamamatsu City conducted by the Center for U.S.-Mexican Studies in 1996 (see Cornelius 1998), nikkeijin immigrants had each worked for an average of 2.9 firms during 3.7 years in Japan. Non-nikkeijin immigrants had worked for an average of 2.7 firms during 3.2 years in Japan.

[8] As mentioned earlier, the exercise of national citizenship rights no longer requires residence in the nation-state since its rights can increasingly be exercised by citizens living abroad or by dual nationals.

unwilling or unable to become engaged, local community citizens by claiming substantive rights and services. There is a measure of irony in the resulting situation: local governments and NGOs regard foreign workers as long-term community residents entitled to citizenship rights, but the migrants view themselves much as does the national government—as temporary, transient outsiders who are in the host society solely for economic gain. Although various municipalities have accorded them local citizenship, many of them have neither felt like nor acted like substantive citizens. This contrasts with more advanced countries of immigration, which have had stable, settled foreign-born populations for decades, along with growing numbers of culturally assimilated second-generation immigrant minorities. Not only have these immigrants developed long-term civic commitments to their local communities, they also have more complex sociopolitical needs and have demanded a further expansion of rights.

Although there are no comprehensive statistics, one can surmise that only a small minority of Japan's total population of foreign workers participates in the programs and services offered by local governments and NGOs. This is certainly true for the Japanese-descent nikkeijin, the most settled and culturally competent immigrant population in Japan.[9] In her chapter, Keiko Yamanaka notes that information about local government policies in Hamamatsu City has not been properly disseminated even to the nikkeijin because of the language barrier. Likewise, other authors represented in this book underscore foreign residents' lack of integration and participation in local civic communities. In fact, many immigrants in Japan are even unaware of the limited rights they are granted under Japanese national law (Terasawa 2000) and the services offered by local governments. In his study of NGOs, Apichai Shipper (2002: 60) claims that most migrant workers have not heard about the approximately two hundred NGOs that assist immigrants in Japan, and similar situations may prevail in other recent countries of immigration. For instance, in his chapter, Timothy Lim states that foreign workers in South Korea are often unaware of their immigrant rights and the services offered by local NGOs. The situation is exacerbated for illegal immigrants, whose fear of apprehension and deportation often dissuades them from using government services or exercising their worker rights even when they are aware of them (see, for example, Terasawa 2000).

---

[9] The author conducted extensive fieldwork among the Japanese Brazilians (see Tsuda 2003).

Demand for local citizenship programs may also be relatively low if local institutions are not delivering the rights and services that truly address immigrants' social needs. Even though some municipal governments in Japan have conducted surveys to identify foreign residents' needs and have created foreigner advisory councils, their social integration programs are run by Japanese officials, with limited immigrant input and participation.[10] Thus far, there has been only limited activism among immigrants to demand rights and services or to pressure local governments to adopt suitable programs (see below). In addition, NGOs that serve immigrants are mainly staffed by Japanese (in contrast to NGOs in Spain, which actively recruit immigrants for their organizations; see Agrela and Dietz, this volume). Many are middle-class Japanese citizens who identify with the marginalized and dispossessed and are committed to social equality and human rights (Stevens 1997; Yamanaka, this volume),[11] turning these NGOs into largely paternalistic organizations that benevolently bestow services based on their own assumptions about what is best for their foreign residents.

To date, Japan has few NGOs created and run primarily by immigrants. Some immigrant-run organizations have had difficulty sustaining activities because of the transient nature of their members, internal conflicts over leadership and organizational objectives, and lack of interest among their own compatriots (see Yamanaka, this volume, for the case of Brazilian nikkeijin in Hamamatsu). In addition, as Belén Agrela and Gunther Dietz point out for Spain, "multicultural" NGOs that use immigrant staff to deliver culturally sensitive services end up running highly specialized programs tailored to a single immigrant group, and these programs tend to be inferior to or duplicate the more generalized services offered by governmental welfare agencies. However, in Japan, where few government welfare agencies are assisting foreign workers, immigrant-run NGOs would

---

[10] Local governments' International Exchange Offices often include an immigrant staff member. Although an increasing number of local governments have foreigner advisory councils, they are not all staffed by foreign residents. Even the members of the Foreigners' Advisory Council in Kawasaki City (the first in Japan composed entirely of foreign residents) are mainly foreign professionals and students (who speak Japanese) and not the unskilled migrant workers who constitute the majority of the immigrant population (Satoko Ando, personal communication).

[11] Some have previous experience with helping Japanese minorities, the poor, and women.

serve a crucial function not covered by Japanese NGOs or local governments. As Keiko Yamanaka documents in her chapter, immigrant NGOs'
objectives are based on the specific cultural needs and ethnic heritage of
their own community, in contrast to the assimilation-oriented service programs of Japanese local governments.

Of course, this is not to deny that Japanese local governments and
NGOs are providing essential rights and services for their foreign residents. For instance, migrant workers obviously require protection from
abusive employers as well as access to basic medical care and other social
welfare services. However, local citizenship in recent countries of immigration tends to be "episodic"; foreign workers claim rights and utilize services not as long-term civic participants, but in response to immediate problems or emergencies.[12] This is partly a result of social integration programs
that are as yet underdeveloped and often limited to crisis management,
and partly attributable to the intention of most foreign workers to repatri-
ate after a temporary sojourn, which causes them to draw on immigrant
services only for short-term, instrumental purposes.

The services Japanese NGOs provide for undocumented immigrants
offer the most visible example of this episodic citizenship. Instead of being
active, contributing members of these organizations, foreign workers only
appear at NGO offices when they need help with a serious problem and
leave quickly once the issue is resolved (Shipper 2002: 60, 63). This is especially true for medical NGOs which tend to focus on emergency assistance
for workplace accidents, sudden illness, or lack of medical access or insurance. For instance, foreign workers enroll in these NGOs' health insurance
programs but stop paying premiums once their illness has been treated
(Shipper 2002: 41–42). Japanese labor unions that welcome foreign workers
have also experienced episodic participation. Instead of becoming active
union members working to improve conditions for all immigrants, foreign
workers join labor organizations when they want to resolve a specific dispute with an employer and then stop paying dues thereafter (Roberts 2000;
Shipper 2002: 22).

Some local-government social integration programs (such as counseling
services) also offer crisis assistance to foreign residents who generally do
not participate in the civic community. However, participation in these
local programs tends to be less episodic. Despite the small number of for-

---

[12] This is similar to what Zanfrini (1998) calls "assistential" immigrant social
integration policies, which mainly aim to address social emergencies and the
socioeconomic marginalization of foreign workers (cited in Koff, this volume).

eign residents who participate in them, these programs (language classes, cultural exchange activities, and foreigners' advisory councils) require some ongoing commitment. For example, local education for immigrant children usually involves a long-term institutional commitment by settled immigrant families. A number of immigrant parents (especially the Latin American nikkeijin) have become actively involved in their children's education and school activities, and even participate in local parent-teacher groups.

THE LIMITS OF LOCAL ACTIVISM

As noted in the introductory chapter, localities in recent countries of immigration are not only the sites where citizenship is conferred and exercised, but also where it is contested though struggles for immigrant rights. According to Joppke (2001), the expansion of immigrant rights in Euro-American countries has often begun at the local level through grassroots political mobilization or judicial activism. Such local activism is especially important in recent countries of immigration given that their citizenship rights and programs for foreign residents are still underdeveloped and insufficient. Again, however, there are a number of constraints on the effectiveness of immigrant activism in these countries.

There has been relatively little political mobilization among immigrants in Japan to protest abuses and injustices or to fight for rights, even compared to other recent countries of immigration. Foreign workers have yet to form active political organizations to promote their interests (Tegtmeyer Pak 2000: 268), and there are few immigrant-run NGOs. In fact, immigrant organizations played only a secondary role in the activist struggles Deborah Milly examines in her chapter in this volume. There have been some scattered protests and demonstrations by migrant workers (including hunger strikes by migrants unjustly detained by the government) and unauthorized immigrants who have petitioned the national government for amnesty, but there has been no sustained political mobilization of a scale to capture the public's attention. Even community labor unions that have welcomed foreign workers have been unable to mobilize them for collective action against employers because of their general lack of interest, episodic participation, and internal conflicts (Roberts 2000: 283–84; Terasawa 2000). Foreign workers are unlikely, therefore, to form their own branch union in the near future (Roberts 2000: 283).

The foreign workers' sojourner mentality and unwillingness to become active civic participants undoubtedly underlie their relative lack of political mobilization. Because they are only in Japan temporarily and for instrumental purposes, they are uninterested in improving the conditions for immigrants in the host society through political activism. In addition, most remain highly mobile and are relatively scattered throughout Japan, and few have developed a strong sense of community identification, which is often a prerequisite for sustained identity politics. The diversity of the immigrant population in terms of national origin, language, ethnicity, and legal status has also made it difficult for immigrants to unite and mobilize collectively around common issues (Miyajima 1997: 137). The relatively large number of unauthorized immigrants in Japan (and other recent countries of immigration), who fear detection by the authorities, also dampens political protest.

Joppke (2001) has noted the importance of the courts in improving the human rights of immigrants in Euro-American countries, and legal activism may offer a promising alternative for expanding immigrants' rights in Japan. Although Japan does not have an effective judicial review process for the government's administrative decisions, as exists in many Euro-American countries, Japan's courts are independent and sometimes willing to rule against the government (Upham 1987: 15). As Amy Gurowitz's chapter makes clear, there have been a number of favorable judicial rulings involving immigrant rights, in which lawyers and judges referred to international human rights conventions and norms to argue their cases or justify their rulings in opposition to government policy.[13] Although some scholars seem to assume that international human rights regimes are incompatible with national sources for the expansion of immigrant rights (see Joppke 2001), it is quite apparent that such international norms influence nation-states through the actions of domestic courts.

In this regard, localities again emerge as the primary site for immigrants' citizenship struggles. In the past, Japan's minority groups (especially the Korean Japanese immigrant minority, but also the Burakumin and Ainu) have succeeded in having a number of discriminatory laws revised or overturned through the courts, partly by appealing to international human rights conventions (see Gurowitz, this volume; Kashiwazaki 2000: 456-59; Shipper 2002: 44). Although most newcomer immigrants have not yet begun to fight for their rights through the courts, there has

---

[13] Japan has ratified a number of United Nations conventions on human rights and antidiscrimination, partly in response to international and domestic pressures (including from NGOs) (see Kashiwazaki 2000: 448-51; Kondo 2001).

been one potentially landmark case involving Ana Bortz. This Brazilian journalist was ejected from a jewelry store in Hamamatsu by the store-owner, who had banned all foreign customers because of his concern about rising foreigner crime. Bortz took the storeowner to court for racial discrimination, claiming that her case represented a violation of the United Nations International Convention on the Elimination of All Forms of Racial Discrimination, which Japan ratified in 1995. The judge ruled in her favor, and awarded her US$12,500 in damages, stating that the international convention was effective as domestic law in the absence of any specific and unequivocal law in Japan (including in the Constitution) barring racial discrimination against foreigners. Although this case seems to have had limited social impact among Japanese residents in Hamamatsu (Yamanaka 2003), it may become a precedent that will enable other foreign residents to fight for their civil rights.

As Deborah Milly notes in her chapter, Japanese courts are beginning to adopt a more activist position toward immigrant rights and offer a means for clarifying foreign workers' rights and reviewing their treatment by the government and employers. NGOs often appeal to the courts when their direct efforts to petition government officials do not produce results, and the number of lawsuits filed on behalf of immigrants has been increasing. In fact, the Japanese courts seem to have become more active recently in defending the rights of visa overstayers. In September and October 2003, the Tokyo District Court repealed deportation orders against the families of two unauthorized immigrants and ordered immigration authorities to grant them special residency permits because they and their children had been living in Japan for a long time (the government appealed the decision to a higher court). In a case with more significant repercussions, the Japanese Supreme Court ruled in January 2004 that it is illegal for authorities to bar all undocumented immigrants from the national health insurance program.

Pressure from NGOs that represent immigrants has been more effective in the struggle for foreigner rights than political mobilization by the migrant workers themselves. In fact, most of the immigrant activism in Japan has come from Japanese citizen NGOs acting on behalf of immigrants (see Milly, this volume).[14] Various local NGOs (including labor unions) representing foreign workers have lobbied local governments. Such local com-

---

[14] NGOs have recently shifted from emergency assistance for foreign workers to services and advocacy for those who have settled in Japan (see Milly, this volume).

munity pressure on municipal governments has undoubtedly been one reason for the development of local citizenship programs for foreign residents (see Tegtmeyer Pak 2000 and in this volume).[15] However, NGO activism that targets local governments tends to be uneven because NGOs cannot pressure all local governments at the same time and municipal officials are not equally responsive to such pressure (see Milly, this volume). As a result, NGOs are increasingly organizing on a national level as well.

Instead of simply fighting for local immigrant citizenship through municipalities, Japanese NGOs have begun lobbying the national government to make policy changes to improve the rights of all foreign workers in Japan. The NGOs have petitioned various government ministries to improve services and welfare programs for foreign workers; abolish unjust government practices (including inhumane detention of undocumented immigrants and asylum seekers); clarify and improve visa issuance, asylum, and amnesty procedures; and change immigration control policies and programs that negatively impact migrant workers (see Milly, this volume; Shipper 2002). Much of the NGO activism seems to be triggered by specific injustices toward foreign workers that highlight a general problem with the national government's treatment of immigrants. NGOs also have used international human rights and norms to legitimate their activities and position (Roberts 2000: 295) and to pressure the national government (Shipper 2002).

Unfortunately, Japan's national government has been much less responsive to local NGO activism than have local governments. As Milly indicates, active lobbying by local NGOs may result in better implementation and clarification of current national government policies, but it has not produced revised and reformed national policies. In fact, the NGOs' impact has often been limited to raising awareness about problems with government policy and engaging officials in dialogue about these issues. Activist NGOs seem to prefer such a cooperative approach over a (possibly more effective) adversarial approach that relies on public protests, demonstrations, and petitions. In addition, much of the pressure seems to focus on the government's micro-policies (the detailed regulations, procedures, and measures through which overall macro–immigration policies are carried out) and not on the macro-policies themselves. In general, it seems that the national government only takes action after there has been some

---

[15] Citizens' movements have a history of influencing local governments in Japan (Steiner 1980: 21).

public and media exposure to abuses of immigrants' human rights. Although NGO conferences have exposed the injustices that foreign workers face, the NGOs' focus on micro-policies means that their activism remains largely beyond direct public awareness.

Local activism's rather limited impact on national immigrant policies in Japan contrasts with the case of South Korea. Timothy Lim notes that political pressure from NGO lobbying and immigrant protests prompted the South Korean government to change a number of abusive policies, dramatically improving the human rights situation for foreign workers. Lim argues that civil society is much more active in Korea because of its history of political opposition to dictatorial governments and the proliferation of civil groups following the collapse of the authoritarian regime. In addition, political mobilization among the immigrants themselves (often organized by NGOs) has been more active and vocal than in Japan. For instance, a recent government crackdown on illegal foreign workers (although preceded by an amnesty) provoked migrant worker rallies, sit-ins, months-long hunger strikes, and NGO protests, causing the government to retreat somewhat. Similar draconian government crackdowns against illegal immigrants in Japan have yet to illicit any mass political protest or civil disobedience.

South Korea has also been more responsive in the area of migrant workers' rights because of the country's past anti-authoritarian, pro-democracy movement, which concentrated on human rights, including workers' rights. South Korea's status as a labor exporter (and its concerns about protecting its emigrants abroad) has also made it sympathetic to the rights of foreign workers in Korea (Seol and Skrentny n.d.). According to Lim, the national government has also been sensitized to international human rights norms because of its concern with South Korea's image abroad and the fact that a past president was a former dissident and leading advocate of human rights, including the rights of immigrants (the country's current president has a similar background).[16]

Despite immigrant activism's limited results in Japan, local governments, which are at the forefront of immigrant citizenship and integration policies, have attempted to influence national immigrant policy. Some municipal governments have assumed an "activist" role by lobbying the national government for policy changes that would improve immigrant

---

[16] However, Seol and Skrentny (n.d.) find that the impact of international human rights has been less prominent in Korea.

rights. Indeed, in other countries of immigration, changes in national immigrant policy have sometimes derived from local political forces and initiatives (Body-Gendrot and Schain 1992; cf. Andrew and Goldsmith 1998: 111). In the past, Japan's local governments and politicians have collectively opposed the central government, submitted alternative policy proposals, and influenced national policies (Muramatsu 1988; Samuels 1983).[17] Local governments have occasionally petitioned the national government on such issues as improving the foreigner registration system, providing better access to health insurance and pension programs, and even creating an office to coordinate policies affecting foreign residents (Tegtmeyer Pak, this volume). However, they have been most active in pressuring the Japanese government to grant local voting rights to foreigners as well as access to public administration jobs.[18] Thus far, foreign residents' political representation at the local level has been restricted to the foreigners' advisory councils established by some local governments. In general, it seems that immigrants are first granted social, civic, and cultural rights, and only later are their political rights seriously considered.[19]

CONCLUSION: TOWARD LOCAL-NATIONAL COLLABORATION IN IMMIGRANT CITIZENSHIP POLICY

We cannot overstate the importance of local citizenship in recent countries of immigration such as Japan. With national governments preoccupied

---

[17] However, Goldsmith (1996) argues that in southern Europe (including Italy and Spain) collaboration and links between national and local governments are stronger and local interests are more easily represented nationally.

[18] A bill submitted to the Diet to grant voting rights in local elections to permanent residents (most of whom are Korean Japanese born and raised in Japan but still not granted Japanese citizenship) has been shelved indefinitely because of strong opposition from members of the dominant Liberal Democratic Party. The bill was introduced and promoted by one of the three parties of the ruling coalition, the Komeito Party (which is supported by Korean Japanese), which calculated that the bill would give it a half-million new voters in local elections. However, hard-liners from the Liberal Democratic Party (which would be politically weakened in certain districts by the new voters) argued that the legislation will harm Japan's national interest and may be unconstitutional, and that Korean Japanese should simply naturalize if they want voting rights.

[19] This contrasts with Marshall's seminal work on citizenship, in which he argues that civic rights develop first, followed by political and then social rights (Marshall 1977). The order seems to be different in the case of immigrants.

with controlling unwanted immigration, local governments and NGOs have been the only official organizations providing essential rights and social services to the foreign residents who have settled in local communities. In the process, they have demonstrated that immigrants can enjoy substantive rights even without the formal citizenship conferred by the nation-state. As localities have taken charge of immigrant integration policy, they have shown considerable ability to independently craft innovative programs and services that are sensitive to local needs and also sufficiently specialized to deal with Japan's increasingly diverse foreign worker population.[20]

Nonetheless, the emerging local citizenship does suffer from some serious limitations. The immigrant integration programs of municipal governments and NGOs are each restricted to a single geographical locality, and they vary widely in quality and coverage from city to city. Although some Japanese cities have provided extensive rights and services, most have been less welcoming to their foreign residents (Komai 2001: 120; Machimura 2000: 191). Even the more supportive municipal governments are hampered by a lack of resources—they have limited local tax revenues, and the national government has generally been unwilling to offer financial support. Likewise, some NGO services are also underfunded and understaffed. These organizations have also tended to become highly specialized, sometimes focusing on a specific group of immigrants or a narrow set of issues. Because, by definition, local citizenship cannot provide the same level of rights to all immigrants nationwide, it remains an uneven and uncoordinated conferral of rights without firm governmental guarantees.

Therefore, the Japanese national government will have to become more engaged in immigrant social integration policy. Local governments, NGOs, and the national government must work together to coordinate the current patchwork of disparate local immigrant policies with a coherent national policy directed by the Japanese government and backed by federal resources.[21] Only the national government can implement policies that provide a uniform set of services and rights for immigrants across localities.

---

[20] One survey found that the kind of administrative services foreign workers demand varies considerably by national origin (cited in Komai 2001: 124).

[21] Some academics and immigrant NGOs have proposed the creation in Japan of an "Integration Bureau" within the federal government which would formulate a comprehensive immigrant integration policy and coordinate efforts by various ministries to provide social services and rights to immigrants.

Even if it does not create an official "immigrant integration policy," the government needs to begin extending formal citizenship rights to immigrants and offering social and welfare programs to assist them. For instance, in 1996 Japan's Ministry of Health and Welfare finally began compensating hospitals for some of the unpaid medical bills of foreign workers who had no health insurance, thus relieving local governments of this costly responsibility. There have also been initial steps toward a national education policy for immigrant children. In the early 1990s the Ministry of Education began a program to increase the number of Japanese-language teachers for foreign students, set aside hours for special Japanese language classes, and issued a language textbook and teaching guide. At minimum, the Japanese government, like those of Italy and Spain, needs to provide some funding to localities for their immigrant service and welfare programs and provide some national coordination and guidance by issuing a pro forma immigrant integration policy or a set of guidelines.

Given the current political climate in recent countries of immigration, it will be some time before immigrant rights and social integration become a priority on national policy-making agendas. Even so, the Italian and Spanish central governments are attempting to regain control of this policy domain.[22] Yet even in cases where national governments are willing to get involved, localities need to retain substantial autonomous power over immigrant citizenship policy, rather than ceding all control to federal authorities. National governments can implement extensive programs that provide the services and rights nationwide that are characteristic of formal citizenship. However, such general (one-size-fits-all) programs may not be sufficiently sensitive to the needs of specific immigrant groups or localities when compared to the particularity of local citizenship. In addition, federal programs and services may be even more underutilized than those offered by localities, especially among the large number of illegal immigrants who are afraid of apprehension by federal authorities. For instance, although the Japanese government has shelters for abused migrant women,[23] the shelters are not fully utilized because most of the women are undocu-

---

However, the government is opposed to this idea and unwilling to reform the immigration policy-making system (Kondo 2001: 433).

[22] In the Italian case, the government is attempting to wrest control from the localities in order to restrict immigrant integration policies in the name of national security.

[23] The Ministry of Health, Labor, and Welfare also plans to open temporary shelters for victims of human trafficking.

mented and hence reluctant to come to the attention of federal authorities (Shipper 2002: 32). Although the Ministry of Justice's Human Rights Bureau has consultation services for foreign residents, it is doubtful that many illegal immigrants use this service, since they fear being reported to the Immigration Bureau (also part of the Ministry of Justice).

Therefore, any coherent, effective immigrant citizenship and social integration policy must strike a balance between national and local policy making and service delivery. If local governments and NGOs are the only political actors, the result is likely to be an uncoordinated and uneven proliferation of specialized programs limited to specific localities and immigrant groups. If national governments have complete control, they may offer more comprehensive, nationwide programs, but these may not respond to local differences and the needs of specific immigrant groups. What is needed is a coordinated and combined effort between the federal government and localities that draws upon the strengths of both formal and local citizenship. It remains to be seen whether recent countries of immigration will find the right policy mix and balance of power between national and local governance for developing citizenship and integration policies that are sensitive to specific localities and various immigrant groups, while at the same time providing a comprehensive and consistent level of services and rights to immigrants nationwide.

References

Andrew, Caroline, and Michael Goldsmith. 1998. From local government to local governance—and beyond? *International Political Science Review* 19 (2):101–17.

Body-Gendrot, Sophie, and Martin A. Schain. 1992. National and local politics and the development of immigration policy in the United States and France: A comparative analysis. In *Immigrants in two democracies: French and American experience*, edited by Donald L. Horowitz and Gerard Noiriel. New York: New York University Press.

Cornelius, Wayne A. 1998. The structural embeddedness of demand for Mexican immigrant labor: New evidence from California. In *Crossings: Mexican immigration in interdisciplinary perspectives*, edited by Marcelo Suárez-Orozco. Cambridge, MA: David Rockefeller Center for Latin American Studies, Harvard University.

Goldsmith, Michael. 1996. Normative theories of local government—A European comparison. In *Rethinking local democracy*, edited by Desmond King and Gerry Stoker. London: Macmillan.

Gurowitz, Amy. 1999. Mobilizing international norms: Domestic actors, immigrants, and the Japanese state. *World Politics* 51 (3):413–45.

Joppke, Christian. 2001. The evolution of alien rights in the United States, Germany, and European Union. In *Citizenship today: Global perspectives and practices*, edited by T. Alexander Aleinikoff and Douglas Klusmeyer. Washington, DC: Carnegie Endowment for International Peace.

Kashiwazaki, Chikako. 2000. Citizenship in Japan: Legal practice and contemporary development. In *From migrants to citizens: Membership in a changing world*, edited by T. Alexander Aleinikoff and Douglass Klusmeyer. Washington, DC: Carnegie Endowment for International Peace.

Komai, Hiroshi. 2001. *Foreign migrants in contemporary Japan.* Trans. Jens Wilkinson. Melbourne, Australia: Trans Pacific Press.

Kondo, Atsushi. 2001. Citizenship rights for aliens in Japan. In *Citizenship in a global world: Comparing citizenship rights for aliens*, edited by Atsushi Kondo. New York: Palgrave.

Machimura, Takashi. 2000. Local settlement patterns of foreign workers in greater Tokyo: Growing diversity and its consequences. In *Japan and global migration: Foreign workers and the advent of a multicultural society*, edited by Mike Douglass and Glenda S. Roberts. London: Routledge.

Marshall, Thomas Humphrey. 1977. *Class, citizenship, and social development.* Chicago: University of Chicago Press.

Miyajima, Takashi. 1997. Immigration and the redefinition of "citizenship" in Japan: "One people-one nation" in question. In *Citizenship and national identity: From colonialism to globalism*, edited by T. K. Oommen. London: Sage.

Muramatsu, Michio. 1988. *Local power in the Japanese state.* Berkeley: University of California Press.

Roberts, Glenda S. 2000. NGO support for migrant labor in Japan. In *Japan and global migration: Foreign workers and the advent of a multicultural society*, edited by Mike Douglass and Glenda S. Roberts. London: Routledge.

Samuels, Richard J. 1983. *The politics of regional policy in Japan: Localities incorporated?* Princeton, NJ: Princeton University Press.

Seol, Dong-Hoon, and John Skrentny. n.d. How do international norms affect domestic politics? A comparison of migrant worker and women's rights in South Korea. Manuscript.

Shipper, Apichai W. 2002. *Pragmatism in activism: Organizing support for illegal foreign workers in Japan.* Cambridge, MA: Program on U.S.-Japan Relations, Harvard University.

Steiner, Kurt. 1980. Toward a framework for the study of local opposition. In *Political opposition and local politics in Japan*, edited by Kurt Steiner, Ellis S. Krauss, and Scott C. Flanagan. Princeton, NJ: Princeton University Press.

Stevens, Carolyn S. 1997. *On the margins of Japanese society: Volunteers and the welfare of the urban underclass.* New York: Routledge.

Tegtmeyer Pak, Katherine. 2000. Foreigners are local citizens, too: Local governments respond to international migration in Japan. In *Japan and global migration: Foreign workers and the advent of a multicultural society*, edited by Mike Douglass and Glenda S. Roberts. London: Routledge.

———. 2001. Towards local citizenship: Japanese cities respond to international migration. CCIS Working Paper No. 30. La Jolla: Center for Comparative Immigration Studies, University of California, San Diego.

Terasawa, Katsuko. 2000. Labor law, civil law, immigration law and the reality of migrants and their children. In *Japan and global migration: Foreign workers and the advent of a multicultural society*, edited by Mike Douglass and Glenda S. Roberts. London: Routledge.

Tsuda, Takeyuki. 1999. The permanence of "temporary" migration: The "structural embeddedness" of Japanese-Brazilian migrant workers in Japan. *Journal of Asian Studies* 58 (3):687–722.

———. 2003. *Strangers in the ethnic homeland: Japanese Brazilian return migration in transnational perspective*. New York: Columbia University Press.

Upham, Frank K. 1987. *Law and social change in postwar Japan*. Cambridge, MA: Harvard University Press.

Yamanaka, Keiko. 2003. A breakthrough for ethnic minority rights in Japan: Ana Bortz's courageous challenge. In *Gender and migration: Crossing borders and shifting boundaries*, edited by Mirjana Morokvasic Muller, Umut Erel, and Kyoko Shinozaki. International Women's University Series. Opladen, Germany: Verlag Leske+Budrich.

Zanfrini, Laura. 1998. *Leggere le migrazioni: I risultati della ricerca empirica, le categorie interpretative, problemi aperti*. Milan: Franco Angeli.

INDEX

activism, by immigrants, 25; in
Japan, 99–100, 281, 283–284;
in South Korea, 30, 255–56,
260, 261, 265, 266, 287;
activism, in support of
immigrants, 6, 7, 23, 27–28;
in Japan, 105, 135, 139, 285–
86; in South Korea, 251, 253,
259, 265, 266, 283, 287
advocacy, in support of
immigrants, 70, 79, 99, 123–
48, 158. *See also* activism, in
support of immigrants;
nongovernmental
organizations
aged dependency ratio, 40–41, 42,
43, 58
Agrela, Belén, 29–30
Ahn Seoung-Guen, 257
Ainu, 116, 158, 284
ALA Brasil (Japan), 108–109, 110–
12, 115
Algeria, migrants from, 208
All Japan Prefectural and
Municipal Workers Union,
69
Alleanza Nazionale, 179, 182, 183
amnesty programs, 136
Andalusia, 217, 218, 219
Andrew, Caroline, 11n21
Asian People's Friendship Society
(APFS), 133

Asian Workers' Problems
Discussion Network, 124
assimilation. *See* social integration
of immigrants
Azurmendi, Mikel, 226

Basque region, 217
Ben Jalloun, Tahar, 180–81
Berlusconi, Silvio, 179
Blue Sky Society (Japan), 110n, 112–
14, 115
Bomme, Michael, 210
border enforcement, 5, 6nn7–8, 18,
176, 177; in Italy, 29, 178; in
Japan, 19; in Spain, 209–10,
211, 212, 215
Bortz, Ana, 164, 285
Bossi, Umberto, 179
Brazilians, in Japan, 13, 14–15, 19,
20n, 24, 27, 46, 48n12, 50n18,
68, 72, 100–102, 103, 106, 107,
108, 109, 110, 111, 124, 126,
154, 280, 283
Brubaker, William Rogers, 7n10
Buddhist Coalition for Economic
Justice (BCEJ, South Korea),
257
Burukumin, 116, 158, 284

Campbell, John C., 38n1
Carens, Joseph, 11
Cassano, Franco, 195

sex workers, 15–16, 130
Shimada, Haruo, 158–59
Shipper, Apichai W., 24, 280
Small and Medium Business
    Administration (SMBA,
    South Korea), 249, 263
social integration, of immigrants,
    6, 7, 19, 20, 22, 23, 26, 27, 275,
    282, 283; in Europe, 45, 177;
    in Italy, 29, 173, 178, 181,
    189, 193, 194, 195, 196–200,
    201–2, 290; in Japan, 22, 43,
    50, 51, 52–53, 66, 67, 68, 71,
    73, 74–76, 77, 97, 99, 101,
    104–5, 111, 133, 289; in
    Spain, 29, 213, 215, 217, 220,
    221–22, 223–24, 227, 290
social welfare industries, 56, 59
South Korea, as homogenous
    society, 236
Soysal, Yasemin, 83
Spain, political system of, 216
students, as immigrants, 15, 46,
    48, 49–50, 125, 154
subcontractors, and foreign
    workers, 52
Switzerland, and immigration,
    45n7

Tanaka, Marisa, 108, 109, 110, 111
Tangentopoli scandal (Italy), 175,
    182
Tarumoto Hideki, 89
Tegtmeyer Pak, Katherine, 22n36,
    26, 159–60, 276n4, 277
terrorism. See security, and
    immigration
Thailand, migrants from, 16, 20
Tokyo, 52, 98, 100

trainee programs, 14, 30; in Japan,
    46, 48–49, 51, 125, 143–47; in
    South Korea, 243–45, 247, 263.
    See also Industrial Technical
    Trainee Program
Treaty of Amsterdam, 177, 211
Treaty on European Unity, 177
Tsuda, Takeyuki, 176

Ukraine, migrants from, 208
unions. See labor unions
United Kingdom, and immigration,
    45n9
United Nations, 8, 42–43
Usui, Chikako, 25

Vogel, Ezra, 157
volunteerism, 105–106, 112, 113–14,
    116, 131

wages. See work conditions
Weiner, Michael, 156
women, in labor force, 3–4, 57–58,
    174
women, and social integration of
    immigrants, 24, 27, 97, 99,
    105–106, 108–9, 110, 112, 113,
    115, 116
women immigrants, 100, 154, 290–
    91. See also sex workers
work conditions, of foreign
    workers: in Japan, 17, 20, 25,
    28, 49, 51, 130, 144–45; in
    South Korea, 30; in Spain, 209,
    256
work permits, 30, 250, 261, 265, 266–
    67
worker rights, 5, 14, 20, 24, 25, 30,
    50, 51, 99, 100

xenophobia, 179, 181, 188, 225–26, 227

Yamanaka, Keiko, 24, 27, 280

Yasuaki Onuma, 155
Yasuhira Ueki, 157
Yokohama, 66, 71, 72, 74, 76, 78, 80, 86

ABOUT THE AUTHORS

Belén Agrela is an Assistant Professor of Social Work at the University of Jaén and a research fellow at the Laboratory of Intercultural Studies, University of Granada, Spain. Both as an academic researcher and as an adviser to public agencies, she has conducted ethnographic research in various subregions of southern Spain on public policies toward immigrants and immigrants' social integration. She is currently finishing a doctoral dissertation on the institutional construction of cultural differences, with special reference to immigration policy in Spain. Among her recent publications are *Inmigración Extranjera en la Provincia de Jaén: Discursos y Prácticas (Immigration of Foreigners in Jaén Province: Discourse and Practice*, coauthor, Diputación Provincial de Jaén, 2002) and *Mujeres de un Solo Mundo: Globalización y Multiculturalismo (Women in One World: Globalization and Multiculturalism*, coeditor, Feminae, 2002).

Gunther Dietz is Professor of Social Anthropology at the University of Granada, Spain. He has conducted ethnographic fieldwork on minority integration, development policies, and ethnic movements in Mexico as well as on ethnicity and multiculturalist movements, nongovernmental organizations, and migrant communities in Spain. Among his recent publications are *Frontier Hybridization or Culture Clash? Trans-national Migrant Communities and Sub-national Identity Politics in Andalusia, Spain* (CCIS Working Paper 35, 2001); *"Door to Door with Our Muslim Sisters": Intercultural and Interreligious Conflicts in Granada, Spain* (in "Studi Emigrazione," 2002); and *Muslim Women in Southern Spain: Stepdaughters of Al-Andalus* (with Nadia El-Shohoumi, CCIS Monograph 4, 2005).

Amy Gurowitz is a Lecturer of Political Science at the University of California, Berkeley. A specialist in International Relations, she received her Ph.D. from Cornell University in 1999. Her doctoral dissertation, "Mobilizing International Norms: Domestic Actors, Immigrants, and the State," is a comparative study of variation in the application of international human rights norms as they pertain to immigration, with particular attention to the cases of Germany, Canada, Malaysia, and Japan. The latter case is also examined in a *World Politics* article, "Mobilizing International Norms: Domestic Actors, Immigrants, and the Japanese State" (April 1999). Prior to receiving her doctorate, Gurowitz was a predoctoral fellow at Harvard University's Center for International Affairs. She now teaches courses on immigration and on international ethics and justice.

Harlan Koff is a Nord Pas de Calais Fulbright Scholar at the Centre Lillois d'Études et de Recherches Économiques et Sociologiques of the Université de Lille 1, France. Previously, he was a Jean Monnet Fellow at the Robert Schuman Centre of the European University Institute and a Visiting Research Fellow at the Center for Comparative Immigration Studies at the University of California, San Diego. His current research focuses on the comparative impact of regional integration on border communities in Europe and the Americas. He has published in the fields of immigration politics, ethnic conflict, and human rights.

Timothy Lim is an Assistant Professor of Political Science at California State University, Los Angeles, and teaches courses in international relations, comparative and East Asian politics, American government, and U.S. foreign policy. He is the author of various interdisciplinary and area studies and a book entitled *Doing Comparative Politics: An Introduction to Approaches and Issues* (Lynne Rienner). Over the past several years he has conducted research on the politics of transnational labor migration, particularly in the Asia Pacific region (primarily Korea and Japan) and is developing an edited volume on this topic, tentatively entitled *Korea and Global Migration*. Before coming to CSLA, he was a postdoctoral research fellow at the Center for Korean Studies at the University of California, Berkeley.

Deborah Milly is Associate Professor of Political Science at Virginia Polytechnic Institute and State University. Her teaching and research interests include Japanese politics, social movements, the politics of immigration, comparative public policy, and comparative and regional Asian political economy. Her book *Poverty, Equality, and Growth: The Politics of Economic Need in Postwar Japan* (Harvard University Asia Council, 1999) received the Masayoshi Ohira Memorial Prize for 2000. Her current research interests include Japanese responses to increased immigration and comparative and global responses to international migration. She has held fellowships from the Abe Fellowship Program (1995–1996) and from the Japan Society for the Promotion of Science (2001). She is currently working on a book manuscript entitled "The State, Immigrants, and Advocacy in Asia and Europe," which places in comparative context the institutional and policy changes brought about by grassroots nongovernmental advocates in Japan on behalf of foreign residents who have settled since the 1980s.

Katherine Tegtmeyer Pak is Freeman Assistant Professor of Asian Politics at St. Olaf College. She earned her M.A. and Ph.D. in Political Science from the University of Chicago. Her research and teaching interests are in Asian politics and comparative politics. Between college and graduate school she worked at Toshiba Corporation's Tokyo headquarters for two years and returned to Japan for sixteen months of field research during graduate school. Before joining the St. Olaf faculty in 2003, she taught for five years at the New College of Florida. She is currently working on a book manuscript on Japanese immigration and citizenship politics from 1945 to the present.

Takeyuki (Gaku) Tsuda is Associate Director of the Center for Comparative Immigration Studies at the University of California, San Diego. After receiving his Ph.D. in anthropology from the University of California, Berkeley in 1997, he taught for three years as a Collegiate Assistant Professor at the University of Chicago. His primary academic interests include international migration, diasporas, ethnic minorities and identity, transnationalism and globalization, ethnic return migrants, the Japanese diaspora in the Americas, and contemporary Japanese society. His publications include numerous articles in anthropological and interdisciplinary journals as well as a book entitled *Strangers in the Ethnic Homeland: Japanese Brazilian Return Migration in Transnational Perspective* (Columbia University Press, 2003). He is the coeditor of *Controlling Immigration: A Global Perspective* (second edition, Stanford University Press, 2004). He is currently working on a field research project that compares peoples of Japanese descent in the Americas. In July 2006 he will move to Arizona State University (Tempe) as Associate Professor in the School of Human Evolution and Social Change (formerly the Department of Anthropology).

Chikako Usui is Associate Professor of Sociology at the University of Missouri at St. Louis and Adjunct Faculty in East Asian Studies at Washington University. She received her Ph.D. in Sociology at Stanford University. Her teaching and research interests are cross-national, comparative social welfare policies, sociology of aging, U.S.-Japan industrial organizations, and gender studies. She is currently engaged in four ongoing research projects: a cross-national analysis of changes in employment patterns among older men and women; a study of female labor force participation in Japan and the United States, 1960–1990; an analysis of the changing pattern of industrial groupings in Japan; and an examination of the changing pattern of bureaucratic retirement in Japan.

Keiko Yamanaka, a sociologist, is a Lecturer in the Department of Ethnic Studies and a Research Associate at the Institute for the Study of Social Change at the University of California, Berkeley. Since 1993, she has studied transnational migration and social transformation in Japan, focusing on two contrasting immigrant populations: authorized resident Brazilians of Japanese ancestry and unauthorized Nepalese. In recent years she has investigated feminized migration and civil actions in Asia. She has published articles and chapters on these topics in both English and Japanese. Her recent publications include: "Migration, Differential Access to Health Services and Civil Society's Responses in Japan" (*Migration and Health in Asia*, Routledge, 2005) and "Changing Family Structures of Nepalese Transmigrants in Japan: Split-Households and Dual-Wage Earners" (*Global Networks*, 2005). She has coedited "Gender, Migration and Governance in Asia" (special issue, *Asian and Pacific Migration Journal*, 2003) and co-authored *Feminized Migration in East and Southeast Asia: Policies, Actions and Empowerment* (Occasional Paper 11, United Nations Research Institute for Social Development, 2006).